ADVANCE PRAISE FOR
Conservative Philanthropies and Organizations Shaping U.S. Educational Policy and Practice

"As I write this endorsement from my COVID-era back porch, I cannot imagine a more timely (and ultimately timeless) text than *Conservative Philanthropies and Organizations Shaping U.S. Educational Policy and Practice.* This text brings together pieces that are always thoughtful, often provocative, and invariably helpful to readers seeking to better understand the complicated web of influence that connects the "good works" of ideologically conservative philanthrocapitalists and their ilk. deMarrais, Herron, and Copple do a terrific job of constructing a narrative arc out of the work of the fine scholars within, and themselves bring this text home with a beautiful, sobering, and fiery call to action for us all to remain informed, participate in dialogue, and work (and vote!) for the preservation of the *public* good. Bravo."

—Pamela J. Konkol, PhD,
Director of Academic Research, Concordia University Chicago

"Building upon their previous work, deMarrais, Herron, and Copple further unravel the tightly connected network of conservative philanthropists shaping policy and practice at all levels of US education. In *Conservative Philanthropies*, contributors pull apart diverse historical and contemporary threads of this network. Chapter by chapter, authors provide more coherent vision of the power and reach of philanthrocapitalism and its hand in dismantling public education. This is essential reading for those committed to the fight for a more just and democratic system of education."

—Amy Stich, PhD, University of Georgia

CONSERVATIVE PHILANTHROPIES

CONSERVATIVE PHILANTHROPIES

AND

ORGANIZATIONS SHAPING U.S. EDUCATIONAL POLICY AND PRACTICE

EDITED BY

KATHLEEN deMARRAIS,

BRIGETTE HERRON,

AND

JANIE COPPLE

Myers Education Press

GORHAM, MAINE

Myers Education Press

Published by Myers Education Press, LLC
P.O. Box 424 Gorham, ME 04038

Myers Education Press is an academic publisher specializing in books, e-books, and digital content in the field of education. All of our books are subjected to a rigorous peer review process and produced in compliance with the standards of the Council on Library and Information Resources.

Library of Congress Cataloging-in-Publication Data available from Library of Congress.

13-digit ISBN 978-1-9755-0300-0 (paperback)
13-digit ISBN 978-1-9755-0299-7 (hard cover)
13-digit ISBN 978-1-9755-0301-7 (library networkable e-edition)
13-digit ISBN 978-1-9755-0302-4 (consumer e-edition)

Printed in the United States of America.

All first editions printed on acid-free paper that meets the American National Standards Institute Z39-48 standard.

Cover design by Teresa Lagrange

CONTENTS

List of Tables and Figures ix

Acknowledgments xi

Preface xiii

1. Benevolence or Tax Avoidance? A Primer for Understanding How Philanthropic Foundations Work 1
KATHLEEN DEMARRAIS, *University of Georgia*
BRIGETTE HERRON, *University of Georgia*
JANIE COPPLE, *University of Georgia*

2. Ideology and the Education Debate: Examining the Powell Memorandum's Influence on Education Policy and Neoliberal Reform Models 17
JAMIE C. ATKINSON, *Missouri State University*

3. *Lochner*'s Redeemers: How the Federalist Society and the Institute for Justice Impact the School Privatization Movement 39
BRIAN DOTTS, *University of Georgia*

4. The Myth of Educational Freedom: The DeVos Family's Influence on Educational Policy 79
JAMIE B. LEWIS, *Georgia Gwinnett College*

5. Tracking Catholic School Funding From K-12 Through Higher Education 97
KEVIN J. BURKE, *University of Georgia*

6. The City Fund Takes It to "The People": How Top-Down Reforms Imposed on New Orleans Will Be Bankrolled as Bottom-Up Initiatives in Cities 119
KRISTEN BURAS, *Georgia State University*

7. The Walton Family Foundation: Key Players, Initiatives, and Its Growing Influence on Colleges and Universities 153
Kathleen deMarrais, *University of Georgia*
Brigette Herron, *University of Georgia*
Janie Copple, *University of Georgia*

8. Conservative Philanthropy and Historically Black Colleges and Universities: Historical Trends and the Current Landscape 185
E. Anthony Muhammad, *Georgia Southern University*

9. Operationalizing Toxic Ideology: How Radical Right-Wing Campus Organizations Undermine Democratic Engagement 202
T. Jameson Brewer, *University of North Georgia*
Amy Swain, *East Carolina University*

10. Miseducation of Communities: Sinclair Broadcasting and the Nationalization of Local News 225
Janie Copple, *University of Georgia*
Kathleen deMarrais, *University of Georgia*
Brigette Herron, *University of Georgia*

Coda 259
Brigette Herron, *University of Georgia*
Kathleen deMarrais, *University of Georgia*
Janie Copple, *University of Georgia*

Author Bios 265

Index 271

LIST OF TABLES AND FIGURES

Tables

Table 3.1 Federalist Society Network 55

Table 3.2 Federalist Society List of Experts in School Choice and Vouchers 63

Table 3.3 School Choice Litigation, 2001–2016 68

Table 8.1 Total Donations of Select Conservative Donors to Historically Black Colleges and Universities, 200?–2017 195

Figures

Figure 6.1 The City Fund Lineage—Partial Chronology of Elite Entrepreneurial Network Development 123

Figure 7.1 Walton Foundation Higher Ed Top Recipients . . . 173

Figure 9.1 Turning Point USA Political Network 217

ACKNOWLEDGMENTS

For all the journalists, whether local, national, or global, who track the activities of conservative philanthropies and their networks. We thank them for their continued efforts to follow the money, sort through the rhetoric, and get to the heart of what is really going on.

PREFACE

This book is about conservative philanthropies and the organizations and individuals within their networks. After publishing *Philanthropy, Hidden Strategy, and Collective Resistance: A Primer for Concerned Educators* (deMarrais et. al., 2019), we had more stories to tell of other philanthropies and interconnected networks of players. This book builds on that previous book and offers further analyses and cases of other efforts in the network. Fligstein and McAdam (2012) remind us that

> fields are constructed in the sense that they turn on a set of understandings fashioned over time by members of the field . . . there is a general, shared understanding of what is going on in the field, that is, what is at stake. (p. 10)

The ideological and philanthropic strategies presented in the following chapters demonstrate a network of what Fligstein and McAdam call *strategic action fields*, defined as meso-level social orders, in which social actors jockey for resources and position to wield power and influence. In Chapter One, we provide an overview of the increasing wealth disparities in the United States and the impact tax laws have had on the accumulation of wealth for a small number of individuals and their families. Explaining tax laws provides a context for understanding a financial infrastructure that rewards the wealthiest citizens by providing safeguards to protect and expand their wealth.

Chapter Two turns attention toward the origins of conservative ideologies shaping educational policymaking today. Specifically, Atkinson addresses free-market principles driving educational reform and Lewis Powell's 1971 memorandum in response to the

New Left and the memorandum's influence on education policy. The chapter chronicles events ushering in neoliberal education reform in the United States and provides historical context for understanding the forces driving federal and state-level education policy.

In Chapter Three, Dotts examines the Federalist Society and the Institute for Justice, the conservative philanthropies that support them, and the educational policies they pursue. The Federalist Society has brandished greater influence as a powerful national organization among state and university chapters, legal professionals, and others seeking to educate policy makers on conservative and libertarian interpretations of the U.S. Constitution and, like the American Bar Association, vets nominees to federal courts and the U.S. Supreme Court. The Institute for Justice, a nonprofit litigation firm funded by conservative-motivated philanthropic giving, litigates conservative causes including school choice and voucher programs. This chapter analyzes how the Institute for Justice and the Federalist Society work in tandem within a network of related organizations to affect public policies. Dotts demonstrates how emergent educational policies from these converging interests contribute to undermine U.S. public education and mobilize efforts toward school privatization.

In Chapter Four, Lewis details the history and context of the DeVos foundations and the impact of their work on education in the United States, particularly as related to school choice initiatives. Lewis begins with a brief history of the DeVos Family Foundation from the 1970s and its funding levels and priorities over time. The chapter turns to an exploration of the role Betsy DeVos's appointment as secretary of the U.S. Department of Education has played in furthering the efforts to erode public education.

Broadly speaking, very little attention is paid to Catholic education in the United States in the educational research literature. Chapter Five chronicles the history of political power and funding behind the Catholic school system and the educational reformers, many of the Catholic variety seeking to save it. In this chapter, Burke looks at the ways in which private foundation money has been harnessed by Catholic universities and the conservative Catholic bishops to drive educational policy toward school choice and push public money into Catholic schools regardless—and often because—of the consequences for public schools and their students.

Chapter Six is a case study of the City Fund, a New Orleans charter school reform organization. In this chapter, Buras traces the history of the City Fund, its leadership and its alliance with New Schools for New Orleans, the Mind Trust, and Education Cities—all pro–charter school organizations. Through a network analysis of philanthropy and political strategy, Buras examines how the City Fund provides a template for charter school expansion in cities across the United States.

In Chapter Seven, deMarrais, Herron, and Copple investigate the origins of the Walton Family Foundation (WFF) and its impact as a philanthropic foundation with giving guided by the personal interests of foundation and Walmart founder Sam Walton's heirs. The authors track strategic funding around the WFF's three primary funding initiatives: the arts, the environment, and education. Like the Charles G. Koch Foundation, the WFF has contributed millions to colleges and universities since 2005. Although extant literature focuses on the WFF's initiatives in K–12 education (specifically, charter school programming), there is little attention devoted to the foundation's investment in higher education. This chapter explores various ways the Walton family, through the tax-deductible WFF, use its wealth to influence specific projects related to family member's interest. The authors examine how the WFF's investment in higher education facilitates special interest funding to colleges and universities for programming in arts education, teacher preparation, and environmental sustainability. The authors argue the Walton family and the WFF exemplify a case of philanthropic elites whose vast wealth provides them with greater access to input in how we build and maintain our society and educational systems.

Drawing from ideological roots dating back to the Powell Memorandum, Chapter Eight examines the current role of conservative philanthropies in historically Black colleges and universities (HBCUs).

Muhammad traces the history of HBCUs in the United States, outlines the (often competing) educational models that have shaped them, and examines conservative philanthropic and political strategies jockeying for influence on HBCU campuses.

For a number of decades, right-wing foundations and nongovernmental organizations funded by a small number of interconnected wealthy benefactors have sought to influence academic and student discourse on college and university campuses. In Chapter Nine, Brewer and Swain explore how Turning Point USA (TPUSA), Campus Reform, and the Foundation for Individual Rights in Education have risen in prominence over the past decade as watchdog agencies that police faculty expression deemed to be radical left in an effort to suppress faculty influence. The authors examine a network of conservative venture philanthropists, political ideologues, and strategists that wield social influence and financial support to sustain such campus watch groups. Brewer and Swain turn specifically to TPUSA and its founding, corporate structure, funding, shared connections, and use of traditional and new forms of media and explore the impacts these tactics have on democratic engagement and campus culture.

Chapter Ten explores the existing scholarship around the changing nature of print and media news consumption in the United States in the 20th and 21st centuries. Copple, deMarrais, and Herron chronicle how contributing factors such as increased channel access and nationalization of print and media outlets led to a decline in local news consumption. The authors investigate the case of the Sinclair Broadcast Group as an example demonstrating the role media organizations play in the conservative ideological network through monopolization strategies of station markets and content control. They argue Sinclair's station acquisition strategies and conservative slanted political commentary undermine the principles of journalistic balance and integrity to conceal propaganda as local news. The purpose of this book is to unveil a broad network of conservative philanthropies and organizations influencing educational policy and practice. We shed light on actors within this network including the courts, philanthropy, the media, and P–12 and higher education in hopes to raise awareness around this complex web of actors and their influence.

References

deMarrais, K., Brewer, T. J., Herron, B., Atkinson, J. C., & Lewis, J. B. (2019). *Philanthropy, hidden strategy, and collective resistance: A primer for concerned educators.* Myers Education Press.

Fligstein, N., & McAdam, D. (2012). *A theory of fields.* Oxford University Press.

Chapter One

BENEVOLENCE OR TAX AVOIDANCE? A PRIMER FOR UNDERSTANDING HOW PHILANTHROPIC FOUNDATIONS WORK

KATHLEEN DEMARRAIS, *University of Georgia*
BRIGETTE HERRON, *University of Georgia*
JANIE COPPLE, *University of Georgia*

> *"Big Philanthropy is definitionally a plutocratic voice in our democracy," Reich told me, "an exercise of power by the wealthy that is unaccountable, non-transparent, donor-directed, perpetual, and tax-subsidized."*
>
> —Madrigal (2018, para. 3, emphasis added)

Each of the chapters in this volume focuses on the relationship of philanthropic foundations to national organizations, think tanks, P–12 and higher educational institutions, and the media. As an introduction to these studies, we begin with a brief overview of how philanthropic foundations work from a tax perspective, specifically focusing on U.S. federal tax codes and tax-exempt guidelines, and pay particular attention to the more recent donor-advised funds. The public may view the work of philanthropists, including the most wealthy and well-known foundations, such as those headed by the Waltons, Bill and Melinda Gates, Kochs, and Broads and many others as benevolent, charitable organizations working for the public good. Foundations are established by individuals, families, and corporations through legal Internal Revenue Service (IRS) tax codes enabling them to transfer income that would otherwise be taxed to the foundations and then use those foundations to promote activities of their choosing. As readers will see in this volume, the activities promoted reflect the ideological views of the foundations' founders and boards and can fund efforts not necessarily in the public good. Callahan (2017) refers to the rise of well-connected and ultra-wealthy family dynasties who use philanthropy as a tool to promote their own personal interests as the "New Philanthropic Power Elite." Although we support and applaud the work of charitable organizations, we question the use of tax codes to benefit this group of elite philanthropic foundations without democratic oversight. Within the context of increasing wealth inequality across the globe, we question the motivations of these privileged few to withhold tax dollars from the U.S. Treasury, where duly elected representatives can determine how tax dollars are used to benefit the society. By allowing these philanthropic organizations tax exemptions under the guise of assumed benevolence, are citizens giving up their ability to hold these organizations accountable for how the money is spent?

As an explanation of how the rich are able to avoid taxation, a 2016 Oxfam report, *An Economy for the 1%*, argued that paying as little tax as possible is a key strategy for many of the superrich and that "a global network of tax havens further enables the richest individuals to hide $7.6 trillion" (Oxfam, 2016, p. 1). This report documented the disparities of wealth distribution as follows:

- In 2015, just 62 individuals had the same wealth as 3.6 billion people – the bottom half of humanity. This figure is down from 388 individuals as recently as 2010.
- The wealth of the richest 62 people has risen by 45% in the five years since 2010 – that's an increase of more than half a trillion dollars ($542bn), to $1.76 trillion. (Oxfam, 2016, p. 2).

In a 2017 Oxfam report, *Economy for the 99%*, Hardoon reported the following:

- Since 2015, the richest 1% has owned more wealth than the rest of the planet.
- Eight men now own the same amount of wealth as the poorest half of the world.
- Over the next 20 years, 500 people will hand over $2.1 trillion to their heirs – a sum larger than the gross domestic product of India, a country of 1.3 billion people. . . .
- In the United States, new research by economist Thomas Piketty shows that over the last 30 years the growth in the incomes of the bottom 50% has been zero, whereas incomes of the top 1% have grown 300%. (p. 2)…
- Big businesses did well in 2015/16: profits are high and the world's 10 biggest corporations together have revenue greater than the government revenue of 180 countries combined. (p. 3)

The result, Oxfam argued, is that "many of the super-rich also use their power, influence and connections to capture politics and ensure that the rules are written for them" (Hardoon, 2017, p. 5). As Rhodes and Bloom (2018) noted,

> essentially, what we are witnessing is the transfer of responsibility for public goods and services from democratic institutions to the wealthy, to be administered by an executive class. In the CEO society, the exercise of social responsibilities is no longer debated in terms of whether corporations should or shouldn't be responsible for more than their own business interests. Instead, it is about how philanthropy can be used to reinforce a politico-economic system

> that enables such a small number of people to accumulate obscene amounts of wealth.

Rhodes and Bloom (2018) further explained the growth of big philanthropy with the term *philanthrocapitalism* to describe

> the application of management discourses and practices from business corporations and adapts them to charitable work. The focus is on entrepreneurship, market-based approaches and performance metrics. The process is funded by super-rich businesspeople and managed by those experienced in business. The result, at a practical level, is that philanthropy is undertaken by CEOs in a manner similar to how they would run businesses. . . . Many firms have sought to resolve this contradiction through high-profile philanthropy. Exploitative labour practices or corporate malpractice are swept under the carpet as companies publicize tax-efficient contributions to good causes. Such contributions may be a relatively small price to pay compared with changing fundamental operational practices. Likewise, giving to charity is a prime opportunity for CEOs to be seen to be doing good without having to sacrifice their commitment to making profit at any social cost. Charitable activity permits CEOs to be philanthropic rather than economically progressive or politically democratic.

As we witness this form of philanthrocapitalism, we see it can not only benefit the few ultra-wealthy family and corporate foundations through legal means to avoid federal and state taxes, but at the same time, it garners high levels of public goodwill and thus benefits the corporate bottom line. As Rhodes and Bloom (2018) remind us,

> there is an even more straightforward financial consideration at play in some cases. Charity can be an absolute boon to capital accumulation: corporate philanthropy has been shown to have a positive effect on perceptions by stock

> market analysts. At the personal level, CEOs can take advantage of promoting their individual charity to distract from other, less savoury activities; as an executive, they can cash in on the capital gains that can be made from introducing high-profile charity strategies (para 24).

So what are the tax mechanisms through which foundations live and work? We turn to a brief overview of relevant tax codes and a more detailed discussion of donor-advised funds, a more recent means of establishing foundations that preserve the intent of the original funder in the use of charitable donations.

U.S. IRS Tax Rules For Nonprofit Organizations[1]

After the legislative and administrative branches of the U.S. government develop and pass the U.S. tax laws, the IRS provides governance to ensure they are followed. These codes include the laws governing how nonprofit organizations work. According to U.S. tax codes, a nonprofit organization is one that "commonly performs some type of public or community benefit, without the purpose of making a profit" ("Starting a Nonprofit," n.d. para2). The codes most relevant to this book are those with 501(c)(3) and 501(c)(4) status that

> may qualify for exemption from federal income tax if it is organized and operated exclusively for one or more of the following purposes: religious, charitable, scientific, testing for public safety, literary, educational, fostering national or international amateur sports competition (but only if none of its activities involve providing athletic facilities or equipment), and the prevention of cruelty to children or animals (Chapter 3 Section 501(c)(3) Organizations, 2018, p. 21).

1 This section of the essay is adapted from a longer, more in-depth version included in deMarrais et al. (2019).

Per IRS regulations, "to qualify, the organization must be organized as a corporation (including a limited liability company), unincorporated association, or trust. Sole proprietorships, partnerships, individuals, or loosely associated groups of individuals won't qualify" (IRS tax map archive, 2018, p. 21). 501(c)(3) organizations, referred to as charitable organizations, can be either a private foundation or a public charity. A private foundation usually has a single major source of funding from a corporation or family funding and uses these funds to contribute to other charitable organizations and individuals. For example, the wealthiest U.S. philanthropists include Warren Buffett, Bill and Melinda Gates, Michael Bloomberg, the Walton Family, and Mark Zuckerberg and Priscilla Chan (Wang, 2019, November). In contrast to family or corporate foundations, a public charity has many sources of funding, including the public, governmental agencies, corporations, private foundations, or other charities, and uses these funds to further the stated purposes of the organization. *Forbes*'s list of America's top charities includes the United Way, Feeding America, the Salvation Army, St. Jude Children's Research Hospital, and Habitat for Humanity, among others (Barrett, 2019). Both private and public foundations are eligible for federal tax-deductible contributions from both individuals and corporations.

> Like federal law, most states allow for deductibility for state income tax purposes . . . many states allow exempt(ion) from sales tax on purchases, as well as exemption from property taxes (and) special nonprofit, bulk rate postage discounts are available from the Post Office to qualifying organizations. (Foundation Group, n.d., "Provisions Unique to 501(c)(3)")

Organizations eligible for 501(c)(3) status are expected to promote some kind of public, not private, benefit and are *not allowed* to engage in political activities. In contrast, a 501(c)(4) organization can engage in "some political activities, so long as that is not its primary activity" IRS, n.d.-b., para 5). IRS (n.d.-b) states:

> Seeking legislation germane to the organization's programs is a permissible means of attaining social welfare purposes. Thus, a section 501(c)(4) social welfare organization may further its exempt purposes through lobbying as its primary activity without jeopardizing its exempt status. (para. 4)

"However, any expenditure it makes for political activities may be subject to tax under section 527(f)" (IRS, n.d.-b, para. 5). Also, "an organization that has lost its section 501(c)(3) status due to substantial attempts to influence legislation may not thereafter qualify as a section 501(c)(4) organization" (IRS, n.d.-b, para. 4). To this point, the legal restrictions on the 501(c)(3) organizations with regard to political activity are articulated clearly on the IRS (n.d.-a) website mentions the following restrictions as follows:

> All section 501(c)(3) organizations are absolutely prohibited from directly or indirectly participating in, or intervening in, any political campaign on behalf of (or in opposition to) any candidate for elective public office. Contributions to political campaign funds or public statements of position (verbal or written) made on behalf of the organization in favor of or in opposition to any candidate for public office clearly violate the prohibition against political campaign activity (para. 1).

All 501(c)(3) organizations are required to operate with a level of transparency so that their annual tax returns using Form 990 are publicly available documents, allowing the public, including researchers like us, access to their annual assets, resources, expenditures, the names of people on boards of directors, and so on. With these reporting requirements, we have been able to access various 501(c)(3) organizations' tax filings over time to observe their donations and spending patterns. The authors of the chapters in this book access the 990 forms on a variety of websites and databases that catalog nonprofit tax filings (e.g., Foundation Directory Online, Guidestar, etc.). However, despite filing annual 990 forms, they are not required to have a website or publicize their work in any way. They are not accountable to the public, and with donor-advised funds, explained in the following, the mission of the original donor must be maintained in perpetuity, even after that donor has died. As Madrigal (2018) argued,

> on top of all this, foundations are tax-subsidized. "We're at a moment in American society in which the winners in the marketplace attempt to diminish their tax burdens, both corporately and individually, as low as they can legally go," Reich told me. "Then having diminished their tax burden as low as it can go, they turn around and set up a private foundation, taking a further tax break." Then, with money that would have otherwise have gone to the government, where at least there is nominal democratic control over spending priorities, the philanthropists use that money on whatever social purpose they've decided to support. (para. 13)

In the late 1990s, a new form of funding became available for use by individuals, families, and organizations in the form of donor-advised funds (DAFs). The next section details how these operate and the advantages for donors.

Donor-Advised Funds (DAFS)

According to the National Philanthropic Trust's 2019 DAF report, a DAF serves as "a philanthropic giving vehicle administered by a charitable sponsor. A donor-advised fund allows donors to establish and fund the account by making irrevocable, tax-deductible contributions to the charitable sponsor. Donors then recommend grants from those funds to other charitable organizations" (National Philanthropic Trust, n.d., p. 9). In recent years, DAFs have become an increasingly popular way for individuals, families, and organizations to contribute to charitable causes. *Consumer Reports* noted that DAFs are "the fastest-growing form of philanthropy today" (Wang, 2019) and a *Nonprofit Quarterly* 2019 article cited a 200% increase in the number of DAFs in the past 5 years (Osborne, 2019) and grants from DAFs totaled more than $23 billion in 2018 (Philanthropy News Digest, 2019). In the paragraphs that follow, we define the purposes and advantages of DAF charitable giving and note the distinctions among the three types of DAFs: single-issue charities, community foundations, and national sponsored organizations. We then turn to a review of academic literature on DAFs operating strategies with specific attention to national charities to give readers a sense of this latest form of philanthropy, one that further benefits the wealthy and enables a level of anonymity.

Financial advisors cite ease, flexibility, and impact as reasons why more people are turning to DAFs for charitable donations. DAFs operate as "a charitable savings account that lets you make a donation without choosing a specific charity right away. You can send the money later, at any time, to a qualified charity, while the account grows tax-free" (Wang, 2019, para. 2). Other benefits include "streamlined" charitable giving. Rather than making separate donations across several organizations, DAFs allow for aggregate donations of cash and noncash assets (e.g., securities) in one location. Allowing for noncash asset donations creates more opportunities for individuals to donate within or across the three categories of DAFs: single-issue charities, community foundations, and nationally sponsored organizations.

Single-issue charities focus charitable work around specific causes or initiatives and include "universities, Jewish federations, other faith-based charities and issue-specific charities, such as those in the environmental, social justice or international relief arenas" (National Philanthropic Trust, 2019, p. 9). According to the National Philanthropic Trust's 2019 DAF report, single-issue charities accounted for the highest grant payout across DAFs. Community foundations fundraise from public donors and qualify as publicly supported charities. Most community foundations engage "separate donors to carry out charitable interests for the benefit of residents of a defined geographic area, typically no larger than a state" (National Philanthropic Trust, 2019, p. 8). Grants from community-foundation DAFs increased 10.2% in 2018 and include grants totaling more than $6.5 billion, with grant payout decreasing from 20% in 2017 to 16.6% in 2018 (National Philanthropic Trust, 2019). Nationally sponsored organizations focus grants and fundraising around national initiatives and programs. Charitable assets in national sponsored DAFs grew more than 22% between 2017 and 2018 increasing from more than $59 billion in 2017 to more than $72 billion in 2018. Heist and Vance-McMullen's 2019 longitudinal study on DAFs found that while nationally sponsored organization DAFs "accounted for about 5% of the number of sponsors in the data, they account for about half (49%) of the assets" (p. 1076). The chief executive officer of the National Philanthropic Trust, Eileen Heisman, believes tax reform laws may account for this recent trend toward DAF philanthropy. In the following quote, Heisman refers to a giving strategy in which an individual combines or "bunches" charitable donations across multiple fiscal years into one donation for itemization purposes during a single fiscal year:

> Contributions to donor-advised funds outpaced grants for the first time in four years, which may indicate donors choosing to "bunch" their giving—essentially pre-funding several years of charitable giving to make their philanthropy more tax effective. (Philanthropy News Digest, 2019, para. 5)

Recent academic literature and financial journalism acknowledge a growing trend toward DAF giving (Daniels & Lindsay, 2016; Frostensen et al., 2013; Heist & Vance-McMullen, 2019; Rooney, 2017). Frostensen and colleagues (2013) noted a substantial uptick in DAF following a slight downturn in 2008 due to the global financial crisis. In 2013, Frostensen and colleagues reported Fidelity Charitable, the largest grossing DAF in the United States, "now holds slightly more in assets than the Robert Wood Johnson

Foundation, the nation's third-largest grant maker" (Frostensen et al., 2013, para. 6). Critique points to a lack of federal regulations around requirements for DAF distribution and tax exemptions that absolve donors from capital gains and protects donor anonymity (Rooney, 2017). In instances in which individuals or families experience liquidity moments (inheritance, sale of business), DAFs provide an easy way to donate to charitable causes while avoiding capital gains taxes. We argue DAFs—specifically nationally sponsored DAFs—provide an increasingly popular giving strategy for big philanthropy to secure philanthropic investment for future generations while depleting national coffers of resources that could otherwise fund federal programs contributing to the public good.

This introductory chapter provides a bare-bones look at the ways tax codes work to benefit individuals and corporations through the establishment of nonprofit organizations. These organizations are granted tax-exempt status if they fulfill the purposes of benefiting the public good and when the primary purpose is not to engage in political activities. For further reading, see the recommended reading list at the end of the chapter. Focused more on the tax codes legislation itself, Saez and Zucman (2019) call for an overhaul of the tax codes that allow this accumulation of wealth through tax havens and loopholes in *The Triumph of Injustice: How the Rich Dodge Taxes and How to Make Them Pay.* They describe the context in which the wealthy can control and generate wealth through legal means and the impact on wealth inequality described at the beginning of this chapter:

> In 1970, the richest American paid, all taxes included, more than 50% of their income in taxes, twice as much as working class individuals. In 2018, following the Trump tax reform, and for the first time in the last hundred years, billionaires have paid less than steel workers, schoolteachers, and retirees. The wealthy have seen their taxes rolled back to levels last seen in the 1910s, when the government was only a quarter

> of the size it is today. It is as if a century of fiscal history has been erased. (Saez & Zucman, 2019, p. xi)

Their text provides an in-depth look at the context of wealth and taxation today and offers solutions for addressing tax inequities as does the website Tax Justice Now (taxjusticenow.org), where readers can try our different tax plans or create their own. We encourage readers to study the ways wealth in this nation and across the globe has been concentrated in the hands of a few, work toward a fair and democratic way to address social needs, and support public programs without reliance on the "benevolence" of private-sector wealth. We conclude with a challenge from Oxfam (2016):

> *Our world is not short of wealth. It simply makes no economic sense—or indeed moral sense—to have so much in the hands of so few. Oxfam believes that humanity can do better than this, that we have the talent, the technology and the imagination to build a much better world. We have the chance to build a more human economy, where the interests of the majority are put first. A world where there is decent work for all, where women and men are equal, where tax havens are something people read about in history books, and where the richest pay their fair share to support a society that benefits everyone.* (p. 9, emphasis added)

Suggested Readings

Arnsburger, P., Ludlum, M., Riley, M., & Stanton, M. (2008, Winter). A history of the tax-exempt sector: An SOI perspective. *Statistics of Income Bulletin*, *27*(3), 105–135. http://irs.gov/pub/irs-soi/tehistory.pdf

Callahan, D. (2017). *The givers: Wealth, power, and philanthropy in a new gilded age.* New York: Penguin Random House.

Chuck Collins's Hidden Wealth Project at the Institute for Policy Studies: https://inequality.org/about/

Madrigal, A. (2018, June 27). Against big philanthropy. *The Atlantic.* https://www.theatlantic.com/technology/archive/2018/06/against-philanthropy/563834/

Oxfam. (2016, January 18). *An economy for the 1%: how privilege and power in the economy drive extreme inequality and how this can be stopped* (210 Oxfam Briefing Paper Summary). https://oi-files-d8-prod.s3.eu-west-2.amazonaws.com/s3fs-public/file_attachments/bp210-economy-one-percent-tax-havens-180116-summ-en_0.pdf

Petegrosky, D. (2018, September 18). *The elephant in the room: What's missing from the recent public conversation about DAFs.* National Committee for Responsive Philanthropy. https://www.ncrp.org/2018/09/the-elephant-in-the-room-whats-missing-from-the-recent-public-conversation-about-dafs.html

Philanthropy News Digest. (2019, November 14). *Grants from donor-advised funds totaled $23.42 billion in FY2018.* http://philanthropynewsdigest.org/news/grants-from-donor-advised-funds-totaled-23.42-billion-in-fy2018?utm_medium=email&utm_source=PND News-All Subscribers&utm_campaign=pnd20191119

Rhodes, C., & Bloom, P. (2018, May 24). The trouble with charitable billionaires. The Guardian. https://www.theguardian.com/news/2018/may/24/the-trouble-with-charitable-billionaires-philanthrocapitalism

References

Barrett, W. P. (2019). America's top charities 2019. *Forbes.* https://www.forbes.com/lists/top-charities/#7b2032965f50

Chapter 3 Section 501(c)(3) Organizations. (2019, October 27). https://taxmap.irs.gov/taxmap2018/pubs/p557-016.htm

Daniels, A., & Lindsay, D. (2016, November). Donor-advised funds reshape the philanthropy landscape. *The Chronicle of Philanthropy*, pp. A26, A32.

deMarrais, K., Brewer, T. J., Herron, B. A., Atkinson, J. C., Lewis, J. B., & Dayton, J. (2019). *Philanthropy, hidden strategy, and collective resistance: A primer for concerned educators.* Myers Education Press.

Foundation Group. (n.d.). *What is a 501(c)(3)?* http://www.501c3.org/what-is-a-501c3

Frostenson, S., Grovum, E. C., & López-Rivera, M. (2013). Donor-advised funds keep up rapid growth. *The Chronicle of Philanthropy*, *25*(13), 7–10.

Hardoon, D. (2017, January). *An economy for the 99%: It's time to build a human economy that benefits everyone, not just the privileged few.* (Oxfam Briefing Paper Summary). Oxford International. https://oi-files-d8-prod.s3.eu-west-2.amazonaws.com/s3fs-public/file_attachments/bp-economy-for-99-percent-160117-summ-en.pdf

Heist, H. D., & Vance-McMullen, D. (2019). Understanding donor-advised funds: How grants flow during recessions. *Nonprofit & Voluntary Sector Quarterly*, *48*(5), 1066–1093. https://doi-org.proxy-remote.galib.uga.edu/10.1177/0899764019856118

Internal Revenue Service. (n.d.-a). *The restriction of political campaign intervention by section 501(c)(3) tax-exempt organizations.* https://www.irs.gov/charities-non-profits/charitable-organizations/the-restriction-of-political-campaign-intervention-by-section-501c3-tax-exempt-organizations

Internal Revenue Service. (n.d.-b). *Social welfare organizations.* https://www.irs.gov/charities-non-profits/other-non-profits/social-welfare-organizations

Madrigal, A. (2018, June 27). Against big philanthropy. *The Atlantic.* https://www.theatlantic.com/technology/archive/2018/06/against-philanthropy/563834/

National Philanthropic Trust. (2019). *The 2019 DAF report.* https://www.nptrust.org/wp-content/uploads/2019/11/2019-Donor-Advised-Fund-Report-NPT.pdf

Osborne, A. Jr. (2019, July 29). Voices from the field: Fidelity's 2019 DAF grants spike-How donor-advised funds changed giving for the better. *Nonprofit Quarterly.* https://nonprofitquarterly.org/fidelity-charitables-2019-daf-grants-spike-how-donor-advised-funds-changed-giving-for-the-better/

Oxfam. (2016, January 18). *An economy for the 1%: how privilege and power in the economy drive extreme inequality and how this can be stopped* (201 Oxfam Briefing Paper Summary). https://oi-files-d8-prod.

s3.eu-west-2.amazonaws.com/s3fs-public/file_attachments/bp210-economy-one-percent-tax-havens-180116-summ-en_0.pdf

Philanthropy News Digest. (2019, November 14). *Grants from donor-advised funds totaled $23.42 billion in FY2018.* http://philanthropynewsdigest.org/news/grants-from-donor-advised-funds-totaled-23.42-billion-in-fy2018?utm_medium=email&utm_source=PND%20News%20-%20All%20Subscribers&utm_campaign=pnd20191119

Rhodes, C., & Bloom, P. (2018, May 24). The trouble with charitable billionaires. Retrieved from https://www.theguardian.com/news/2018/may/24/the-trouble-with-charitable-billionaires-philanthrocapitalism

Rooney, P. M. (2017, November 7). Have donor-advised funds and other philanthropic innovations changed the flow of giving in the United States? *Nonprofit Quarterly.* https://nonprofitquarterly.org/have-donor-advised-funds-and-other-philanthropic-innovations-changed-the-flow-of-giving-in-the-united-states/

Saez, E., & Zucman, G. (2019). *The triumph of injustice: How the rich dodge taxes and how to make them pay.* W. W. Norton.

Starting a Nonprofit. (n.d.). Retrieved from https://www.usa.gov/start-nonprofit

Wang, J. (2019, November 20). America's Top Givers: The 50 Philanthropists that Gave the Most in 2018. Retrieved from https://www.forbes.com/top-givers/

Wang, P. (2019, December 7). 5 things to know about donor-advised funds. *Consumer Reports.* https://www.consumerreports.org/charitable-donations/donor-advised-funds-things-to-know/

Chapter One

IDEOLOGY AND THE EDUCATION DEBATE:

EXAMINING THE POWELL MEMORANDUM'S INFLUENCE ON EDUCATION POLICY AND NEOLIBERAL REFORM MODELS

Jamie C. Atkinson, *Missouri State University*

> The plain fact of the matter is the right-wing in the United States has been much more successful in mobilizing the "people" than either the Democrats or what remains of the left. Absent a viable left alternative or a political party willing to address the grievances of the "people," the political landscape has shifted very significantly to the right in recent years.
>
> —Seybold (2013, p. 289)

Seybold's matter-of-fact statement bemoans our current state of affairs—conservatism and market nationalism have permeated the core of our social, political, economic, and cultural institutions. Rugged individualism, choice, market valuation, and competition have come to define norms of being, thinking, and meaning-making. Those normative antecedents infiltrate our educational institutions—reifying free-market ideology as a way of life and providing an impetus for ideologically motivated educational reforms. How has education arrived in such a place? How have these ideological principles shaped educational policy? There is no one right answer. It requires examinations of federal and state-level educational policy making and the associated political maneuvers to control education. One must understand the broader history of education, realizing it is primarily parsed in the ongoing ideological battle of the sociopolitical and cultural wars—which have become increasingly pronounced and have driven education policy since the nation's founding.

Deeply entrenched ideologies have acted as kindling for battles over the purpose, goals, and aims of education throughout our nation's history. This chapter first attends to a discussion of culturally conservative and free-market ideologies permeating the sociocultural and political order of society and associated belief systems held by adherents to those ideologies that currently dominate the direction of educational reforms. I examine Lewis Powell's memorandum to the United States Chamber of Commerce in 1971 as a response to the New Left and how that memorandum was indicative of a larger, much more ominous, ideological endeavor to influence education policy. Turning to Powell's other speeches and writings (Powell, 1970a-d, 1971), I provide an understanding of the broader ideological discussion. Finally, I chronicle how events from the 1970s to the 1990s ushered in and firmly rooted current neoliberal reform models in American education. Although this chapter does not address every issue and ideologically related machination, it provides the reader with a general understanding of the ongoing ideological battle over the control of educational policy in the United States.

Ideology And The Culture Wars

Education is inherently political and never neutral. The goals and aims of education are encapsulated within sociocultural struggles for the future—often driven by ideological motivations. Most recently, we have witnessed politically and ideologically driven educational reforms making way for the growth of charter schooling and the retraction of various federal education policies under Secretary of Education Betsy DeVos. The history of education in the United States is replete with examples of ideological struggles regarding the purpose and aims of education. One only has to examine the many tomes on the history and politics of education to understand the political-ideological nature of education policy such as Jennings (2015), Saltman (2018), Spring (2011), and Urban et al. (2019), to name just a few. Politically and culturally conservative education policy reform models have a history in both the neoliberal and neoconservative revolution of the 1960s and 1970s. Neoliberal ideology is not unique to any one party in the United States, with both Democrats and Republicans embracing various tenants of neoliberalism. Charles Krauthammer (2005), in a piece on neoconservatism in *Commentary*, stated that "the vast right-wing conspiracy has grown even more vast than liberals could imagine" (p. 1), and as Phillip Kovacs (2008) has noted,

> the neoconservative/neoliberal revolution is the evolving product [of now 40 years] of well-planned, well-funded, concentrated action" whose ideologues' mission is to infiltrate educational discourse at all levels, promoting rugged individualism, choice, and market-oriented language, which is centered on one's patriotic duty to the American free enterprise system. (p. 229)

In other words, the goal is to inculcate the next generation of students with ideas that rugged individualism, competition, choice, market fundamentalism, and consumerism are the only way forward.

In a wonderful examination of the social and psychological basis for ideology, Hulda Thorisdottir et al. (2009) argued that "ideology has been described as one of the most elusive constructs in all of the social sciences, largely because it has been enormously difficult for researchers to agree on a compact, yet comprehensive definition" (p. 4). There are many resources referencing the psychological bases for ideology and politics. More particular to this chapter, a few resources that examine ideology from psychosocial and cultural perspectives include Eagleton (1991); Gerring (1997); Feldman (2003), Hennes, et al. (2012); Jost (2006); Jost, Frederico, et al. (2009); Jost et al. (2008), McLellan (1995); and Mullins (1972). Thorisdottir et al. (2009) define two aspects of ideology necessary to understanding the ideological motivations in educational policy formations: (1) an ideology is a "body of ideas reflecting the social needs and aspirations of an individual, group, class, [institution], or culture" and (2) "a set of doctrines or beliefs that form the basis of a political, economic, or other system" (p. 4). With this general understanding of ideology, I turn to an examination of two extremely influential ideological frameworks: neoliberalism and neoconservatism. Each framework has had a significant impact on education reform policies yet seems to be quite hidden from the public because of how seamlessly society seems to incorporate the ideas espoused in each.

Neoliberalism

Neoliberalism, and its associative root term *neoliberal*—those who adhere to this framework or the policies they espouse—has become somewhat amorphous due to its multitudes of possible meanings (Au & Ferrare, 2015, p. 2; Ball, 2012). Words such as *neoliberal* and *neoliberalism* and *neoconservativism* and *neoconservative* can become "sliding signifiers whose exact meaning shifts depending on who is using it, where they are using it, when they are using it, and to what audience they are speaking" (Au & Ferrare, 2015, p. 2; Gee, 1996). Although these terms can shift in their "temporal, spatial, cultural, and geographic contexts" (Au & Ferrare, 2015, p. 2), our current understandings of neoliberalism are encapsulated in the U.S.-led coup d'état of Chile's president in 1972, which ushered in extremist right-wing conservatism (going well beyond neoconservatism), corporatism, and fascism via the new ruler, Pinochet (Davies, 2014; Harvey, 2004). We next turn to a definition of neoliberalism in its current form.

For the purpose of this chapter, I turn primarily to Harvey's (2004, 2005, and 2007) research for a working definition of neoliberalism and draw further support from Au and Ferrare (2015), Brown (2006, 2015), Down (2009), Lipman (2011), Fabricant and Fine (2013), Mirowski and Plehwe (2009), and Walpen (2004).

Harvey explained: "Neoliberalism is a theory of political economic practices proposing that human well-being can be best advanced by the maximization of entrepreneurial freedoms within an institutional framework characterized by private property rights, individual liberty, unencumbered markets, and free trade" (2005, p. 2; 2007, p. 22). Lipman (2011) defined neoliberalism as

> an ensemble of economic and social policies, forms of governance, and discourses of ideologies that promote self-interest, unrestricted flows of capital, deep reductions in the cost of labor, and sharp retrenchment of the public sphere. Neoliberals champion privatization of social goods and withdrawal of government from provision for social welfare on the premise that competitive markets are more effective and efficient. (p. 6)

As an ideology, neoliberalism includes "a spectrum of social, political, and economic phenomena at different levels ranging from highly abstract, to concrete examples, but all are committed to the idea that the market should organize all political, social, and economic decision making" (deMarrais et al., 2019, p. 3; Down, 2009; Hursh, 2008, Saad-Filho & Johnston, 2005). What makes the American, and much of the Western world's, version of neoliberalism so influential is its roots in the "doctrines of competition and entrepreneurship" combined with an outright "rejection of advancing socialist ideas" (deMarrais et al., 2019, p. 4; Mirowski & Plehwe, 2009; Walpen, 2004). This "neoliberal thought collective" is rooted in unifying political-economic philosophy as the underlying driving mantra in a society (Brown, 2006, p. 698; Mirowski & Plehwe, 2009). Many scholars look to Harvey (2005) for a complete history of neoliberalism around the world, although Mirowski and Plehwe (2009) provide a more nuanced history tracing neoliberalism's roots to ordoliberalism, a German variation of economic liberalism formulated in Germany after World War II and with the influence of Austrian and American economists.

There is currently a radical shift from government to governance while "responsibilities for governing are increasingly being shifted from democratically elected state governments towards private bodies that are unelected and unaccountable to the voting public" (Au & Ferrare, 2015, p. 4). Lipman (2011) notes this radical shift is the "triumph of market ideology," which is "coupled with an erosion of the idea that informed citizens should make decisions based on general welfare" (p. 13). Furthermore, Lipman (2011) notes,

> the shift from government by elected state bodies and a degree of democratic accountability to governance by experts and managers and decision making by judicial authority and executive order is central to neoliberal policy making… public-private partnerships, appointed managers, and publicly accountable bodies comprised of appointed state and corporate leaders make decisions about urban development, transportation, schools, and other public infrastructure using business rationales. In these arrangements, the state acts as an agent of capital. (p. 13)

A key outcome of shrinking the state under this neoliberal model is "the opening of new markets through the privatization of public goods and services" (Au & Ferrare, 2015, p. 5).

Fabricant and Fine (2013) specifically discuss the impacts on education, stating,

> In public education, we have witnessed the ascent of charter schools, virtual learning, market curricula development, and an expansive number of firms engaged in the measurement and assessment of teachers, with a host of entrepreneurs making large and small profits. More specifically, profit making extends from publishers capitalizing on the new standards-based testing curricula, to high-tech companies experimenting and testing their curricula interventions, to real estate operators leasing property at exorbitant fees, to

> alternative certification programs [like the Relay Graduate School; see Atkinson & Dotts, 2019], and finally for-profit schools. Each of these fragments, pieces of profit-making, are part of a new "gold rush" to capitalize $500 billion of public assets being redistributed away from neighborhood K–12 public schooling to the marketplace. (p. 25)

Another outcome is how neoliberal policies "reconfigure key aspects of education policy and practice," such that public education is now seen as an additional "competitive market where students, teachers, schools, and administrators are ranked against each other using high-stakes, standardized test scores as a primary metric of comparison" (Au & Ferrare, 2015, p.6). Unfortunately, this neoliberal model of schooling is endorsed by members on both sides of the aisle in Congress and has become reified as the means of school reform. In addition to neoliberal models, there has been a rise in right-wing conservatism resulting from a reaction to the social advances of the 1960s and the perceived failure of old conservatism. Next, I briefly address neoconservatism as an ideological influence on educational governance.

Neoconservatism

The amalgamation of both market-driven and culturally-driven ideologies—neoliberalism and neoconservatism—became the dominant rightist ideological platform countering the New Left as we exited the 1960s. A budding neoconservative ideological movement that "[drew] from and produce[d] a particular political culture and political subject" appeared to grab hold and dominate the narrative of the political Right (Brown, 2006, p. 697). Authors such as Fukuyama (2006), Thompson and Brook (2010), and Vaïse (2010) have written extensively about the history of neoconservatism, yet it is seldom discussed alongside neoliberalism. Buras and Apple (2008) discussed neoconservatism as a form of anti-utopianism meant to counter and correct the "assumed naïveté of leftist cultural and economic desires" and whose adherents have become a powerful force in domestic policy (p. 291; deMarrais et al., 2019). Buras (2008) described neoconservatism as a "rightest formation" consisting of multiple groups whose aim is a political restoration of nostalgic American ideals, whether real or imagined. Additionally, neoconservatism has been characterized by the "undermining [of] the limited, progressive gains of the past several decades" using tools such as "narratives of crisis, discourses of fear and instability, and nostalgic desires to restore cultural integrity and the foundations of 'American' [and Western] civilization (Buras, 2008, p. 3; see also Ball, 2012; deMarrais et al., 2019).

Although many conservatives argue against a strong state, neoconservative ideology relies on the support of a strong state utilizing its power to enforce traditional and conventional values and behaviors on its citizens (Atkinson, 2017; deMarrais et al., 2019). In other words, a strong state is acceptable as long as it forces the citizenry to adhere to traditional conservative canon. Interestingly, neoconservatives view market ideology as fundamental to American exceptionalism and value our market economy as sacrosanct. It is within this context—the blending of neoliberalism with the anchoring of neoconservatism to further a moral cause—that education policy, specifically, and schooling have faced its greatest challenge. These ideas emerge slowly but eventually reach critical mass. One example of these blending ideologies related to education reforms is present in the writings and speeches of Lewis F. Powell Jr., especially his memorandum decrying a war against the American free-enterprise system.

Pushing Back Against The New Left: The Powell Memorandum

At any point in the history of schooling, one can see sociocultural, political, and ideological motivations in education policy. However, pronounced changes began in the 1960s and accelerated in the 1970s as America was experiencing rapid changes and social upheaval. Conservatives of all types (political, cultural, religious, etc.) and powerful members of corporate America were threatened by sociocultural and political reforms espoused and implemented by the New Left, such as President Johnson's Great Society initiatives. Activism in the 1960s increased unionization and organized social justice initiatives challenging America's capitalist-market system, resulting in fears over declining rates of profit. America's economic elite became increasingly worried about a continuation of this trend and sought ways to combat the New Left's momentum. Conservatives organized against liberal socioeconomic and sociopolitical policies, which included strategies to undermine democratic participation, all while promoting these efforts as a form of American freedom of thought.

The United States witnessed a broad range of social, political, and economic changes at the end of the 1960s. The country was in the midst of the civil rights movement, with massive resistance to desegregation occurring in the southern states; the Vietnam conflict was raging; the feminist movement, the American Indian Movement (AIM), and fears of a communist wave still gripped the United States long after the Second Red Scare of the 1950s. President Johnson's Great Society initiatives caused great consternation among conservatives and business elite. As mentioned earlier in this chapter, by the early 1970s, "a new conservative establishment set a counter-movement in motion to replace the institutions and expunge the ideas of American liberalism" (Landay, 2002, "The Greatest Power Grab," para. 1), which dominated the social, political, and economic thought of the New Left.

As the 1970s began, Richard Nixon was elected president, ushering in a new conservative agenda, and "several high-profile conservatives saw the need for an institutionalized platform from which conservative ideas could make their way into policy discourse" (McDonald, 2013, p. 3) to counter various progressive policies. One of those conservatives was a southern corporate attorney, Lewis F. Powell Jr., who served on the Virginia Board of Education—a position he held from 1961 through 1969. In addition to his time on the Board of Education, Powell served on numerous corporate boards—up to 11 at one point. In a confidential memorandum written to his friend and neighbor Eugene B. Sydnor, Jr., who at that time was chair of the U.S. Chamber of Commerce's Education Committee, Powell urged the chamber to "mount a campaign to counter criticism of the free enterprise system in the schools and the news media" (Kerr, 2010, p. 103).

At the time Powell authored this memorandum, he was shocked by what he called an "attack on the American free enterprise system," not just from a few "extremists of the left" but also from "perfectly respectable elements of society" (Moyers, 2011, para. 10), including the media, politicians, and leading intellectuals:

> Powell imagined the Chamber of Commerce as a council of war. Since business executives had "little stomach for hard-nosed contest with their critics" and "little skill in effective intellectual and philosophical debate," they should create think tanks, legal foundations, and front groups of every stripe. These groups could, he said, be aligned into a united front through "careful long-range planning and implementation. . . consistency of action over an indefinite period of years, in the scale of financing available only through joint effort, and in the political power only through united action and united organizations." (Moyers, 2011, para. 11)

Leading up to the memorandum in 1971, Powell, a corporate attorney, wrote and gave numerous speeches expressing his opinions on the subject. This illuminates his ideological persuasion—a mixture of neoliberalism and neoconservatism—although he was regarded as a somewhat neutral justice during his Supreme Court tenure (Anderson, 1972, September 28 and 29; Blum, 2017). For instance, on July 15, 1970, Powell opened the 51st Annual Session of the Southern Industrial Relations Conference in Blue Mountain, North Carolina. His opening statements were titled *The Attack on*

American Institutions. Addressing the delegates, he stated, "You are the front line of the free enterprise system; also you are dedicated Americans who believe that our economic and political system – free American democracy—is the best ever conceived by man" and continued by warning them that American democracy "and the values it sustains are under broad and virulent attack," going so far as to claim concern for potential revolution (Powell, 1970c, p. 2).

Powell's (1970a) speech titled *An Education Program FOR America* exemplifies his ideology. Powell's speech was a response to a letter dated May 25, 1970, from Harrison Mann, a corporate attorney and friend of Powell. Powell and Mann had become concerned over the "growing role of the American Civil Liberties Union [ACLU], believing the ACLU was encouraging a "disruption in our national and state life" (Powell, 1970a; Grimsley, 1972). They believed the ACLU to have its roots in the Communist Party and was directly influencing the dialogue and instruction occurring on university campuses around the country. In the opening of the speech, Powell lamented the "anti-American syndrome evidenced by the unending barrage of criticism leveled by Americans against America itself, our institutions, our system of government, and upon the values which for centuries have sustained western civilization" (Powell, 1970a, p. 2). While although arguing that criticism is good for debate and that

> no rational person would wish to inhibit criticism or dissent . . . criticism can be destructive, extreme, irrational, and slanderous. If this type of criticism continues long enough, without a balance of constructive responses, it can tear down and destroy our most cherished institutions. (Powell, 1970a, p. 2)

Later in this speech, Powell listed many cherished institutions he felt were under indictment from the New Left, including the free-enterprise system—or free-market system, noting that "a significant part of this criticism comes from organizations and individuals who wish to destroy the American free enterprise democratic system" (Powell, 1970a, p. 3). Powell proposed founding an educational corporation called the Virginia Committee for America, whose purpose would be "to engage in educational activities as to our democratic system of government, the free enterprise system . . . , and the contrast between our system of freedom under law and totalitarianism" (Powell, 1970a, p. 7). This corporation promoted American exceptionalism and the rugged individualism promoted by the free-market economy and qualified for tax-deductible gifts and provided its purpose is solely educational, and it is operated consistently for that purpose (Powell, 1970a, p. 7). In many ways, the Virginia Committee for America was a forerunner for many of the philanthropic organizations and think tanks influencing educational policy today, such as the American Enterprise Institute, the Heritage Foundation, the American Legislative Exchange Council (ALEC), the Koch brothers, and many others (see deMarrais, 2006; deMarrais et al., 2019; Waterhouse, 2014).

There are two other speeches to note, one dated July 11, 1970 (given on July 15, 1970) and one dated November 17, 1970 (given as the convocation address to Longwood College), both of which are prior to Powell's famous memorandum. The July 1970 speech titled *The Attack on American Institutions* (Powell, 1970c) was referenced earlier in this section. The November 1970 speech is titled *The Ideological Assault on America* (Powell, 1970d). In this speech, Powell targeted leftist groups, radicals, and social justice organizations, among others, as threats to America. He viewed the college campuses as the base for this leftist revolutionary spirit. He stated:

> Lacking the traditional popular base of oppressed workers and peasants, the radicals who focus on the campus believe our society can be overthrown by new techniques. They understand that the levers of power—especially the means of influencing thought and emotion—are different in the modern world. They believe these levers can best be manipulated from the college campus, with a base of support among students, faculty, and other intellectuals. Their first

target, therefore, has been the major universities. (Powell, 1970d, p. 7)

Quoting from the *Washington Post* from an article dated March 14, 1968, Powell recalled a passage stating that "the New Leftists . . . regard the universities as the soft spot in a society they are trying to bring down" (1970d, p. 7). Powell's language here demonstrated his push against the New Left, arguing that American universities were the root of power for the political left, the conservative tag line that colleges and universities act as *liberal seminaries*.

Education Policy, Ideology, And The Legacy of Powell's Memorandum

The influence of the Powell memorandum, and its ideological anchoring in neoliberal and neoconservative thought, can be seen in the birth of organizations such as the Business Roundtable (founded in 1972) and the Philanthropy Roundtable (founded in 1987), in President Reagan administration's education policies (1980–1988), the publication of *A Nation At Risk* (1983), the work of groups such as the ALEC providing model bills, the growth of charters and school-choice propaganda in the 1990s, the *Citizens' United v. Federal Election Commission* (2010) Supreme Court case, and the continuing efforts of many organizations to promote the privatization and economization of education (Dayton & Lewis, 2019). Powell's memorandum was the beginning swell of the eventual ideological tidal wave of actors endeavoring to commercialize and economize education, tie education to the market, undermine traditional state-funded public education, and convince many to equate the free market with overall personal liberty. Socioculturally and politically motivated actors understand that individuals who hold power and influence to change educational policy and the curriculum taught in schools can significantly influence the next generation of leaders and society for decades to come. This has not been lost on the political right. What began in the 1960s and 1970s as a grassroots movement to battle the New Left, has led to one of the most damaging Supreme Court decisions in the January 2010 *Citizens' United v. Federal Election Commission* decision. This 5–4 split ruling provided corporations, philanthropic organizations, media, and many other associations and entities unfettered access to the political process, allowing ideologically driven actors with vast capital to influence and, at times, completely drive policy decisions at all levels of governance (*Citizens United v. Federal Election Commission*, 2010). With this ruling, corporate and philanthropic actors now had more leverage to advance educational policy reform measures, increasing the number of charter schools, advocating for vouchers and tax scholarships, and influencing fights over curriculum standards and even the textbooks utilized in classrooms. An example of the ideological struggle over curriculum can be seen in the documentary *The Revisionaries* (Thurman, 2012).

Apple (2006), Au and Ferrare (2015), deMarrais (2006), deMarrais et al. (2019), Fabricant and Fine (2012), Lubienski and Brewer (2019), Saltman (2012), and Tompkins-Stange (2016) are just a few of the educational theorists, scholars, and educational activists currently examining impacts on educational policy reforms by various philanthropic and corporate entities. The scholars named earlier have found that conservative philanthropic and corporate entities have influenced education in the United States in the following summarized ways:

1. Regressive tax policies and parallel systems such as charter schools are defunding traditional state-run public education.
2. Already-limited public funds are going to private companies to provide educational services such as testing services, test preparation services, textbook publishing, accreditation mandates, and increasing levels of administrative roles.

3. A continual push for charter schools, private-school voucher programs, tax scholarships, and so on have pulled students away from traditional state-level public education.

4. Disempowering teacher labor unions, decreasing criteria for teacher certification, and fostering a favorable climate for alternative teacher certification programs (e.g., Relay Graduate School, Teach for America, etc.)

5. Data-driven comparison models shape and redefine the goals, purposes, and aims of education in terms of competition, productivity, accountability, and economic growth.

6. A "narrowing of the purpose" of education- and educational-related issues to "that of solely meeting the needs of the business community and/or that of the economy" and devaluing "humanistic, civic, cultural, and environmental goals" found in educational practice (Au & Ferrare, 2015, p. 8)

7. Continual movement toward reliance on "democratically unaccountable" nongovernment agencies, philanthropic organizations (often considered nonprofits), and corporations (private entities) to guide and implement education policies

8. A continued marginalization of social and cultural foundations in institutions of higher education teacher preparation programs while pushing for more practitioner-based applied models and less on theory, often evaluated by outside reviewers such as edTPA, and meant to thwart critique.

Although most of the preceding points are specifically rooted in the "neoliberal thought collective," embedded within the curriculum is also a culturally conservative assumption that supporting free-market thinking and maintaining conservative values are patriotic duties.

Conclusion

Although Lewis Powell, Jr. did not have direct control over educational policy, other than his short stint on the Virginia Board of Education, he was highly influential in garnering the urgency of the political (conservative) right to attack public education and higher institutions to counter social and cultural reforms instigated by the New Left. His ideas regarding how education should support and defend the free-market economy and push back against more socialistic ways of engaging (e.g., regulations, higher corporate taxes, social programs, etc.) became rooted in the neoconservative and neoliberal movements extending from the 1960s and 1970s to the present. One only has to examine the continual push to align education to market rationalities, which is then emphasized by politically and culturally conservative-oriented philanthropic entities, corporations, and activists. I argue that Powell's memorandum to the U.S. Chamber of Commerce, while not specifically identified in educational policy legislation, was the catalyst and/or ammunition sparking the conservative revolution that swept the nation in the 1980s during the Reagan administration and continues to define educational policy, especially at the federal and state levels of governance.

References

Anderson, J. (1972, September 28). Powell's lesson to business aired. *The Washington Post.* https://vault.fbi.gov/lewis-f.-powell-jr/lewis-f.-powell-jr.-part-04-of-1

Anderson, J. (1972, September 29). FBI missed blueprint by Powell. *The Washington Post.* https://vault.fbi.gov/lewis-f.-powell-jr/lewis-f.-powell-jr.-part-04-of-1

Apple, M. W. (2006). *Educating the "right" way: Markets, standards, god, and inequality* (2nd ed.). Routledge.

Au, W., & Ferrare, J. J. (2015). *Mapping corporate education reform: Power and policy networks in the neoliberal state.* Routledge.

Atkinson, J. C. (2017). Countering the neos: Dewey and the democratic ethos in teacher education. *Democracy and Education, 25*(2), Article 2.

Atkinson, J. C., & Dotts, B. W. (2019). Impacting education through privatized graduate schools: Strategic fields, charter networks, and the relay graduate school of education. In T. J. Brewer & C. Lubienski (Eds.), *Becoming a teacher in an age of reform: Global lessons for teacher preparation and the teaching profession* (pp. 91–111). Teachers College Press.

Ball, S. J. (2012). *Global Education Inc.: New policy networks and the neo-liberal imaginary.* Routledge.

Blum, B. (2017, August 15). The right-wing legacy of Justice Lewis Powell and what it means for The Supreme Court today. *The Huffington Post.* https://www.huffpost.com/entry/the-rightwing-legacy-of-j_b_11521804

Brown, W. (2006). American nightmare: Neoliberalism, neoconservatism, and dedemocratization. *Political Theory, 34*(6), 690–714.

Brown, W. (2015). *Undoing the demos: Neoliberalism's stealth revolution.* Zone Books.

Buras, K. (2008). *Rightist multiculturalism: Core lessons on neoconservative school reform.* Routledge.

Buras, K., & Apple, M. (2008). Radical disenchantments: Neoconservatives and the disciplining of desire in an anti-utopian era. *Comparative Education, 44*(3), 291-304.

Citizens' United vs. Federal Elections Commission. 540 U.S. 93, 203–209 (2010).

Davies, W. (2014). Neoliberalism: A bibliographic review. *Theory, Culture, and Society, 31*(7–8), 309–317.

Dayton, J, & Lewis, J. B. (2019). Citizens United and the disuniting of the United States. In K. deMarrais, T. J. Brewer, B. Herron, J. C.

Atkinson, & J. B. Lewis, *Philanthropy, hidden strategy, and collective resistance* (pp. 115-137). Meyers Education Press.

deMarrais, K. (2006). "The have and the have mores": Fueling a conservative ideological war on public education (or tracking the money). *Educational Studies, 39*(3), 201–240.

deMarrais, K., Brewer, T. J., Herron, B., Atkinson, J. C., & Lewis, J. B. (2019). *Philanthropy, hidden strategy, and collective resistance: A primer for concerned educators*. Myers Education Press.

Down, B. (2009). Schooling, productivity, and the enterprising self: Beyond market values. *Critical Studies in Education*, *50*(1), 51–64.

Eagleton, T. (1991). *Ideology: An introduction*. Verso.

Fabricant, M., & Fine, M. (2012). *Charter schools and the corporate makeover of public education: What's at stake?* Teachers College Press.

Feldman, S. (2003). Values, ideology, and the structure of political attitudes. In D. O. Sears, L. Huddy, & R. Jervis (Eds.), *The Oxford handbook of political psychology* (pp. 477–508). Oxford University Press.

Fukuyama, F. (2006). *America at the crossroads: Democracy, power, and the neoconservative legacy*. Yale University Press.

Gee, J. P. (1996). *Social linguistics and literacies: Ideology in discourses* (2nd ed.). Routledge.

Gerring, J. (1997). Ideology: A definitional analysis. *Political Research Quarterly*, *50*(4), 957-994.

Grimsley, J. E. (1972, October 4). The Powell memo. *Richmond Times-Dispatch*, p. 18. https://vault.fbi.gov/lewis-f.-powell-jr/lewis-f.-powell-jr.-part-04-of-1

Harvey, D. (2004). The "new" imperialism. Accumulation by dispossession. *Socialist Register, 40*, 63–87.

Harvey, D. (2005). *A brief history of neoliberalism*. Oxford University Press.

Harvey, D. (2007). Neoliberalism as creative destruction. *The Annals of the American Academy of Political and Social Science, 610*(1), 22-44.

Hennes, E. P., Nam, H. H., Stern, C., & Jost, J. T. (2012). Not all ideologies are created equal: Epistemic, existential, and relational needs predict system-justifying attitudes. *Social Cognition*, *30*, 669–688.

Jennings, J. (2015). *Presidents, Congress, and the public schools: The politics of education reform*. Harvard University Press.

Jost, J. T. (2006). The end of the end of ideology. *American Psychologist, 61*(7), 651–670.

Jost, J. T., Fredrico, C. M., & Napier, J. L. (2009). Political ideology: Its structure, functions, and elective affinities. *Annual Review of Psychology, 60*, 307–337.

Jost, J. T., Kay, A. C., & Thorisdottir, H. (Eds.). (2009). *Social and psychological bases of ideology and system justification.* Oxford University Press.

Jost, J. T., Nosek, B. A., & Gosling, S. D. (2008). Ideology: Its resurgence in social, personality, and political psychology. *Perspectives on Psychological Science, 3*(2), 126–136.

Kerr, R. L. (2010). The attack memorandum and the First Amendment: Adjudicating a stronger voice for business in the marketplace of ideas. *Journal of Media Law and Ethics, 2*(3/4), 102–138.

Kovacs, P. (2008). Think tanks, foundations, and institutes. In D. Gabbard (Ed.) *Knowledge and power in the global economy: The effects of school reform in a neoliberal/neoconservative age* (pp. 229–238). Erlbaum.

Krauthammer, C. (2005, July/August). The neoconservative convergence. *Commentary*, p. 1. https://www.commentarymagazine.com/articles/the-neoconservative-convergence

Landay, J. (2002). *The attack memo that changed America*. Environmental Research Foundation. http://www.rachel.org/?q=en/node/3348

Lipman, P. (2011). *The new political economy of urban education: Neoliberalism, race and the right to the city.* Routledge.

Lubienski, C., & Brewer, T. J. (2019). *Learning to teach in an era of privatization: Global trends in teacher preparation.* Teachers College Press.

McClellan, D. (1995). *Ideology* (2nd ed.). University of Minnesota Press.

McDonald, L. (2013). In their own words: U.S. think tank "experts" and the framing of education policy debates. *Journal of Critical Education Policy, 11*(3), 1-28.

Mirowski, P. & Plehwe, D. (Eds.). (2015). *The road from Mont Pelerin: The making of the neoliberal thought collective.* Harvard University Press.

Moyers, B. (2011, November 2). How Wall Street occupied America: Why the rich keep getting richer and our democracy is getting poorer. *The Nation*. https://www.thenation.com/article/how-wall-street-occupied-america

Mullins, W. A. (1972). On the concept of ideology in political science. *American Political Science Review*, *66*(2), 498–510.

Powell, L. F. Jr. (1970a, May 28). *An education program FOR America*. The Lewis F. Powell Jr. Papers. Washington & Lee University School of Law, Lexington City, VA.

Powell, L. F. Jr. (1970b, June 30). *Political warfare*. The Lewis F. Powell Jr. Papers. Washington & Lee University School of Law, Lexington City, VA.

Powell, L. F. Jr. (1970c, July 11). *The attack on American institutions*. The Lewis F. Powell Jr. Papers. Washington & Lee University School of Law, Lexington City, VA.

Powell, L. F. Jr. (1970d, November 11). *The ideological assault on America*. The Lewis F. Powell, Jr. Papers. Washington & Lee University School of Law, Lexington City, VA.

Powell, L. F. Jr. (1971, August 23). *Attack on American free enterprise system*. The Lewis F. Powell Jr. Papers. Washington & Lee University School of Law, Lexington City, VA.

Saad-Filho, A. & Johnston, D. (2005). Introduction. In A. Saad-Filho & D. Johnston (Eds.), *Neoliberalism: A critical reader* (pp. 1–6). Pluto Press.

Saltman, K. (2018). *The politics of education: A critical introduction* (2nd ed.). Routledge.

Seybold, P. (2013). Radical legacies: Antonio Gramsci and contemporary American politics. *Humanity & Society*, *37*(4), 286–305.

Spring, J. (2011). *The politics of American education*. Routledge.

Thompson, C., & Brook, Y. (2010). *Neoconservatism: An obituary of an idea*. Paradigm Publishers.

Thorisdottir, H., Jost, J. T., & Kay, A. C. (2009). On the social and psychological bases of ideology and system justification. In J. C. Jost, A. C. Kay, & H. Thorisdottir (Eds.), *Social and psychological bases of ideology and system justification* (pp. 3–26). Oxford University Press.

Thurman, S. (Director). (2012). *The revisionaries* [Film]. Silver Lining Films; Magic Hour Entertainment; Naked Edge Films.

Tompkins-Stange, M. E. (2016). *Policy patrons: Philanthropy, education reform, and the politics of influence*. Harvard University Press.

United States. National Commission on Excellence in Education. (1983). *A nation at risk: The imperative for educational reform*. Washington, D.C: The National Commission on Excellence in Education.

Urban, W., Wagoner Jr., J. L., & Gaither, M. (2019). *American education: A history* (6th ed.). Routledge.

Vaïse, J. (2010). *Neoconservatism: The biography of a movement*. Harvard University Press.

Walpen, B. 2004. *Die offenen Feinde und ihre Gesellschaft: Eine hegemonietheoretische Studie zur Mont Pèlerin Society*. Hamburg: VSA

Waterhouse, B. C. (2014). *Lobbying America: The politics of business from Nixon to NAFTA*. Princeton University Press.

Chapter Three

LOCHNER'S REDEEMERS: HOW THE FEDERALIST SOCIETY AND THE INSTITUTE FOR JUSTICE IMPACT THE SCHOOL PRIVATIZATION MOVEMENT

Brian Dotts, *University of Georgia*

In the Judiciary Committee, we see the result over and over—meaningless committee hearings where nominees parrot empty words about applying law to fact and respecting precedent. Then, once confirmed and on the bench, those nominees deliver dependably for the partisan and corporate donors behind this Federalist Society operation.

—Sheldon Whitehouse, Rhode Island Senator Speech, Senate, Congressional Record, March 27, 2019

On October 6, 2018, the Senate voted 50–48 to confirm the lifetime appointment of Brett M. Kavanaugh to the U.S. Supreme Court after a combative confirmation battle made more contentious over sexual assault and sexual misconduct allegations against Kavanaugh by three women (Hauser, 2018). Six weeks later, the Federalist Society gave Kavanaugh a lengthy standing ovation during their annual convention in Washington, D.C. Kavanaugh had been active in the society since 1988 while a student at Yale Law School. Thoroughly cultivated in the Federalist Society's libertarian and conservative jurisprudence, the society played an active role in shepherding Kavanaugh's nomination and confirmation. The society also managed the nomination and confirmation process for Chief Justice John Roberts and Justices Samuel Alito and Neil Gorsuch. The late justice Antonin Scalia served as an advisor to the society from its establishment in 1982, and Justice Clarence Thomas has been actively involved in the organization for decades (Bowden, 2018; Grayer, 2018; Hollis-Brusky, 2015, pp. 155, 181n3; Toobin, 2017). Former and current members of the society include numerous federal judges and members of the legislative and the executive branches, illustrating the depth and breadth of the Federalist Society's influence in American politics today. The society's academic and deliberative functions are often praised and rarely develop criticism beyond differences of opinion, which are welcomed by the society.

This chapter begins with a brief history of the Federalist Society and the Institute for Justice (IJ), including their ideological influences. Thereafter, I provide an analysis of the conservative donors that fund their activities and the specific school-choice litigation agenda pursued by the IJ, which aligns with the Federalist Society's aversion to government programs and regulation generally and what it refers to as the government "monopoly" over public schooling specifically.[1] The Federalist Society and the IJ are only two organizations of a much larger epistemic network, but both organizations are significant actors in a decades-long battle to return constitutional jurisprudence to a pre–New Deal era.

The Federalist Society Today

The Federalist Society (n.d.-a), according to its website, "is a group of conservatives and libertarians interested in the current state of the legal order" (para. 2). The society

> is founded on the principles that the state exists to preserve freedom, that the separation of governmental powers is central to our Constitution, and it is emphatically the province and duty of the judiciary to say what the law is, not what it should be. (Federalist Society, n.d.-a, para. 2)

The latter assumption, of course, assumes the existence of a straightforward, explicitly clear Constitution. Furthermore, "the Society seeks both to promote an awareness of these principles and to further their application through its activities" (Federalist Society, n.d.-a, para. 2).

The Federalist Society's Student Division, according to its website, "includes more than 10,000 law students," and "the national office provides speakers and other assistance to" its 214 chapters "in organizing their lectures, debates, and educational activities" (Federalist Society, n.d.-b, para. 3). During "the 2017-2018 academic year . . . student chapters hosted 1,123 events, with a total attendance of about 63,395 students" (Federalist Society, n.d.-b, para. 3). The society's "Lawyers Division is comprised of over 65,000 legal professionals and others interested in current intellectual and practical developments in the law" with "active chapters in ninety cities," an "annual National Lawyers Convention, a Speakers Bureau for organizing lectures and debates, and 15 Practice Groups" (Federalist Society, n.d.-b, para. 5). The Federalist Society "established its Faculty Division in early 1999 with a conference that was attended by many of the rising stars in the legal academy" (Federalist Society, n.d.-b, para. 5). "The objective of the Faculty Division," according to the website, "is to provide events and other tools to help encourage constructive academic discourse. This encouragement will help foster the growth and development of rigorous traditional legal scholarship" (Federalist Society, n.d.-b, para. 5).

Senator Mitch McConnell, a member of the Federalist Society, has expedited the conservative turn in judicial appointments as the Senate's Majority Leader with the aim of "transform[ing] the federal judiciary," according to David Montgomery (2019). McConnell refers to this effort as his "judges project" (para. 7). Other members of the Federalist Society who acquired national attention include Leonard Leo, current executive vice president of the society; Don McGahn, former White House attorney for Donald Trump; Rod Rosenstein, former U.S. deputy attorney general; Matthew Whittaker, former acting attorney general; and Jeff Sessions, former U.S. attorney general during the Trump administration (Montgomery, 2019). William

Barr, the current U.S. attorney general, has also been involved in the society (*United States Senate Committee on the Judiciary, Questionnaire for Nominee to the Supreme Court*, 2018).

As Majority Leader, Mitch McConnell has expedited the nomination of many federal judges during the Trump administration, nearly 90% of whom have been proselytized in Federalist Society jurisprudence (Whitehouse, 2019). According to a recent NPR analysis of data from the Federal Judicial Center and the United States Courts, as of August 5, 2019, Trump has appointed 25% of current "federal appeals court judges" in 11 of the 13 circuits. The same data show that 78% of Trump's appointments are male, and 87% are White (Johnson, 2019). Based on my calculations, out of the 51 Trump appointments to the Circuit Courts of Appeal, eight of which are pending, 42 (82%) are affiliated with the Federalist Society. Trump has appointed 105 district court judges, 39 of which are affiliated with the Federalist Society (37%). Fifteen of his 49 pending appointments (31%) are affiliated with the Federalist Society.[2] Like most presidents before him, Trump exercises great influence in remaking federal appellate courts, which are well represented by members of the Federalist Society today.

As a conservative and libertarian advocacy group challenging established federal civil rights laws and affirmative action,[3] it is not surprising to find criticism directed toward the Federalist Society's states' rights agenda, which is harmful to people of color. As Lynn Adelman, U.S. district court judge in the Eastern District of Wisconsin explains,

> it is becoming clear . . . that the practical consequences of the conservatives' attachment to [states' rights] federalism are far from benign. For African Americans, particularly those living in states of the former Confederacy, the impact of federalist doctrine as implemented by the Supreme Court,

meaning the justices associated with the Federalist Society, "has been no less than devastating" (Adelman, 2018, para. 4). The kind of jurisprudence supported by the society and actualized through U.S.

Supreme Court decisions on "voting rights and healthcare," justified by "the guise of 'federalism'" has significantly weakened "hard-won progress toward racial justice," she concludes (Adelman, 2018, para. 1; see also Brennan Center for Justice, 2018). Adelman provides two important U.S. Supreme Court decisions to support her claims, including *Shelby County v. Holder* (2013) and *National Federation of Independent Business v. Sebelius* (2012). In the former case, the court's conservative majority annulled the portion of the 1965 Voting Rights Act intended to protect minority voting. In the latter case, the conservative majority found the Affordable Care Act's "inducement" for "states to participate in . . . Medicaid . . . expansion" unconstitutional (Adelman, 2018, para. 4). The court's majority justified its decisions in support of "states' rights" jurisprudence (Adelman, 2018). Of course, opposition to civil rights is not restricted to the judiciary. According to Sidney Blumenthal (2008), George W. Bush's Justice Department pushed out "60 percent of the professional staff" in its "civil rights division . . . and not a single discrimination case was filed" (Blumenthal, p. xi). In addition, several cabinet officials, Attorney General John D. Ashcroft, former solicitor general Ted Olson, and "five of the eleven lawyers in the White House Counsel's Office were members" of "or active participants" in the "Federalist Society" (as cited in Avery & McLaughlin, 2013, p. 11; Blumenthal, 2008, p. xix).

Despite the society's claim that it is a "nonpartisan organization," according to its current president and former executive director, Eugene Meyer, it is clearly a partisan—conservative and libertarian—advocacy group (Hollis-Brusky & Terbeek, 2019).[4] According to Sheldon Whitehouse, a Democratic senator from Rhode Island, although he does not oppose the society's academic and deliberative functions, he takes exception to its excessive partisanship and advocacy. During a March 27, 2019, Senate hearing, Whitehouse declared,

> The Society is the nerve center for a complicated apparatus that does not care much about conservative principles like judicial restraint, or originalism, or textualism. [The] Society is the vehicle for powerful interests, which seek not to

> simply "reorder" the judiciary, but to acquire control of the judiciary to benefit their interests. This [function of the] Federalist Society understands the fundamental power of the federal judiciary to rig the system in favor of its donor interests . . . and as the Kavanaugh confirmation so clearly illustrated, it is willing to go to drastic lengths to secure that power. ("The Federalist Society," 2019, paras. 7–8)

Anyone familiar with constitutional jurisprudence today easily recognizes the fact that judicial activism has transcended ideological factions on the court. As shown in the following, the Federalist Society focuses on two comprehensive goals: (1) to increase corporate and business liberties, what I refer to as their selective libertarianism, and (2) to scale back government regulation to the extent necessary to achieve the first goal.

Federalist Society Origins

The Federalist Society for Law and Public Policy Studies was established in 1982 "by a small group of conservative and libertarian law students at Yale Law School and the University of Chicago Law School" as "an alternative to the perceived liberal orthodoxy that dominated . . . law school curriculum, the professoriate, and most legal institutions at the time," according to Amanda Hollis-Brusky (2015, p. 1). Three of the society's principal founders were Steven Calabresi and Lee Liberman Otis, both of whom "had worked on the Reagan campaign before" entering "law school" (Hollis-Brusky, 2015, p. 1, 16), as well as David McIntosh, a former member of the House of Representatives from Indiana (Avery & McLaughlin, 2013, p. 1). McIntosh served as assistant to former attorney general Edwin Meese during the Reagan administration and is the current president of the Club for Growth, a free-enterprise advocacy group (The Club for Growth, n.d.). With the help of ideologically friendly public interest law firms, the Federalist Society's libertarian and conservative agenda "challenge[s] government regulation of the economy," contests "affirmative action," works to "invalidate laws providing access to the courts by aggrieved workers, consumers, and environmentalists," fights to "expand state support for religious institutions and programs," resists "marriage equality," and labors to restrict abortion rights for women, "defend[s] state's [*sic*] rights," and acts to "increase presidential power," according to Michael Avery and Danielle McLaughlin (2013, pp. 2–3). The society currently enjoys a total membership of approximately 70,000 (Montgomery, 2019), made up largely from law school students and faculty, practicing lawyers, judges, chief executive officers, conservative philanthropists, and members of conservative advocacy groups.

The motives that structure the ideological framework of the Federalist Society predate Reagan and the society's founding. The motivations behind the ideology are exemplified in Richard S. Weaver's 1948 publication *Ideas Have Consequences* and in the 1905 Supreme Court case *Lochner v. New York* (overturned in 1937 in *West Coast Hotel Company. v. Parrish*; Hollis-Brusky, 2015, p. 1; see also Teles, 2008), viewed nostalgically by members who long for an unregulated capitalist economy and an absolute constitutional right to contract. In fact, I find the Federalist Society's libertarian focus to be highly selective in application by its prioritizing business and corporate liberties over other liberties. This ideological inconsistency is easily detectible in their litigation strategies. *Lochner*, for example, is celebrated by the society for rejecting state regulations intended to protect workers' (and, concomitantly, consumers') health and safety while safeguarding an employer's unconditional right to contract with employees, even when doing so results in common standards of exploitation and abuse, which is discussed in more detail later.

Ideas Have Consequences

Richard Weaver's (1948) *Ideas Have Consequences* resonates with Leo Strauss's neoconservatism or Allan Bloom's cultural ethnocentrism of Western philosophy and culture. Throughout

Ideas, Weaver sounds resentful and distraught with modernity, with Franklin Delano Roosevelt's New Deal programs, progressive education reforms, and relativism. Weaver begins his polemic by declaring that "modern man [is] an idiot," and "our present state may be a fallen state" (p. 1). He goes on by demurring the "attack upon universals [absolutism]" and "the defeat of logical realism" (Weaver, 1948, p. 3), the belief that facts exist outside human experience, much like Plato's theory of the Forms. "With the denial of objective truth," according to Weaver, "there is no escape from the relativism of 'man [as] the measure of all things'" (p. 4). Longing for "metaphysical certitude," Weaver asks, "what relief will this not bring to those made seasick by the truth-denying doctrines of the relativists!" (p. 131). Weaver opposed the idea of equality, believing that some people are better than others in a variety of ways, and he believed that modern society undermined his ideals by prioritizing democracy and a social welfare state.

In the chapter titled "Distinction and Hierarchy," Weaver (1948) illustrates his Platonic influence when he reflects on the American Constitution, concluding "that democracy cannot exist without aristocracy" and that aristocratic leadership "must be constantly recruited from democracy" (p. 19) with no consideration of how that leadership is subjectively chosen. Moreover, Weaver argues, "we have failed to provide against corruption of the system of recruitment by equalitarian dogma and the allurements of materialism," both of which are a result of education in America that "neither encourages reflection nor inspires a reverence for the good" (p. 49). This "good," of course, is circumscribed by Weaverian ethnocentrism. It is not surprising, therefore, that Weaver includes a chapter titled "The Spoiled-Child Psychology," which he views as the foundation of mid-20th-century public education. "The spoiled child has not been made to see the relationship between effort and reward," he declares (Weaver, 1948, p. 113). Rather, "the child expects everything to be given to him, and he abuse[s] those who do not gratify him" (Weaver, 1948, p. 113). Critical of John Dewey's educational philosophy, Weaver (2000) condemns "progressive education," for its focus on "pragmatism, optimism and romanticism about the nature of man, [its] rejection of . . . enduring truth, and [its] politics based upon an expected triumph of collectivism," all of which "represents a very radical departure from the traditional Judaic-Christian-classical concepts of man and the world and the nature of knowledge" (pp. 490–491), he protests. Weaver criticizes state-controlled education, "the final form of which" was headed toward a centralized "federal educational system directed out of Washington and used to instill . . . collectivist political notions" in children (p. 192). Likewise, Weaver expresses strong disdain toward the justices on the Supreme Court for having developed a progressive jurisprudence during the New Deal that he describes as "the crisis of our times" (pp. 99–100).[5]

Perhaps typical of reactionaries generally, Weaver (1948) criticizes a changing America initiated by progressive responses to the Great Depression and school reforms heralded by progressives that emerged during his lifetime. In hindsight, it is not surprising that an absolutist like Weaver would criticize the multifarious and relativistic progressive schools of thought transpiring among political, economic, and educational voices at the time. For Weaver, America did not need progressive reform; rather, it needed to return to an era that appreciated aristocratic political and corporate leadership untethered by needless government regulations. With much the same gusto that Weaver expressed toward corporate and elite rule, "much of the Federalist Society's influence," according to Montgomery (2019), "comes not from its very public Washington victories but from its behind-the-scenes, grass-roots ability to shift the law at the idea level, even the cultural level" (para. 9). A pillar of this cultural support can be found in an early 20th-century Supreme Court decision.

Lochner v. New York *and Selective Libertarianism*

The 1905 *Lochner* decision offers a conservative beacon to modern-day members of the Federalist Society (and the IJ). They nostalgically look back to a moment in Supreme Court history when government's (in this case, the state of New York's) regulatory restrictions on business activity were spurned and the liberty of contract triumphed. According to the *Lochner* decision, New York violated the liberty of contract when it prohibited bakers from working their employees more than 10 hours a day and more than 60 hours a week. At issue was New York's 1895 Bakeshop Act (see Syllabus in *Lochner v. New York*, 198 U.S. 45 (1905), which was intended to protect the health and safety of employees and, thus, public health. In other words, individuals who worked in bakeries often suffered from the excessive inhalation of "flour and sugar particles and excess heat," from ovens which increased the possibility for unsanitary conditions, unsanitary consumer goods, and workplace accidents (Bernstein, 2011, p. 31). The liberty of contract established in *Lochner* combined with the court's rejection of class legislation, as it was called at the time, inspired free-market advocates while forsaking the working class. "In the three decades following *Lochner*," according to Avery and McLaughlin (2013), "the Supreme Court . . . struck down nearly two hundred regulations on economic due process grounds" (p. 55).[6]

This began to change, however, when *Lochner* was overturned by a progressive court during Franklin Roosevelt's administration. Not one justice from the *Lochner* era remained on the court when *Lochner* was overturned in 1937 in *West Coast Hotel Company v. Parrish*. The majority in this case concluded that government "restraint or regulation" supersedes the liberty to contract "if reasonable in relation to its subject and if adopted for the protection of the community against evils menacing the health, safety, morals and welfare of the people" (see Syllabus in *West Coast Hotel Co. v. Parrish*, 300 U.S. 379 (1937). Paraphrasing Steven Teles's (2008) research, Amanda Hollis-Brusky (2015) explains that the Federalist Society "sought to build a counter-network that would" (p. 166) revive *Lochner*-era jurisprudence. Longing for *Lochner*'s resurrection, the Federalist Society highlights its selective prioritization of business libertarianism—the liberty of contract, in particular—even when state legislation attempts to protect the health and safety of workers who are dependent on the whims of their employers.

This selective libertarian view favors employers and supports the presumption that employees enjoy liberty only when such liberty does not conflict with employers' entrepreneurial freedoms. For instance, in this view, the liberty of employees consists of their freedom to either comply with their employer's lawful demands or to quit and seek employment elsewhere. Although workers are free to accept or reject such employment, *Lochner* gave employers the ability—or, rather, a right protected by law—to use contracts as justification for worker exploitation. The extent to which the liberty of contract informs and serves as a fundamental pillar for libertarian jurisprudence today may be best understood in Devin Watkins's (2016) blog post, which is located on the Federalist Society's website. A legal associate in the Cato Institute's Center for Constitutional Studies, Watkins (2016) argues that "our Constitution is in many ways a contract between us—the people—and those we *hire* [emphasis added] to run the government on our behalf" (para. 9). In an atypical strategy, Watkins infuses his natural law argument with agency law, which is an area of law related to commercial or contractual dealings between individual parties thereby imposing an instrumental, means-end rationalization of the Constitution that validates the society's prioritization of contractual liberty and natural rights as they apply to corporations. Such an absolutist commitment to contractual liberty is at odds with modern protections for public health and safety often identified in jurisprudence as a compelling government interest. Yet the influence of *Lochner* can be seen in a variety of contemporary cases decided by the court's conservative majority.

Daniel J. H. Greenwood (2017) argues that in the 2014 *Burwell v. Hobby Lobby Stores* case that challenged the Affordable Care Act's requirement that health insurance plans cover contraceptives in contradistinction to the 1993 *Freedom Restoration Act*, the court's "majority simply assumes away the conflict at the core of the case" (p. 216) namely, "the conflict between agency law's authoritarian grant to the master, and a free citizenry's demand for personal agency" (p. 216). In other words, Greenwood asserts that "the common law of agency granted masters (here, the corporation) the authority to direct servants (here, the employees) and required servants to accept those directions" (p. 216). However, "the feudal age is over," and "agency law in its full ancient form is untenable [today]," he concludes (Greenwood, 2017, p. 216). Greenwood traces the widely accepted view that corporations are human beings to the "unarticulated—and ultimately indefensible—view that business corporations are entitled to comity as if they were semi-sovereign foreign bodies within our polity: 'wormes in the entrayles' of the state, in Hobbes's memorable description" (p. 166). Conservatives on the Court who support this view of corporate personhood, as evidenced in decisions like *Citizens United* (2010), according to Greenwood (2017),

> "atavistically recapitulate . . . feudal doctrines limiting the sovereign's authority over the medieval corporations of Aristocracy, Church, guilds, universities, and cities, as if business corporations were fundamental units of our polity or foreign states we must respect to avoid war" (p. 166). [7]

Greenwood concludes that *Citizens United* redeemed *Lochner* in at least one important sense; namely,

> Lochner lives when the Court holds that laissez-faire free-speech principles require that we allow corporations to use corporate funds to influence tastes or politics so as to generate more corporate funds or to refuse to disclose information that citizens or consumers seek to know in order to control corporate officials. (p. 181)

Greenwood describes in great detail what I refer to throughout this chapter as a selective libertarian perspective favoring business or corporate liberty vis-à-vis workers. It is largely this corporate liberty that the Federalist Society (and the IJ) prioritizes, despite its occasional disagreements.[8]

The conservative members of the court were inculcated in the libertarian jurisprudence that serves as a pillar of the Federalist Society's primary principles, and this majority has consistently supported corporate liberty by endowing corporations with natural human rights. Cloaking corporations with such language expanded the rights of corporations to contract in *Lochner* by extending additional constitutional rights to corporations. These include free speech and the freedom to worship. This reconfiguration of citizenship grants great power to corporations that can, in turn, ignore or challenge government regulations in order to protect First Amendment freedoms. In other words, the conservative majority on the court today has gone beyond protecting a corporation's liberty to contract by imbuing corporations with natural rights.

Corporations may now reject or challenge government regulation that interferes with the religious beliefs (*Hobby Lobby*) or free speech rights (*Citizens United*) of corporate owners even when doing so disadvantages workers and voters. Likewise, the Federalist Society and "the dominant strain of conservative legal thought for the last half-century," according to Brian Beutler (2015), "has largely been shaped by the right's backlash to the social revolution stemming from the 1960s and the Warren and Burger Courts' use of the Constitution to further progressive ends like desegregation and access to abortion" (para. 19). The contemporary court has not only swung the pendulum back toward *Lochner*; it has also extended the periphery beyond *Lochner*.

It should not go unnoticed that opposition to a woman's right to choose, which appears to be the overwhelming position of the Federalist Society and the IJ, is considered by many to be antithetical to libertarian ideology, illustrating the inconsistency between their libertarian and conservative ideals. Another important decision was decided in 2015 in *Obergefell v. Hodges* when liberals on the court were joined by Justice Anthony Kennedy in declaring same-sex marriage a constitutional right protected by the Fourteenth Amendment's Equal Protection Clause. On the other hand, three of the four dissenting justices who were inculcated by the

Federalist Society's selective libertarianism chose to step into their conservative roles when making their decisions in this case. For instance, Justice Scalia (2015), an original member of the Federalist Society, explained his dissent by prioritizing states' rights over and above the protection of equal liberty as follows:

> The Constitution places some constraints on self-rule—constraints adopted by the People themselves when they ratified the Constitution and its Amendments. Forbidden are laws "impairing the Obligation of Contracts," denying "Full Faith and Credit" to the "public Acts" of other States, prohibiting the free exercise of religion, abridging the freedom of speech, infringing the right to keep and bear arms, authorizing unreasonable searches and seizures, and so forth. Aside from these limitations, those powers "reserved to the States respectively, or to the people" can be exercised as the States or the People desire. (para. 3)

Dissenters in the *Obergefell* case show an example of libertarianism and conservatism in conflict. When confronted with a liberty they oppose, they shift from a libertarian to a conservative ideological stance. A right to marry, including marriage licenses, is not viewed in the lexicon of contract rights. Rather, they are constructed through the prism of states' rights. This jurisprudence tethers liberty to the dictates of each individual state thereby circumscribing libertarian ideology. They generally view corporate and business interests through a libertarian lens while deeming other individual liberties through a conservative lens. In order to circumvent this inconsistency, they appeal to states' rights arguments when doing so protects conservative, as opposed to libertarian principles.

Although the Federalist Society does not litigate cases, its goals overlap numerous other organizations. Political scientists refer to the network of institutions of which the Federalist Society is a part as a "political epistemic community," according to Amanda Hollis-Brusky (2015). She defines an epistemic community as "an interconnected network of experts with policy-relevant knowledge who share certain beliefs and work to actively transmit and translate those beliefs into policy" (p. 10). The Federalist Society grooms its members to adopt libertarian and conservative interpretations of the Constitution, preparing them for positions in the private sector, the federal courts, and work in public interest law firms. Steven Teles (2008) cites a report to the Scaife Foundation written by Michael Horowitz (often referred to as the Horowitz Report) that summoned "a conservative legal movement" that "needed to stretch beyond the courts to the institutions that supported legal activism and generated movement reputations and intellectual distinction," including "the Federalist Society" (p. 68). According to Teles, "conservatives had to adapt to the regime they sought to dismantle" (p. 68). It appears that the Horowitz Report had the same effect in igniting a legal conservative networking movement in the same way that the 1973 Powell Memo initiated the neoliberal crusade. However, the Federalist Society does not litigate cases. Public interest law firms like the IJ have taken on this useful responsibility.

The Federalist Society lists seven projects on its website. The first is its Article I Initiative, which is intended to teach its members about the "powers and responsibilities for [*sic*] Congress," and to critique how this institution has strayed from its founding principles. As of the writing of this chapter, this project's webpage includes videos, podcasts, and blogs related to the Electoral College, the administrative state, "Litigation to Overturn the Administrative State," and "Executive Power in the Trump Era." The society's Regulatory Transparency Project critiques "the benefits and costs of federal, state, and local regulatory policies" (Project initiatives may be accessed through the following link: https://fedsoc.org/projects). The society's Global Governance Watch

> is designed to raise awareness about global governance trends and developments, to monitor how the work of transnational organizations influence domestic policies and outcomes . . . transparency and accountability within the United Nations,

> related intergovernmental organizations, and other non-state actors. (https://www.globalgovernancewatch.org/about/

Its State Attorney General Guide (https://stateags.com/) is a database providing ideological and contact information for each of the country's 50 state attorneys general. The State Courts Guide provides similar information as well as an interactive map explaining how each state selects its judges. The society's Pro Bono Project focuses on "the cause of liberty and the rule of law" (https://fedsoc.org/probono) when matching lawyers with potential clients throughout the country. Their clients are overwhelmingly small business owners frustrated with local or state regulations. The society's No. 86 Project offers 86 courses on the *Federalist Papers*, one for each paper and an introductory video. This "project provides different perspectives on key concepts and cases throughout the law school curriculum" intended to "challenge . . . thinking" (https://fedsoc.org/no86). The Federalist Society's official journal is the *Harvard Journal of Law & Public Policy*. Notable alumni include Justice Neil Gorsuch; Senators Ted Cruz and Tom Cotton; five Circuit Court of Appeals judges; former Central Intelligence Agency director and current Secretary of State Michael Pompeo; and David Frum, senior editor of *The Atlantic*.

The Federalist Society network is large and includes a number of conservative think tanks, public interest law firms, advocacy groups, philanthropies, and elected government officials and appointed federal judges, as detailed in Table 3.1. Well-known federal representatives include Richard Cheney; Orrin G. Hatch; John Ashcroft; Samuel Alito, Jr.; Robert Bork; Neil Gorsuch; Brett Kavanaugh; John Roberts; Antonin Scalia; Clarence Thomas; Steven G. Calabresi; and Kenneth Starr.

Table 3.1
Federalist Society Network

Conservative Think Tanks	Public Interest Law Firms	Advocacy Groups	Sample of Conservative Philanthropies[1]
Heritage Foundation	Institute for Justice	American Federation for Children	John M. Olin Foundation
Hoover Institution	Pacific Legal Foundation	Focus on the Family	Lynde and Harry Bradley Foundation
Goldwater Institute	Small Business Legal Center	National Federation of Independent Businesses	Sarah Scaife Foundation
American Enterprise Institute	Center for Individual Rights	Becket Fund for Religious Liberty	Claude R. Lambe Charitable Foundation (Koch family)
Hudson Institute	Americans United for Life (anti-abortion focus)	EdChoice (formerly the Friedman Foundation for Educational Choice)	Charles G. Koch Charitable Foundation (Koch family)
Center for Equal Opportunity	Center for Individual Freedom (Founded by former Tobacco Industry Executives)	The Heartland Institute	DeVos Urban Leadership Initiative (formerly the Richard and Helen DeVos Foundation)
American Civil Rights Institute		Summit Power Group (opposed to environmental regulations and headed by the Christian Right)	National Philanthropic Trust
Georgetown University Law Center		Committee for Justice	The Rosenkranz Foundation, Inc.
		Norton Regulatory Strategies	Searle Freedom Trust
Cato Institute		Faith and Freedom Coalition (Ralph Reed, Jr. is president)	David H. Koch Charitable Foundation
Manhattan Institute for Policy Research		American Center for Law and Justice (founder is Pat Robertson, who also founded the Christian Coalition, Christian Broadcasting Network, and International Family Entertainment)	Hickory Foundation
			Searle Freedom Trust
			Ed Uihlein Family Foundation
			John Templeton Foundation
		Independent Women's Forum	Mercer Family Foundation
		U.S. Chamber of Commerce	National Christian Charitable Foundation Inc.

[1] The number of conservative philanthropies donating to the Federalist Society is too numerous to list. Therefore, this list includes a selection of the society's largest donors over the past 4 years. This information was obtained from the Foundation Directory Online (2019).

Yet, although most members of the Federalist Society are lawyers, judges, and law school students who have been immersed in business and corporate libertarianism, the Federalist Society does not try cases, nor does it serve as a public interest law firm battling progressives in the courts to protect the liberty of contact or other libertarian business interests. Such like-minded pursuits are the responsibility of a number of other institutions including, but not limited to, the IJ, which is one of the most active organizations pursuing libertarian business and individual libertarian interests when the latter aligns with the interests of the former. This unbalanced libertarian view is similarly reflected in the inequitable protection of business owners' liberties in relation to their employees in *Lochner*.

Funding The Federalist Society

The Federalist Society has enjoyed funding from numerous conservative groups and philanthropies (too many to list here). A database search of the Candid (2020) (formerly known as the Online Foundation Directory) illustrates the millions of dollars given to the Federalist Society by conservative philanthropies. "Between 2014 and 2017," according to a *Washington Post* analysis, the Federalist Society's executive director, Leonard Leo, and others "collected more than $250 million in . . . donations . . . known as 'dark money,'" whose donors remain anonymous (O'Harrow Jr. and Boburg, 2019, para. 8). As O'Harrow and Boburg further assert, "the groups in Leo's network often work in concert and are linked to Leo and one another by finances, shared board members, phone numbers, addresses, back-office support and other operational details" (para. 9). Leo considers himself as "engaged in the battle of ideas" (O'Harrow & Boburg, 2019). With the same diligence sought by Richard Weaver (mentioned earlier), Leonard Leo knows that ideas have consequences, especially when they are sanctioned by the nation's highest court. Jeffrey Toobin (2017) has described this epistemic network as a "conservative pipeline to the Supreme Court."

Total funding of the Federalist Society from 1985 through 2019, including dark money from the Donors Trust and the Donors Capital Fund, according to the Foundation Center's (2019) records (2003–2019) totals $55,957,327 (Candid, 2020) and Conservativetransparency.org (2019) (1985–2002) (accessed July 2, 2019) totals: $60,542,550.[9] Aligned with their libertarian beliefs, the Koch brothers are among the largest contributors to the Donors Trust, followed by the Lynde and Bradley Foundation's direct donations to the Federalist Society (Whitehouse, 2019). The Mercer family is also a large contributor to the society, although not listed in Table 3.1, giving about $6 million as of 2019, according to Debra Cassens Weiss (2019). The Mercer family gave millions of dollars to support Breitbart News and its former editor, Steve Bannon, according to *Deutsche Welle* (Janjevic, 2018), a German-based international news organization. Jane Mayer (2017), from *The New Yorker*, reports that Robert Mercer, a hedge-fund manager, not only helped bankroll Donald Trump's presidential campaign; he also "funded an array of political projects [many through his foundation] that helped pave the way for Trump's rise" (para. 2). In addition, she describes Mercer as a denier of climate change, a libertarian, and critical of the Republican establishment for its corruption and for "ruin[ing] the country" (Mayer, 2017). Mercer's daughter, Rebekah, runs the foundation, and she gave "millions of dollars to interconnected nonprofit groups, several of which played crucial roles in propagating attacks on Hillary Clinton" (Mayer, 2017, para. 21). Moreover, "by 2015, the most recent year for which federal tax records [were] available" to Mayer, "the foundation had grown into a $24.5-million operation that gave large sums to ultraconservative organizations" (para. 21), including the Federalist Society as mentioned earlier. Christopher Ruddy, who owns "the conservative outlet Newsmax" and who knows Rebekah Mercer, told Mayer, "She is the First Lady of the alt-right" (para. 45). He explained that Rebekah is "respected in conservative circles, and clearly Trump has embraced her in a big way" (Mayer, 2017, para. 43), Mayer explains that "Rebekah Mercer is on the board of the Moving Picture Institute, a conservative group devoted to countering Hollywood liberalism with original online entertainment" (para. 69), which is akin to the Federalist Society's relentless attempts to undermine what it views as the previous dominance of liberal jurisprudence and liberal-leaning law schools. In what will sound very familiar to Richard Weaver's ideas mentioned earlier, Mayer quotes a *Wall Street Journal* article wherein David Magerman, "a senior employee at Renaissance Technologies," Mercer's company, "said that Mercer wants the U.S. government to be 'shrunk down to the size of a pinhead'" (para. 16). According to Mayer, "several former colleagues of Mercer's said that his views are akin to objectivism, the philosophy of Ayn Rand" (para. 16). For instance, "Magerman told me," Mayer explains, that "Bob believes . . . human beings have no inherent value other than how much money they make" (para. 16). However, "if someone is on welfare they have negative value" (Mayer, 2017, para. 16), according to Mercer's thinking. "If he earns a thousand times more than a schoolteacher [sic], then he's a thousand times more valuable" (Mayer, 2017, para. 16). Magerman is quoted by Mayer as adding, "[Mercer] thinks society is upside down—that government helps the weak people get strong, and makes the strong people weak by taking their money away, through taxes" (para. 16).

Origins of The IJ

Self-proclaimed as "the National Law Firm for Liberty," the Institute for Justice (n.d.-a) was established as a public interest law firm in 1991 by William (Chip) Mellor and Clint Bolick, both former members of the Reagan administration, according to Brian Beutler (2015), "with $350,000 a year in seed money from the oil and gas magnate Charles Koch" (p. 40). William Mellor served as the IJ's president and general counsel from 1991 to 2015. Mellor describes his work as protecting "individual rights." He explains in his brief biography that "he grew IJ from a five-person startup into the National Law Firm for Liberty with a staff of nearly 100, including over 40 attorneys, and an annual budget of $20 million" (Institute for Justice, n.d.-d, para. 2). Headquartered in Arlington, Virginia,

IJ has offices in Arizona, Florida, Illinois, Minnesota, Texas, and Washington state. Mellor highlights the Supreme Court's 2002 decision, *Zelman v. Simmons-Harris,* which upheld a Cleveland, Ohio, voucher program, and *Arizona Christian School Tuition Organization v. Winn* (2011), whereby the Supreme Court upheld Arizona's scholarship tax credit program (Institute for Justice, n.d.-d).

Mellor refers to a co-authored book with Robert Levy (the Cato Institute) titled *The Dirty Dozen: How Twelve Supreme Court Cases Radically Expanded Government and Eroded Freedom* (2008). Half of the landmark decisions known as the "dirty dozen" were decided during the New Deal's Progressive Era, and Mellor highlights how they infringed on economic liberties. Deceptively, he refers to these as "individual liberties," giving the perception that they transcend corporate and business liberties. Other cases in Levy and Mellor's list of "terrible decisions" include *Grutter v. Bollinger* (2003), wherein the court upheld the use of race as one of many variables that can be utilized in college admissions. *Roe v. Wade* (1973) is included in the book's postscript because the right to an abortion should be left to individual states, they argue. Other decisions are criticized for the court's upholding a prohibition against double-barrel sawed-off shotguns (*United States v. Miller*, 1939) and campaign finance regulations (*McConnell v. Federal Election Commission*, 2003; Levy & Mellor, 2008). Although members of this political epistemic community sometimes disagree, their disagreement appears to be limited to the inherent conflicts one would expect between groups trying to balance the inevitable inconsistencies between libertarian and conservative ideologies. In other words, the nearly unlimited freedom supported by libertarians can easily clash with an ideology that also seeks to regulate the freedom of individual lifestyles. Nevertheless, the IJ's traditional libertarianism appears to prioritize corporate and entrepreneurial liberties.

Mellor also launched the IJ's Clinic on Entrepreneurship at the University of Chicago in 1998 and the IJ's Center for Judicial Engagement in 2011 (Institute for Justice, n.d.-d). The Clinic on

Entrepreneurship and Center for Engagement missions underscore the IJ's selective libertarianism intended to protect the rights of businesses and corporations. The Clinic on Entrepreneurship, for example, touts its accomplishments (on or before 2013) as having "represented over 15 small businesses last year," including "a painting service, a toy manufacturer, a children's language class provider, a tax preparation service, and a tour guide business" (University of Chicago Law School, 2013, para. 1). Moreover, this clinic consists of "student teams" who

> assisted these businesses and others with their transactional legal needs—setting up business entities, drafting and negotiating contracts and commercial leases, securing intellectual property protections, and navigating city and state licensing laws—so that the business owners could focus on growing their enterprises. (University of Chicago Law School, 2013, para. 1)

The IJ's Center for Judicial Engagement, while promoting freedom abstractly on its website's home page, focuses its commitment to protecting entrepreneurial liberties, primarily for small business owners and startups. Its website home page features three court cases, which include *Florida ex rel. Attorney General v. US Dept. of Health and Human Services* (2011), subsequently identified as *National Federation of Independent Business v. Sebelius* (2012); *Edwards v. District of Columbia* (2014); and a U.S. Court of Appeals case, *St. Joseph Abbey v. Castille* (2013), which involved retail casket sales in Louisiana (Institute for Justice, n.d.-c). The first case involved challenges to the Patient Protection and Affordable Care Act of 2010, otherwise known as Obamacare, by the states of Florida, South Carolina, Nebraska, Texas, and Utah challenging the law's expansion of Medicaid and individual mandate as unconstitutional.[10] The 2014 *Edwards* case challenged a local law unfairly regulating a Segway tour business in Washington, D.C. The IJ litigated the *Edwards* and *St. Joseph Abbey* cases but merely declared support for the multistate litigation against the U.S. Department of Health and Human Services. The courts in all three cases favored the IJ's legal interpretations with the exception of the Obamacare provision related to Medicaid expansion.

The co-founder of the Institute for Justice is Clint Bolick, who currently serves as an associate justice of Arizona's Supreme Court. Previously, he served as a research fellow at the Hoover Institute, a think tank promoting economic freedom, and vice president of litigation at the Goldwater Institute, another think tank devoted to libertarian and conservative causes where he was responsible for litigating against government regulation and specializing in school choice cases (Alexander, 2014). In an opinion piece he authored for the Federalist Society's *Harvard Journal of Law & Public Policy*, Bolick (2017) referred to America's "educational system [as] a national catastrophe" (p. 17) while praising the Khan Academy's Internet school and charter schools. "Thousands if not millions of kids, and for that matter, adults, have learned through the Khan Academy" (Bolick, 2017, pp. 17–18). The Khan Academy is well funded by wealthy donors, with philanthropic donations to the Khan Academy from 2010 through 2018 totaling $86,048,633. According to data obtained from the Candid (2020) some of the Khan Academy's largest donations come from the Bill and Melinda Gates Foundation and the Silicon Valley Community Foundation Bolick declares, "We have charter schools that are absolutely eye-popping in their success, not just for high-performing students but for low-income kids as well" (2017, pp. 18-19). Bolick's diatribe includes condemnation of school districts as unnecessary bureaucracies, which "are prone to capture by special interest groups" (2017, p. 20). He supports education savings accounts, "an idea . . . born in [his] former organization, the Goldwater Institute" (2017, p. 20). Likewise, Bolick praises school vouchers and other choice programs and is critical of Blaine Amendments, which have thwarted many choice programs when choice includes religious institutions. Although most state constitutions prohibit public funding for sectarian schools in their respective constitutions, Blaine Amendments were adopted in 37 states during the 19th century to add additional prohibitions against direct state funding for sectarian education. IJ often refers to Blaine Amendments as discriminatory because they prevent religious schools from receiving government funding. Moreover, IJ "considers as a Blaine Amendment any provision that specifically prohibits state legislatures (and often other governmental entities) from appropriating funds to religious sects or institutions, including religious schools" (Komer et al., n.d., "What Are Blaine Amendments?" para. 1). Although Blaine Amendments are often referred to as anti-Catholic, it is important to consider the historical context that led to their adoption. Conflicts over public funding of common schools during the 19th century became a matter of conflict when Catholic leaders, who correctly viewed the common schools as Protestant in nature, fought to obtain a share of common school funds in New York City. Although the Blaine Amendments were a response to this Catholic/Protestant conflict, these amendments were intended to prevent states from funding any sectarian schools (see, e.g., Ravitch, 2000). One of the historical lessons gleaned from this conflict confirmed the importance of protecting a strict separation of church and state by prohibiting public funds from going to religious institutions.

Bolick (2017) concludes by describing one of his most important victories, the 2002 U.S. Supreme Court decision *Zelman v. Simmons-Harris*, wherein a bare majority agreed with his arguments as co-counsel in this case upholding a Cleveland, Ohio, voucher program. Finally, with a court that included supporters and former members of the Federalist Society, advocates of school choice were able to breach what Joseph Viteritti (1998) referred to in 1998 as a "Wall of Intolerance" toward religious freedom. *Zelman* served as a turning point for the Institute for Justice, igniting a growing focus on school choice litigation at the state level. Bolick also served as the first director of the Alliance for School Choice (now chaired by Betsy DeVos), an organization that also served as a member of the American Legislative Exchange's Education and Workforce Task Force. Bolick's depth of involvement in and leadership of school choice organizations is unparalleled. Now an associate justice of the Arizona

Supreme Court, Bolick will be able to impact education litigation in that state based on his ideological beliefs.

Today, the IJ's board of directors includes William Mellor (mentioned earlier), James Lintott (Freedom Management Group LLC and chairman of the Sterling Foundation Management LLC), Robert Levy (chairman of the Cato Institute's board of directors), Abigail Thernstrom (U.S. Commission on Civil Rights under George W. Bush and now an adjunct scholar for the American Enterprise Institute), Arthur Dantchik (Susquehanna Investment Group and Sig Asia Investment LLLP), Robert Gelfond (MagiQ Technologies, Inc.), Stephen Modzelewski (Maple Engine L.L.C. and an officer for the Reason Foundation), Ken Levy (Community Volunteer), Mary Stiefel (Community Volunteer and wealthy donor contributing to right-wing causes), and Scott Bullock, former president of IJ. The list of "experts" in school choice and voucher litigation provided by the Federalist Society includes the individuals listed in Table 3.2, some of whom are members of the IJ.

Table 3.2
Federalist Society List of Experts in School Choice and Vouchers

Name	Affiliation
Dana Berliner	Institute for Justice
Clint Bolick	Associate Justice of the Arizona Supreme Court, previously with the Goldwater Institute
Laurence D. Cohen	Cohen Communications and former executive director of the Yankee Institute for Public Policy, a pro-business think tank
Donald A. Daugherty, Jr.	A Wisconsin lawyer specializing in business litigation and senior counsel at the Wisconsin Institute for Law and Liberty
George W. Dent, Jr. (now deceased)	Case Western Reserve University School of Law, specializing in the religious rights of students and affiliated with the conservative Claremont Institute
David N. Mayer	Capital University Law School, a former Salvatori Fellow of the Heritage Foundation, specializing in libertarian interpretations of the Constitution
Charles E. Rice (now deceased)	University of Notre Dame Law School, specializing in natural law
Ronald D. Rotunda (now deceased)	Chapman University School of Law, Visiting Senior Fellow in Constitutional Studies at the Cato Institute
Abigail Thernstrom	Senior Fellow, Manhattan Institute, provided Senate testimony supporting striking down the preclearance provision of the 1965 Voting Rights Act
Eugene Volokh	University of California, Los Angeles School of Law, Founder and coauthor of the Volokh Conspiracy, a libertarian and conservative weblog
Gerald Walpin (now deceased)	Former U.S. assistant attorney, and former inspector general of the Corporation for National and Community Service
Russell L. Weaver	Louis D. Brandeis School of Law, specializing in comparative constitutional law
Christopher Wolfe	Marquette University (emeritus), specializing in natural law and original interpretations of the Constitution. Also president of the American Public Philosophy Institute, headquartered at the University of Dallas

Funding The IJ

The IJ's annual budget has grown substantially from $5,946,763 in 2001 to $25,656.698 in 2017, according to Internal Revenue Service (IRS) 990 forms. The list of donors is too large to include here, but the highest and most numerous donations have come from the Donors Trust and the Donors Capital Fund, both established in 1999 to distribute donations to conservative and libertarian causes. This untraceable or dark money consists of hundreds of millions of dollars that have been distributed to a variety of specific groups including the Federalist Society and the IJ.[11] According to IRS 990 forms for organizations claiming tax-exempt status, income for the IJ from 2002 through 2016 totaled $220,443,090.

According to the Foundation Directory Online, "83 percent" of donations to the IJ are from "independent foundations," totaling over $91 million (Candid, 2020). The IJ's largest donors (giving $1 million or more per donation) include Fidelity Charitable, one of the nation's largest donor funds, according to Richard Eisenberg (2018) of *Forbes* magazine. William Dunn's Foundation for the Advancement of Right Thinking focuses much of his philanthropy on libertarian causes and like-minded think tanks. The Claws Foundation, established by Jeff Yass provides large contributions, but most of its organizational structure and mission are not public. One of the directors of Claws, Arthur Dantchik, also serves on the board for the IJ. Dantchik has also helped fund the Cato Institute; the Competitive Enterprise Institute; the Foundation for Individual Rights in Education, which focuses on protecting free speech on university campuses; the Ayn Rand Institute; the Reason Foundation; and the Niskanen Center, a think tank established by William A. Niskanen, a former economic adviser to President Ronald Reagan. Also included are the Galashiels Fund, Ltd., and the Robert W. Wilson Charitable Trust, neither of which publishes mission statements.

The IJ selectively chooses state constitutional language in its amicus briefs. For instance, in its 2011 amicus curiae brief filed in *State of Washington v. McCleary* (Brief of Amicus Curiae, Institute for Justice, State of Washington v. McCleary, 2011) the IJ selectively and exclusively cites Section 1 of Article IX in the state constitution, which states, "It is the paramount duty of the state to make ample provision for the education of all children residing within its borders, without distinction or preference on account of race, color, caste, or sex" (Legislative Information Center, 2011). The IJ claims that this section does not preclude the state from choosing to fund schools other than the public school system. "The State's 'primary duty' under Article IX, section 1, is to provide 'for the education' of Washington's children—not to provide a public school system" (Brief of Amicus Curiae, Institute for Justice, State of Washington v. McCleary, 2011, p. 3). Moreover, "in discharging this 'paramount duty,' the State relies not only on its public schools, but also on private schools and private education providers . . . to place students in private schools for special education services" (Brief of Amicus Curiae, Institute for Justice, *State of Washington v. McCleary*, 2011, p. 3), in accordance with state law. Washington's superintendent of public instruction is also authorized to contract with private educational providers "for the delivery of education services [not only] to juvenile inmates," but also to "common school dropouts," and "voucher programs that allow low-income and seasonal workers to choose private preschools or other child care providers for their children" (Brief of Amicus Curiae, Institute for Justice, State of Washington v. McCleary, 2011, p. 3). What the institute fails to mention in its amicus brief is that Article IX, Section 2 of Washington's state constitution includes the following language:

> The legislature shall provide for a general and uniform system of public schools. The public school system shall include common schools, and such high schools, normal schools, and technical schools as may hereafter be established. But the entire revenue derived from the common school fund and the state tax for common schools shall be exclusively applied to the support of the common schools. (Legislative Information Center, 2011, Article IX, Section 2)

Moreover, Section 4 of Article IX declares that "all schools maintained or supported wholly or in part by the public funds shall be forever free from sectarian control or influence" (Legislative Information Center, 2011).

Although disagreements are inevitable in a political epistemic network, the Federalist Society and the IJ represent an example of this network's primary goals. These include forging an interpretation of the U.S. Constitution and state constitutions that favor the expansion of corporate liberty and a simultaneous effort to deregulate federal and state power in order to achieve this outcome. Another, more recent goal is to weaken the institutions of public education to facilitate the transfer of as many public school students as possible, and the public money that follows them, to private religious schools. This requires delegitimizing previous constitutional decisions upholding a strict separation of church and state confirmed by the Supreme Court's 1962 decision in *Engel v. Vitale*.

Conclusion: A Political Epistemic Community

The Federalist Society and the IJ serve as part of a much larger national and international network of shared libertarian and conservative interests. The American Legislative Exchange Council (ALEC), for example, provides model legislation related to school choice, according to a joint publication by the IJ and ALEC. According to this publication, "the model legislation reflects the experience of ALEC members involved in drafting various sorts of school choice programs, and IJ has developed significant expertise in making any modifications necessary to respond to individual state constitutional provisions" (Komer & Grady, 2017, pp. 6, 104–106). Because many state legislators are members of ALEC and other groups within this network, they often welcome and facilitate the passage of ALEC's model legislation. The Federalist Society also provides a number of forums and publications related to the goals of the ALEC, which include ALEC's positions on voter fraud, voter identification laws, questioning climate change, and criticisms of consumer and environmental protections that burden corporations just to name a few. As shown earlier, there are numerous conservative philanthropists who financially support and belong to multiple organizations that make up this network. Although the Federalist Society serves as an intellectual forum for debate, deliberation, and the vetting of federal judges, the IJ has actualized many of the society's (and the network's) goals through litigation, often in state and federal courts that embrace shared jurisprudence.

The IJ's most recent school choice success is highlighted in the 2018 case *Asociación de Maestros v. Departamento de Educación*, which focused on school vouchers. Following Hurricanes Irma and Maria in 2017, Puerto Rico's devastation opened the door to a number of privatization schemes reminiscent of New Orleans. According to Naomi Klein (2018), Puerto Rico's "vulnerability was aggravated by Washington's imposition of the Financial Oversight and Management Board, an unelected body pushing for the privatization of electricity and schools, increased costs of basic services," and "massive cuts in public education" (p. viii). This board was created in 2016 by Congress and given authority to restructure targeted sectors in Puerto Rico including "the privatization and commercialization of entities within the territorial government" (Puerto Rico Oversight, Management, and Economic Stability Act, 2016, Sec. 205[a][10]).

This newer emphasis by the Institute for Justice includes a variety of school-related cases focusing on vouchers, tax scholarship credits, school choice, educational savings accounts, school funding, and college admissions. According to its website, the IJ has closed a total of 209 cases since 1991, with a majority of those cases focusing on "economic liberty," and 58 cases pending as of September 2019. I reviewed 23 court cases at the state and federal levels from 2001 through 2016. Most of these cases were litigated or co-litigated by the IJ. A few other cases involved the filing of amicus briefs by (or joined by) the IJ. The 23 court cases listed in Table 3.3 include a variety of school choice litigation. The IJ has four pending cases in Nevada (challenging the legislature's cap on educational tax scholarships), Maine (school choice), Washington (student work-study programs excluding options in sectarian institutions), and Montana (school choice).[12]

Indisputably, the Federalist Society has become a very powerful ideological force in American politics influencing the three branches of government, particularly the judiciary. For nearly 25 years, this organization has grown from a student club at Yale University to a nationwide network responsible for turning the tide away from the more liberal Warren and Burger courts and returning it to more conservative *Lochner*-like court, represented by numerous activist decisions handed down by the Rehnquist and the Roberts courts. Since the 1980s, federal judges and legislators have diligently worked

Table 3.3
School Choice Litigation, 2001-2016

Case & Decision Date	State	Issue
Asociación de Maestros v. Departamento de Educación (2018)	Puerto Rico	Vouchers
Thomas et al v. Douglas County BOE (2016) IJ dismissed when state program abolished	Colorado	Exclusion of religious choice
Schwartz v. Lopez (Nev. 2016)	Nevada	Education savings accounts
Citizens for Strong Schools, Inc. v. Florida State Board of Education (2019)	Florida	Tuition tax credits
Gaddy Et Al. V. Georgia Department of Revenue (2017)	Georgia	Tax credit scholarships
Hart et al v. State of North Carolina (2015)	North Carolina	Education scholarships
Richardson v. State (2015)	North Carolina	Education scholarships
Magee v. Boyd (2015)	Alabama	Tax credit scholarships
Duncan v. State of New Hampshire (2014)	New Hampshire	Tax credit scholarships
Louisiana Federation of Teachers v. State of Louisiana (2014)	Louisiana	Tax credit scholarships
Niehaus v. Huppenthal (2013)	Arizona	Education savings accounts
Meredith v. Pence (2013)	Indiana	Education scholarships
Taxpayers for Public Education v. Douglas County School District (2018)	Colorado	Education scholarships
DeBoom et al v. Bergeson (2008)	Washington	Disability education services in religious schools
Cain v. Horne (2009)	Arizona	School choice for special needs children
Garriott v. Winn (2011)	Arizona	Tax credit scholarships
Harrison v. University of Washington (2002) *Thurmond County Superior Court*	Washington	Student teaching in religious schools
Anderson v. Town of Durham (2006)	Maine	Religious school choice
Arizona Christian School Tuition Organization v. Winn	Arizona	Tax credit scholarships
John Ellis "Jeb" Bush v. Holmes (2006)	Florida	Vouchers
Bagley v. Town of Raymond (1999)	Maine	School choice
Chittenden Town School District v. Department of Education (1999)	Vermont	School choice
Giacomucci v. Southeast Delco School District (1999)	Pennsylvania	Tax benefits for private education

to redirect many of the nation's policies back toward the *Lochner* era when corporate constitutional rights reached a zenith in American legal history.

But despite the society's support for and the IJ's limited successes in corporate liberties and school privatization, their efforts have created what many conclude to be harmful results (e.g., *Citizens United v. Federal Election Commission*, *Shelby County v. Holder*, and *National Federation of Independent Business v. Sebelius*) and school choice cases that have apparently not improved education, and in some cases, made education worse. It is clear that the goals of both groups and their epistemic network are fundamentally devoted not just to developing a return to *Lochner* but to reinterpreting the Constitution in new directions. The Federalist Society and the IJ, for example, support the expansion of their notions of corporate citizenship and expanding corporate liberties that rival at the very least, and displace at most, the liberties enjoyed by human beings, whether protected by the Constitution or by legislative fiat. In order to accomplish these goals, they selectively utilize libertarian arguments when advocating and litigating corporate and business interests and conservative arguments when working to weaken federal regulation. Ironically perhaps, the interpretation of economic liberty among members of the Federalist Society, the IJ, and feasibly this entire epistemic network is so radical today that it appears to rupture any conservative or conventional understanding of the Constitution by going well beyond the principles established in *Lochner*. As Justice Oliver Wendell Holmes, Jr. declared in his *Lochner* (1905) dissent, "a constitution is not intended to embody a particular economic theory, whether of paternalism and the organic relation of the citizen to the State or of laissez faire."

References

Acton Institute. (n.d.). (See Endnote No. 4) *Our mission and core principles*. Retrieved September 9, 2019, from https://acton.org/about/mission

Adelman, L. (2018, Summer). Laundering racism through the court: The scandal of states' rights. *Dissent*. https://www.dissentmagazine.org/article/laundering-racism-through-court-scandal-states-rights-federalism

Alexander, R. (2014, October 7). *Clint Bolick and the Goldware Institute quietly transforming the country*. The Goldwater Institute. https://goldwaterinstitute.org/article/clint-bolick-and-goldwater-institute-quietly-trans/

Anderson v. Town of Durham 127 S.Ct. 661 (2006).

Anderson v. Town of Durham, 895 A. 2d 944—Maine Superior Court (2006).

Arizona Christian School Tuition Organization v. Winn, 563 U.S. 125 (2011).

Asociación de Maestros v. Departamento de Educación, 2018 TSPR 150

Asociación de Maestros v. Departamento de Educación, WL 4039855 (2018)

Avery, M., & McLaughlin, D. (2013). *The Federalist Society: How conservatives took the law back from liberals*. Vanderbilt University Press.

Bagley v. Town of Raymond, ME 60, 728 A.2d 127 (1999).

Bernstein, D. E. (2011). *Rehabilitating Lochner: Defending individual rights against progressive reform*. The University of Chicago Press.

Beutler, B. (2015, August 30). The rehabilitationists: How a small band of determined legal academics set out to persuade the Supreme Court to undo the New Deal—and have almost won. *The New Republic*. https://newrepublic.com/article/122645/rehabilitationists-libertarian-movement-undo-new-deal

Blumenthal, S. (2008). *The rise of the counter-establishment: The conservative ascent to political power*. Union Square Press.

Bolick, C. (2017). Jump-starting K–12 education reform. *Harvard Journal of Law & Public Policy*, *40*(1), 17–24.

Bowden, J. (2018, November 15). Federalist Society welcomes Kavanaugh with standing ovation. *The Hill*. https://thehill.com/blogs/blog-briefing-room/news/417054-federalist-society-welcomes-kavanaugh-with-standing-ovation

Brennan Center for Justice. (2018, August 6). *The effects of* Shelby County v. Holder. https://www.brennancenter.org/analysis/effects-shelby-county-v-holder

Brief of amicus curiae for respondents, Institute for Justice, State of Washington v. McCleary (2011) (no. 84362-7). https://ij.org/wp-content/uploads/2015/07/McCLeary-Amicus-Brief.pdf.

Brief of amicus curiae, Institute for Justice, in support of petitioners, Obergefell v. Hodges, 576 U.S. 644 (2015) (nos. 14-566, 14-562, 14-541, 14-574). http://sblog.s3.amazonaws.com/wp-content/uploads/2015/03/14-556-14-562-14-571-14-574-tsac-IFJ.pdf

Burwell v. Hobby Lobby Stores, Inc. 573 U.S. 682 (2014).

Bush v. Holmes, 919 So. 2d 392 (Fla. 2006).

Cain v. Horne, 202 P.3d 1178 (Ariz. 2009).

Candide. (2020). About. https://fconline.foundationcenter.org/

Cassens Weiss, D. (2019, May 23). Federalist Society's Leonard Leo helped raise $250m to promote judges and causes. *ABA Journal.* http://www.abajournal.com/news/article/honcho-worked-with-separate-nonprofits-to-help-raise-250m-for-conservative-judges-and-causes

Category: Federalist Society members. (2019). In *Wikipedia.* Retrieved September 25, 2019, from https://en.wikipedia.org/wiki/Category:Federalist_Society_members

Chittenden Town School District v. Dept. of Educ., 169 Vt. 310 (Vt. 1999), 738 A.2d 539.

Citizens for Strong Schools, Inc. v. Florida State Board of Education, SC18-67 (Fla. 2019).

Citizens United v. Federal Elections Commission, 558 U.S. 310 (2010).

Club for Growth, The. (n.d.). *David McIntosh.* https://www.clubforgrowth.org/staff/david-mcintosh/

Conservativetransparency.org. (2019). Database.

DeBoom v. Bergeson (2008). http://www.ij.org/images/pdf_folder/school_choice/washington/idea_complaint.pdf

Duncan v. State of New Hampshire, 166 N.H. 630 (N.H. 2014).

Edwards v. District of Columbia, 765 F. Supp. 2d 3, 6, 11–12 (D.D.C. 2011).

Eisenberg, R. (2018, August 2). There's a target on charity's booming donor-advised funds. *Forbes.* https://www.forbes.com/sites/nextavenue/2018/08/02/theres-a-target-on-charitys-booming-donor-advised-funds/#b9a0f1d7a327

Engel v. Vitale, 370 U.S. 421 (1962).

Federalist Society. (n.d.-a). *About us.* https://fedsoc.org/about-us

Federalist Society. (n.d.-b). *Our background.* https://fedsoc.org/our-background

Florida ex rel. Attorney General v. U.S. Department of Health & Human Services, Nos. 11-11021 & 11-11067 (11th Cir. Aug. 12, 2011).

Foundation Center (2019). About. https://fconline.foundationcenter.org/

Gaddy v. Ga. Dep't of Revenue, 802 S.E.2d 225 (Ga. 2017).

Garriott v. Winn, 563 U.S. 125 (2011).

Giacomucci v. Southeast Delco School District, 742 A. 2d 1165, Pa: Commonwealth Court (1999).

Grayer, A. (2018, August 19). *Brett Kavanaugh was concerned with his Federalist Society membership in 2001, emails show.* CNN. https://www.cnn.com/2018/08/19/politics/brett-kavanaugh-federalist-society-emails/index.html

Greenwood, D. J. H. (2017). Neofeudalism: The surprising foundations of corporate constitutional rights. *University of Illinois Law Review, 163*(1), 163–223. https://scholarlycommons.law.hofstra.edu/faculty_scholarship/1077

Grutter v. Bollinger, 539 U.S. 306 (2003).

Harrison v. University of Washington (2002) https://ij.org/case/harrison-v-gregoire/

Hart v. State, 774 S.E.2d 281 (N.C. 2015).

Hauser, C. (2018, September 26). The women who have accused Brett Kavanaugh. *The New York Times.* https://www.nytimes.com/2018/09/26/us/politics/brett-kavanaugh-accusers-women.html

Hobbes, T. (1991). *Leviathan* (R. Tuck, Ed.). Cambridge University Press. (Original work published 1651)

Hollis-Brusky, A. (2015). *Ideas with consequences: The Federalist Society and the conservative counterrevolution.* Oxford University Press.

Hollis-Brusky, A., & Terbeek, C. (2019, August 31). *The Federalist Society says it's not an advocacy organization. These documents show otherwise.* Politico.https://www.politico.com/magazine/story/2019/08/31/federalist-society-advocacy-group-227991

Institute for Justice. (n.d.-a). *About us.* https://ij.org/about-us/

Institute for Justice. (n.d.-c). *Center for Judicial Engagement.* https://ij.org/center-for-judicial-engagement/

Institute for Justice. (n.d.-d). *William H. Mellor.* https://ij.org/staff/william-h-mellor/

Janjevic, D. (2018, October 1). Who are the Mercers, the wealthy backers of Breitbart? *Deutsche Welle.* https://www.dw.com/en/who-are-the-mercers-the-wealthy-backers-of-breitbart/a-42100407

Johnson, C. (2019, August 5). *Trump's impact on federal courts: Judicial nominees by the numbers*. NPR. https://www.npr.org/2019/08/05/747013608/trumps-impact-on-federal-courts-judicial-nominees-by-the-numbers

Klein, N. (2018). *The battle for paradise: Puerto Rico takes on the disaster capitalists*. Haymarket Books.

Komer, D., Bindas, M., & Keller, T. (n.d.). *Answers to frequently asked questions about Blaine Amendments*. Institute for Justice. https://ij.org/issues/school-choice/blaine-amendments/answers-frequently-asked-questions-blaine-amendments/

Komer, R. D., & Grady, O. (2016). *School choice and state constitutions: A guide to designing school choice programs* (Reference Guide, 2nd ed.). A Joint Publication of the Institute for Justice and the American Legislative Exchange Council. https://ij.org/report/school-choice-and-state-constitutions/

Legislative Information Center. (2011). Constitution of the state of Washington. https://www.google.com/url?sa=t&rct=j&q=&esrc=s&source=web&cd=4&ved=2ahUKEwj57tr78dzjAhUGyFkKHV9c-BOMQFjADegQIAhAC&url=http%3A%2F%2Fleg.wa.gov%2Flawsandagencyrules%2Fdocuments%2F12-2010-wastateconstitution.pdf&usg=AOvVaw2C-oeAgRtEyvR_V8l5UUd1

Levy, R. A., & Mellor, W. (2008). *The dirty dozen: How twelve Supreme Court cases radically expanded government and eroded freedom*. The Cato Institute.

List of federal judges appointed by Donald Trump. (2019). In *Wikipedia*. Retrieved September 25, 2019, from https://en.wikipedia.org/wiki/List_of_federal_judges_appointed_by_Donald_Trump

Lochner v. New York, 198 U.S. 45 (1905).

Louisiana Federation of Teachers v. State, 118 So. 3d 1033 (La. 2013).

Magee v. Boyd, 175 So. 3d 79 (Ala. 2015).

Mayer, J. (2017, March 17). The reclusive hedge-fund tycoon behind the Trump presidency. *The New Yorker*. https://www.newyorker.com/magazine/2017/03/27/the-reclusive-hedge-fund-tycoon-behind-the-trump-presidency

McConnell v. Federal Election Commission, 540 U.S. 93 (2003).

Meredith v. Pence, 984 N.E.2d 1213 (Ind. 2013).

Montgomery, D. (2019, January 2). Conquerors of the courts: Forget Trump's Supreme Court picks. The Federalist Society's impact on the law goes much deeper. *The Washington Post Magazine*. https://www.washingtonpost.com/news/magazine/wp/2019/01/02/feature/conquerors-of-the-courts/

National Association for the Advancement of Colored People. (2018, August 31). *Brett Kavanaugh poses a severe threat to civil rights: The Senate must reject his nomination*. https://www.google.com/url?sa=t&rct=j&q=&esrc=s&source=web&cd=2&ved=2ahUKEwicy-7TtuzkAhUShuAKHfNHDVgQFjABegQICRAC&url=https%3A%2F%2Fwww.naacp.org%2Fwp-content%2Fuploads%2F2018%2F09%2FNAACPKavanaughTPs.pdf&usg=AOvVaw1yDwTZbbQLSRNoJYLs73Kr

National Federation of Independent Business v. Sebelius, 567 U.S. 519 (2012).

Niehaus v. Huppenthal, 310 P.3d 983 (Ariz. Ct. App. 2013).

O'Harrow, R., Jr., & Boburg, S. (2019, May 21). A conservative activist's behind-the-scenes campaign to remake the nation's courts. *Washington Post*. https://www.washingtonpost.com/graphics/2019/investigations/leonard-leo-federalists-society-courts/?wpisrc=nl_most&wpmm=1

Obergefell v. Hodges, 576 U.S. 644 (2015).

Puerto Rico Oversight, Management, and Economic Stability Act, S. bill 2328, 114th Cong. (2016). https://www.govtrack.us/congress/bills/114/s2328/text/enr#link=II_205_a_10_~T1&nearest=HAE7EAC52B864465EB3CC7F84DDCDCEE7

Ravitch, D. (2000). *The great school wars: a history of the New York City public schools*. Johns Hopkins University Press.

Richardson v. State, 774 S.E.2d 304 (N.C. 2015).

Roe v. Wade, 410 U.S. 113 (1973).

Scalia, A. Dissent in *Obergefell v. Hodges*, 576 U.S. 644 (2015). https://supreme.justia.com/cases/federal/us/576/14-556/

Schwartz v. Lopez, 382 P.3d 886, 891 (Nev. 2016).

Shelby County v. Holder, 570 U.S. 529 (2013)

Smith, E. (2016, December 19). Blaine amendments and the unconstitutionality of excluding religious options from school choice programs. *Federalist Society Review*. Advanced online publication. https://fedsoc.org/commentary/publications/blaine-amendments-and-the-unconstitutionality-of-excluding-religious-options-from-school-choice-programs

St. Joseph Abbey v. Castille, 712 F. 3d 215 (2013).

Taxpayers for Public Education v. Douglas County School District, 351 P.3d 461 (Colo. 2015).

Teles, S. M. (2008). *The rise of the conservative legal movement: The battle for control of the law*. Princeton University Press.

Thomas et al v. Douglas County BOE (2016) Case 1:16-cv-00876, United States Disctrict Court, District of Colorado.

Toobin, J. (2017, April 17). The conservative pipeline to the Supreme Court. *The New Yorker*. https://www.newyorker.com/magazine/2017/04/17/the-conservative-pipeline-to-the-supreme-court

United States. Congress. House. Committee on the Judiciary. (1993). Religious Freedom Restoration Act of 1993 : report together with additional views (to accompany H.R. 1308) (including cost estimate of the Congressional Budget Office). [Washington, D.C.] :[U.S. G.P.O.].

United States Senate Committee on the Judiciary, Questionnaire for Nominee to the Supreme Court, 115th Congress (2018, July 21) (Brett M. Kavanaugh). https://www.judiciary.senate.gov/download/07/21/2018/brett-m-kavanaugh-sjq-public

United States Senate Committee on the Judiciary, Questionnaire for Non-Judicial Nominees, 115th Cong. (2018, December 18) (William Pelham Barr). https://www.google.com/url?sa=t&rct=j&q=&esrc=s&source=web&cd=1&cad=rja&uact=8&ved=2ahUKEwiLr_uLobfkAhUIVt-8KHcoDDeMQFjAAegQIBRAC&url=https%3A%2F%2Fwww.judiciary.senate.gov%2Fdownload%2Fwilliam-barr-senate-questionnaire-public&usg=AOvVaw2Fnpdq5apynpPx1lYKHdNr

United States v. Miller, 307 U.S. 174 (1939).

University of Chicago Law School. (2013, November 4). *Institute for Justice clinic on entrepreneurship: Significant accomplishments*. https://www.law.uchicago.edu/news/institute-justice-clinic-entrepreneurship-significant-accomplishments

Viteritti, J. (1998). Blaine's wake: School choice, the First Amendment, and state constitutional law. *Harvard Journal of Law & Policy*, *21*(3), 657–718.

Watkins, D. (2016, October 5). The natural law foundation of the Constitution. *FedSoc Blog*. https://fedsoc.org/commentary/blog-posts/the-natural-law-foundation-of-the-constitution

Weaver, R. M. (1948). *Ideas have consequences*. University of Chicago Press.

Weaver, R. M. (2000). *In defense of tradition: Collected shorter writings of Richard M. Weaver, 1929–1963* (T. J. Smith, III, Ed.). Liberty Fund.

West Coast Hotel Co. v. Parrish, 300 U.S. 379 (1937)

Whitehouse, S. (2019, March 27). *The Third Federalist Society: Within the Federalist Society is an operation funded by dark money and designed to remake our judiciary on behalf of a distinct group of very wealthy anonymous funders* [Speech]. https://www.congress.gov/congressional-record/2019/03/27/senate-section/article/S2011-6.

Zelman v. Simmons-Harris, 536 U.S. 639 (2002).

Endnotes

1 The Federalist Society and the IJ repeatedly use the terms *government monopoly* or *public school monopoly* in their libertarian literature, and they often refer to state constitutional amendments that prohibit public funding of religious schools as discriminatory toward religion. See, for example, Smith (2016).

2 My calculations were based on biographical data and Federalist Society membership (past and present) roles provided by Wikipedia; see "List of Federal Judges Appointed by Donald Trump" (2019) and "Category: Federalist Society Members" (2019).

3 See, for example, Justice Antonin Scalia's majority opinion, joined by Roberts, Thomas, and Alito, in *Shelby County v. Holder* (2013) invalidating Section 5 of the 1965 Voting Rights Act, intended to protect racial discrimination in elections. See also the National Association for the Advancement of Colored People's (2018) public statement.

4 Eugene B. Meyer is also a member of the Philadelphia Society, whose past members include F. A. Hayek, Milton Friedman, and Ronald Coase. The current president of the Philadelphia Society is Samuel Gregg, also a member of the Acton Institute, a think tank devoted to individual liberty and religious freedoms. See Acton Institute (n.d.).

5 Weaver specifically criticizes Oliver Wendell Holmes, Jr., and Chief Justice Fred Vinson. This chapter is titled "Relativism and the Crisis of Our Times."

6 Economic due process was a constitutional doctrine used by courts during the *Lochner* era to eliminate numerous government regulations

that limited business freedoms, especially the liberty of contract, which assumes an equal relationship between employer and employee.

7 Greenwood (2017) quotes Thomas Hobbes's (1651/1991) *Leviathan* (nonstandard spelling in original): "Another infirmity of a Common-wealth, is . . . the great number of Corporations; which are as it were many lesser Common-wealths in the bowels of a greater, like wormes in the entrayles of a natural man" (p. 230). See Greenwood (2017, n10). Justice John Paul Stevens, who concurred in part and dissented in part in *Citizens United* (2010), declared, "The conceit that corporations must be treated identically to natural persons in the political sphere is not only inaccurate but also inadequate to justify the Court's disposition of this case" (para. 2).

8 The IJ, for example, filed an amicus curiae brief in *Obergefell v. Hodges* supporting a constitutional right for same-sex marriage (Brief of Amicus Curiae, Institute for Justice, 2015).

9 Funding data was obtained from annual IRS 990 forms. Provide Link < https://candid.org/research-and-verify-nonprofits/990-finder.>

10 As a side note, Chief Justice John Roberts, the only conservative on the Supreme Court who has no known affiliation with the Federalist Society, cast the deciding vote upholding the Affordable Care Act.

11 The website for the Donors Trust is https://www.donorstrust.org/?cn-reloaded=1. The website for the Donors Capital Fund is http://donorscapitalfund.org/.

12 The four state court cases are *Morency v. State of Nevada*, A-19-800267-C (2019), *Carson v. Makin*, 401 F.Supp.3d 207 (2019), *Summit Christian Academy v. Meotti* (3:18-cv-05656), and *Espinoza v. Montana Department of Revenue* (18-1195)

Chapter Four

THE MYTH OF EDUCATIONAL FREEDOM: THE DEVOS FAMILY'S INFLUENCE ON EDUCATIONAL POLICY

Jamie B. Lewis, *Georgia Gwinnett College*

Who is Betsy DeVos?

"A privatization extremist. A religious zealot. A culture warrior. Secretary of Education, Betsy DeVos, was painted as any or all of these" during her confirmation hearing (McShane, 2017, p. 27). However, according to McShane, DeVos is "a fairly traditional, center-right, education reformer" (2017, pp. 27–28). Elisabeth Dee DeVos was born on January 8, 1958, and is the 11th and current U.S. Secretary of Education. She is the daughter of Edgar Prince, the founder of the successful auto parts manufacturer, Prince Corporation, and grew up in Holland, Michigan, a suburb of Grand Rapids. She earned her bachelor's degree from Calvin College and is married to Dick DeVos, the former chief executive officer of the multilevel marketing company Amway, and is the daughter-in-law of Amway's billionaire co-founder, Richard DeVos. Her brother, Erik Prince, is a former U.S. Navy SEAL officer and founder of Blackwater USA (now known as Academi; McShane, 2017).

DeVos is a Republican and served as Republican National Committeewoman for Michigan from 1992 to 1997 and as chair of the Michigan Republican Party from 1996 to 2000. During her political career, she has been a staunch advocate for school choice, school vouchers, and charter schools. In the 1990s, she was on the boards of two organizations that promoted school choice, Children First America and the Education Reform Council (McShane, 2017).

In the early 2000s, she created the Great Lakes Education Project, which was a political action committee devoted to influencing educational policy in Michigan and played a major role in Michigan's school choice law and was involved in the school turnaround efforts in Detroit, Michigan. DeVos is a former member of the board of the Foundation for Excellence in Education, has served as chair of the board of the Alliance for School Choice and the Acton Institute, and has headed the All Children Matter political action committee. This chapter traces the DeVos family's involvement in shaping education in the United States from its early involvement with the Philanthropy Roundtable (deMarrais, 2006) and the Heritage Foundation to its current focus on school choice and the neoliberal agenda of privatizing education. Furthermore, it examines Betsy DeVos's efforts in the area of school choice, as exemplified by her focus on educational freedom as secretary of education.

History Of Philanthropic Giving And The Conservative Agenda to Save Free Enterprise And White Privilege

Early proponents of public education, such as Horace Mann, recognized the role education could play as "the great equalizer" and the importance of equal access to educational opportunities that cut across race, class, and gender. The U.S. Supreme Court's decision in *Brown v. Board of Education* (347 US 483 1954), the civil rights movements, the enactment of progressive legislation, and efforts to integrate public schools resulted in measures seeking to address racial and social class inequities and to alleviate and dismantle a system built on White privilege. Strides toward equality resulted in attempts to reallocate resources and governmental regulation, which proved perplexing to White conservatives as they saw the fabric of their existence unravel and their status and power erode. "Opponents also took note of how such legal changes were led by a 'liberal establishment' that was organized and strategic in ways that conservatives were not yet" (Kumashiro et al., 2012, p. 11). In response, two national groups, the Philanthropy Roundtable and the Business Roundtable, emerged whose focus on protecting "free enterprise" and White privilege would influence both public policy and educational policy in the following decades.

In 1971, Lewis Powell described a concerted liberal attack on the American free-enterprise system and on American democracy itself in a document which has become known as the Powell Manifesto. In response to this manifesto, a group of conservative philanthropists with family business fortunes formed a national roundtable to develop a strategy to combat the liberal attack on free enterprise (deMarrais, 2006; deMarrais et al., 2019). "Their project was as much legislative as it was ideological. They aimed to influence legislation and policy as well as to shape 'common sense' in society" (Kumashiro et al., 2012, p. 13). The strategy utilized an interconnected system of funding to influence public policy in ways that would preserve White privilege and allow the maintenance of social, political, and economic advantages. Dismantling public education through privatization and choice was a top priority because public education was "considered by some to be a drain on the government and a crutch for society not only because it was the most expensive of domestic enterprises but also because it exemplified what they considered to be a socialist enterprise" (Kumashiro et al., 2012, p. 13).

Initially, the Bradley, Olin, Scaife, and Smith Richardson Foundations, referred to as the Four Sisters, wielded the most influence through their funding of conservative think tanks, such as the American Enterprise Institute for Public Policy Research, the Heritage Foundation, and the Hoover Institution (deMarrais, 2006; deMarrais et al., 2019). However, between 1998 and 2004, the Walton Family Foundation (WFF) and the DeVos Foundation became major players.

Several other foundations gave more than $100 million to conservative causes between 1998 and 2004, including the WFF, the Charles Koch Foundation, and the DeVos foundations. Other chapters in this book focus on the Walton family and the influence of Lewis Powell, so I turn now to a discussion of the DeVos Foundation.

The Richard And Helen DeVos Foundation

According to Rick Doksai (2016), "one of the top families in philanthropy to watch these days is the conservative DeVos family" (para. 2). The Richard and Helen DeVos Foundation is an American conservative nonprofit organization and grant-making body formed in 1970. Based in Grand Rapids, Michigan, the organization was founded by Richard DeVos, Sr., co-founder of the multilevel marketing company Amway and former finance chair of the Republican National Committee, and his wife, Helen. As of 2014, the foundation had a total revenue of $54.9 million (ProPublica, n.d.). It is one of five nonprofit organizations established and operated by the DeVos family; the others, all founded by siblings of Richard DeVos Jr., include the Dick and Betsy DeVos Foundation, the Daniel and Pamela DeVos Foundation, Cheri DeVos's CDV5 Foundation, and the Douglas and Maria DeVos Foundation. Therefore, when talking about the DeVos foundations' impact on school choice it is important to consider their collective efforts. "The DeVos family, which operates three philanthropic foundations and has a remarkable talent for moving money by the truckload into socially conservative causes to shift voters' and lawmakers' mindsets in a rightward direction" (Doksai, 2016, para. 5).

The Richard and Helen DeVos Foundation provides funding to various organizations across three broad categories: political, religious, and educational. The founders, Richard and Helen, were awarded the William E. Simon Prize for Philanthropic Leadership in 2006. In 2019, the DeVos family was listed by *Forbes* as the 26th-top giver in America, with their gifts totaling $112 million in 2018 (Wang, 2019). Between 2003 and 2017, their gifts to their top 10 recipients totaled more than $195 million. The American Enterprise Institute received over $1.3 million dollars. During this same period, the Richard and Helen DeVos Foundation made contributions in the self-designated category of Elementary and Secondary Education in over $66 million. Turning Point USA (see Chapter 9), received donations in the amount of $10,000. In the following sections, I highlight specific recipients who have connections to efforts to protect free enterprise and/or privatize public education, including the Education Freedom Fund, the Alliance for School Choice, Step Up for Students, and the Alliance Defending Freedom.

Education Freedom Fund

According to MediaMouse (n.d.), a Grand Rapids progressive left news blog, the Education Freedom Fund is an organization based in Grand Rapids, Michigan, offering scholarships to low-income youth, allowing them to attend private schools. Heavily funded by the religious right foundations in Western Michigan, Betsy DeVos and Dick DeVos are members of the board of directors (GuideStar, n.d.). Scholarship recipients can receive a maximum of $1,000 annually. Parents are required to pay a minimum of $500 in tuition per year, which may restrict access to economically disadvantaged students. The Dick and Betsy DeVos Foundation, the Edgar and Elsa Prince Foundation, and the Douglas and Maria DeVos Foundation also contribute to the Education Freedom Fund. The Education Freedom Fund has received $54,000 from the Richard and Helen DeVos Foundation.

Alliance for School Choice

The Alliance for School Choice (ASC) received $300,000 from the Richard and Helen DeVos Foundation and is a conservative 501(c)(3) nonprofit group. The ASC pursues a school privatization agenda and is a member of the Education Task Force of the American Legislative Exchange Council (ALEC; The Center for Media and Democracy, n.d.-a).

Step Up for Students

In 2001, the Florida Legislature created the Florida Tax Credit (FTC) Scholarship Program to provide lower income Florida families more choices in the education options available for their children. "The program gave corporations credit for redirecting their state tax obligations toward K–12 scholarships that helped low-income families send their children to participating private schools or to public schools outside their districts" (Step Up for Students, n.d., para. 2). The Florida Department of Revenue gives dollar-for-dollar tax credits to companies that contribute their eligible tax dollars to the FTC Scholarship Program to fund K–12, income-based education scholarships. The Richard and Helen DeVos Foundation has contributed $225,000 to this fund.

Alliance Defending Freedom

Alliance Defending Freedom (ADF) is an American conservative Christian nonprofit organization. Founded in 1994 by 30 Christian ministries, it has a stated goal of advocating, training, and funding on the issues of "religious freedom, sanctity of life, and marriage and family" (Alliance Defending Freedom, n.d., para. 1). According to the Center for Media and Democracy, "ADF was intended to be a response to the progressive legal groups that had won important victories at all levels of the courts in the previous decades, such as the Anti-Defamation League and the American Civil Liberties Union" (Center for Media and Democracy, n.d.-a). ADF has been identified as a hate group by the Southern Poverty Law Center. The ADF "has supported the recriminalization of homosexuality in the United States. and criminalization abroad; has defended state-sanctioned sterilization of trans people abroad; has linked homosexuality to pedophilia and claims that a 'homosexual agenda' will destroy Christianity and society" (Southern Poverty Law Center, n.d., para. 1). The ADF has advocated against gender-inclusive school policies and practices that protect the rights of transgender students. "An ADF attorney represented Texas and a handful of other states when they challenged guidance issued by the Obama administration that transgender students are protected from discrimination under Title IX" (Ford, 2018, "Education," para. 2). One of Betsy DeVos's first actions as secretary of education was to rescind this guidance. The

ADF received $460,000 from the Richard and Helen DeVos Foundation. The ADF also runs the Center for Academic Freedom, which touts that it has accumulated 385 campus victories against attacks on students' free speech and/or religious freedom on public university and college campuses (Alliance Defending Freedom, n.d.).

The Dick And Betsy DeVos Foundation

Founded in 1979, the Dick and Betsy DeVos Foundation is located in Holland, Michigan. According to Dick and Betsy, "following in the footsteps of our parents, we aim to be faithful servants. Our work focuses on education, community, the arts, justice, and leadership" (Dick and Betsy DeVos Foundation, n.d.). Based on their analysis of the Dick and Betsy DeVos Family Foundation's tax filings from 2000 to 2014, as well as the 2001–2014 filings from her parents' charitable organization, the Edgar and Elsa Prince Foundation (the Prince Foundation listed Betsy DeVos as a vice president during those years; however, DeVos claimed this was "a clerical error" during her confirmation hearing), *Mother Jones* found that "during that period, the DeVoses spent nearly $100 million in philanthropic giving, and the Princes spent $70 million" (Rizga, 2017, para. 9). In their most recent reporting year ending June 2018, the foundation reported assets of $18,302,734 (ledger value) and an income of $20,279,234. The foundation provides funding in the following areas: education, social and human services, religion, arts and culture, and health. However, "the couple's philanthropic record makes clear that they view choice and competition as the best mechanisms to improve America's education system. Overall, their foundation gave $5.2 million from 1999 to 2014 to charter schools" (Rizga, 2017, para. 10). The Dick and Betsy DeVos Foundation made contributions to the American Enterprise Institute (more than $2.2 million), the Heritage Foundation ($95,000), the Federalist Society ($40,000), the Education Freedom Fund (over $1.4 million), the ASC (almost $1.3 million), and Step Up for Students

($150,000). In addition to funding their own charter school, West Michigan Aviation Academy, in the amount of $4.7 million, they contributed more than $15 million to Young America's Foundation, which I briefly describe in the following section.

Young America's Foundation

The Young America's Foundation (YAF) was founded on September 11, 1960, by William F. Buckley, Jr. The YAF (n.d.) describes itself as "the principal outreach organization of the Conservative Movement." According to the Center for Media and Democracy, the YAF is a State Policy Network affiliate. One of its main initiatives, which began in 1969, was to bring conservative speakers to college and university campuses (YAF, n.d.). In May 2017, Stephanie Saul noted in her *New York Times* article that these "speakers have gotten edgier, more in-your-face and sometimes even mean-spirited" (para. 7). Sponsored speakers include Robert Spencer, Ann Coulter, David Horowitz, and Ben Shapiro (The Center for Media and Democracy, n.d.-b). "The speeches are a part of the group's mission of grooming future conservative leaders—Attorney General Jeff Sessions and Stephen Miller, a White House adviser, are among its alumni" (para. 5).

In 2006, the YAF reopened the newly renovated Reagan Ranch Center in downtown Santa Barbara. According to Brown (2018), "the facility is the most important hub of conservative activity outside of Washington, D.C., and is often touted as the 'Schoolhouse for Reaganism,' complete with classrooms, conference space, a theater, a library, a boardroom, interactive exhibits and galleries, and offices to house our Reagan Ranch team members" (para. 5). A $10 million gift from Dick and Betsy DeVos was used to endow the Reagan Ranch (Saul, 2017).

Betsy DeVos And School Choice

In this section, I examine Betsy DeVos's efforts in the area of school choice. Teasley (2017) notes that

> school choice, as a component of market-based reform, is touted as the solution to the bureaucracy and long-standing problems within public education. Although the storm of school choice casts a shadow over the federal landscape, the successful nomination of Betsy DeVos is not a new movement within school reform; it is, however, a major indication that the profit motive of education reform is gaining momentum. (p. 131)

Tracing the roots of market-based school reform movement takes us back to the 1970s. President Jimmy Carter launched an investigation into southern states' practices of providing parent subsidies for private, parochial schools, thus allowing them to avoid sending children to integrated schools. School privatization gained footing during the Reagan years through rhetoric, such as that found in *A Nation at Risk* (Gardner, 1983) that framed our system of public education as failing and in need of reform. Educational policy reforms, such as No Child Left Behind and Race to the Top, bolstered the efforts to privatize education. For example,

> charter schools and school vouchers expanded under Race to the Top. Yet, at that time, there were no major research studies that demonstrated the superiority of charters schools in comparison with traditional public schools, particularly in solving the unabated problems of urban school systems populated by African American and Hispanic students. (Teasley, 2017, p. 132)

For decades, DeVos has supported vouchers and similar programs that use public money for private and religious education.

A leader in the "school choice" movement, DeVos has used her pulpit as education secretary to extol alternatives to traditional public schools. Before her appointment to secretary of education in the Trump administration, DeVos called public schools "a dead end" and has made clear, as has Trump, that the administration's key education priority is expanding "choice" options (Strauss, 2019). Her home community of Holland, Michigan, has been heavily impacted by the state's school choice law—a law DeVos was instrumental in getting enacted. In the two decades since Michigan adopted school choice, "Holland's White enrollment has plummeted 60%, with 2,100 fewer White students. Today, Whites compose 49% of school-aged children living in the district but only 38% of the school population (Hispanics compose 47% of Holland school enrollment)" (Wilkerson, 2017, p. 20). "The outcomes we can measure show it's leading to increased segregation and increased burdens for districts, said Gary Miron, a researcher and education professor at Western Michigan University who studies school choice data" (Wilkerson, 2017, pp. 21-22). The Michigan Department of Education has begun using a data-driven approach to evaluate the effectiveness of the state's charter and choice programs (Wilkerson, 2017). According to Vanessa Kessler, "initial research indicates that students who used choice to change districts do not perform better, on average, academically and that many students who left for another district often return" (Wilkerson, 2017, p. 23). DeVos's most recent project as secretary of education involves garnering support for federal tax-credit programs, similar in nature to some state-level tax credit programs, such as the Education Freedom Fund and Step Up for Students, supported by the DeVos Foundations. The following section discusses the Education Freedom Scholarships and Opportunity Act.

Betsy DeVos And Education Freedom

Federal tax credit scholarships were highly publicized initiatives during Devos's summer 2019 Back-to-School bus tour. DeVos started referring to "education freedom" rather than school choice. At a kickoff event at St. Marcus Lutheran School in Milwaukee, DeVos stated that "doing better begins by expanding freedom," and she referred to Milwaukee as "the 'birthplace of education freedom' because of its long-running voucher program" (Blad, 2019, para. 6). Education freedom is touted as going beyond providing parents and students with a choice of the brick-and-mortar school they will attend, as it allows parents and students the freedom to develop their individual educational experiences:

> "If you don't like to study behind a desk and learn better in a lab or in a garden or between skyscrapers, you can do that," [DeVos] told students in Milwaukee. "If you want hands-on experiences to help decide your learning pathway, you can have those. You should be free to learn in any way and in any place that works for you." (Blad, 2019, para. 10)

The proposed legislation, titled the Education Freedom Scholarships and Opportunity Act, introduced by Senator Ted Cruz in March 2019, would "establish a new, nationwide federal tax-credit scholarship program allowing federal taxpayers to receive a dollar-for-dollar federal tax credit for contributions made to nonprofit scholarship-granting organizations (SGOs), which would in turn provide scholarships for eligible children" (Burke & Michel, 2019, p. 1). The price tag for this initiative is estimated to be $5 billion annually (Blad, 2019). However, this legislation has met with mixed reviews from conservative think tanks, civil rights groups, and teachers' unions.

The Heritage Foundation has expressed its opposition to this federal initiative, believing that school choice decisions, such as vouchers and tax-credit scholarships, should be decided at the state, rather than federal, level (Burke & Michel, 2019). According to Burke and

Michel (2019), education freedom scholarships constitute an overstep of federal authority over education and threaten school choice because it would expose private schools to more federal oversight. Although the federal government lacks constitutional authority over education, states possess this authority and are in a better position to develop legislation and initiatives that support school choice, such as vouchers and educational savings accounts. The federal government's attempt to establish federal tax-credit scholarships would undermine the school choice advances that have been made at the state level and would expand the federal government's authority over K–12 education. The Heritage Foundation argued that

> tax-credit scholarship programs are smart state-level education policy. The public education trifecta that defines state education systems—that education is publicly funded, compulsory, and assigned based on a family's zip code—makes the pursuit of education choice policies critical. State-based tax-credit scholarship programs and their cousins—voucher options and education savings accounts (ESAs)—achieve what Nobel Prize–winning economist Milton Friedman recommended: separating the financing of public education from the delivery of services. As Friedman observed, the government "administration of schools is neither required by the financing of education, nor justifiable in its own right in a predominantly free enterprise society." (citing Friedman, 1955, p. 14, in Burke & Michel, 2019, p. 3)

According to Burke and Michel, in 2010, only four states had school choice programs. Today, there are school choice programs in 29 states; Washington, D.C.; and Puerto Rico. Some fear federal tax-credit programs would shift the state-level donations away from state school-choice initiatives to federal tax credit scholarships, resulting in crowding out state-level programs (Burke & Michel, 2019). Civil rights groups and teachers' unions oppose tax-credit scholarships because of their impact on tax revenues. They believe tax-credit scholarships would have a detrimental impact on resource-deprived schools due to inequitable school financing structures (Blad, 2019). There are currently 22 tax credit scholarship programs in the United States, which, during the 2016–2017 school year alone, awarded more than 250,000 scholarships worth nearly $1 billion (Blad, 2019). The bill has not yet made it out of committee and has only a slight chance of being enacted (GovTrack, n.d.).

Assessing Secretary Of Education Betsy DeVos's Influence

Since assuming her role as secretary of education, DeVos has "proposed billions of dollars in cuts to her own department, hitting class size reductions, after-school program, full-service community schools and student loan forgiveness" (Smith, 2019, para. 7). However, it appears DeVos has retreated from her agenda of new private-school choice programs. The retreat was due, in part, to pushback from Republicans in Congress who rebuffed the public- and private-school choice proposals included in the administration budget request, along with pleas from conservative education policy experts not to pursue private school choice (Camera, 2017).

In the early months of the Trump presidency, many proponents of private-school choice believed if President Trump could work successfully with Congress to score early legislative victories on major policy issues, he and Secretary DeVos would be able to stir up enough goodwill to seriously pursue private-school choice. However, the proponents have seen this idea evaporate into thin air (Camera, 2017). According to Michael Petrilli, president of the Fordham Foundation, "her bully pulpit is pretty damaged because of her unpopularity and because of Trump's unpopularity" (Camera, 2017, para. 18). DeVos has even stated that she believes school choice is a matter for state, rather than federal, government:

> The slow slide to this new reality comes after months of political pushback from both sides of the aisle to directing any new federal funding toward private school choice, a chorus of conservative education policy experts voicing their concerns over such a program opening up private schools to federal oversight, and a more realistic understanding of what's possible to achieve given the political landscape. (Camera, 2017, para. 4)

Her focus has turned to state control/state-level decision making that would be facilitated via a provision in the federal tax reform bill that would allow states to institute tax-credit scholarships. However, even this initiative seems to be losing traction at the federal level.

Perhaps the place in which DeVos has garnered the most success is in the area of shaping "common sense" through her coining of the term *educational freedom*. On January 31, 2010, DeVos stated that "educational freedom is inevitable" (Vondracek, 2020). Transitioning to *educational freedom* rather than *school choice* creates a rhetorical space where it becomes more difficult to express opposition. After all, who is not in favor of educational freedom? Such rhetoric facilitates engagement with the "common sense" of Trump's base and brings them along to support initiatives that promise freedom but have a track record of keeping economically and racially disadvantaged groups "in their place." The education freedom scholarship winners will not be the recipients of the scholarships but the wealthy elite, like Dick and Betsy DeVos, who can glean a dollar-for-dollar tax credit for their donations.

References

Alliance Defending Freedom. (n.d.). *About the Center for Academic Freedom*. https://www.adflegal.org/about-us

Blad, E. (2019). Betsy Devos tests a rhetorical twist on 'school choice': Recent speeches twin 'education' with 'freedom.' *Education Week*, *39*(7), 7.

Brown, S. (2018). Leading conservatives celebrate 20 years of YAF's preservation of Ronald Reagan's western White House. *The New Guard Blog.* https://www.yaf.org/news/leading-conservatives-celebrate-20-years-of-yafs-preservation-of-ronald-reagans-western-white-house/

Brown v. Board of Education of Topeka. 347 U.S. 483 (1954).

Burke, L., & Michel, A. (2019). *Why a federal tax-credit scholarship program will not advance school choice in America* (The Heritage Backgrounder, No. 3395). https://www.heritage.org/sites/default/files/2019-03/BG3395.pdf

Camera, L. (2017). The evolution of Betsy DeVos: The Education Secretary came in as a federal private school choice champion. What happened? *U.S. News and World Report.* https://www.usnews.com/news/the-report/articles/2017-10-02/the-evolution-of-betsy-devos-and-private-school-choice

Center for Media and Democracy. (n.d.-a). *Alliance Defending Freedom.* Source Watch. https://www.sourcewatch.org/index.php?title=Alliance_Defending_Freedom#cite_note-inside-27

Center for Media and Democracy. (n.d.-b). *Young America's Foundation.* Source Watch. https://www.sourcewatch.org/index.php?title=Young_America%27s_Foundation#cite_note-nyt-7

deMarrais, K. (2006). "The haves and the have mores": Fueling a conservative ideological war on public education. *Educational Studies, 39*(3), 204–242.

deMarrais, K., Brewer, T. J., Atkinson, J. C., Herron, B. A., & Lewis, J. B. (2019). *Philanthropy, hidden strategy, and collective resistance: A primer for concerned educators.* Myers Education Press.

Dick and Betsy DeVos Foundation. (n.d.). *About.* https://www.dbdvfoundation.org/about

Doksai, R. (2016). School choice, but much more: Making sense of DeVos family philanthropy. *Inside Philanthropy.* https://www.insidephilanthropy.com/home/2016/3/1/school-choice-but-much-more-making-sense-of-devos-family-phi.html

Education Freedom Scholarships and Opportunity Act. S.634 (2019). https://www.congress.gov/bill/116th-congress/senate-bill/634

Ford, Z. (2018). *Is Alliance Defending Freedom a hate group? Just look at their work.* ThinkProgress. https://thinkprogress.org/adf-hate-group-3302dd95ace4/

Friedman, M. (1955). *The role of government in education*. http://homepage.fudan.edu.cn/jfeng/files/2011/08/role-of-government-in-education_Friedman.pdf

Gardner, D. P. (1983). A nation at risk. *Washington, DC: The National Commission on Excellence in Education, US Department of Education*.

GovTrack. (n.d.). S. 634: Education Freedom Scholarships and Opportunity Act. https://www.govtrack.us/congress/bills/116/s634

GuideStar. (n.d.). *Education Freedom Fund*. https://www.guidestar.org/profile/38-2999840

Kumashiro, K. K., Miller, K. S., Bellamy, R., Melehy, H., Priesmeyer, M., & Goodwin, S. A. (2012). When billionaires become educational experts. *Academe*, *98*(3), 10–16.

McShane, M. Q. (2017). Betsy Devos, the (relatively mainstream) reformer: A long record refutes the radical image of the education secretary. *Education Next*, *17*(3), 26–34.

Media Mouse. (n.d.). *Education Freedom Fund*. https://mediamousearchive.wordpress.com/resources/right/orgs/education-freedom-fund/

Powell, L. (1971). Powell memorandum: The attack on the free enterprise system. Book I: Powell papers.

Propublica. (n.d.) Helen and Richard DeVos Foundation. *NonProfit Explorer*. https://projects.propublica.org/nonprofits/organizations/456659303

Rizga, K. (2017). Betsy DeVos wants to use America's schools to build 'God's Kingdom'. *Mother Jones*. https://www.motherjones.com/politics/2017/01/betsy-devos-christian-schools-vouchers-charter-education-secretary/

Saul, S. (2017). The conservative force behind speeches roiling college campuses. *The New York Times*. https://www.nytimes.com/2017/05/20/us/college-conservative-speeches.html

Smith, D. (2019). Betsy DeVos: The billionaire Republican destroying public education. *The Guardian*. https://www.theguardian.com/us-news/2019/dec/27/betsy-devos-trump-republicans-education-secretary

Southern Poverty Law Center. (n.d.). *Alliance Defending Freedom*. https://www.splcenter.org/fighting-hate/extremist-files/group/alliance-defending-freedom

Step Up for Students. (n.d.). *History*. https://www.stepupforstudents.org/about-us/history/

Strauss, V. (2019). The single most telling sentence Betsy DeVos said to Congress this week. *The Washington Post.* https://www.washingtonpost.com/education/2019/03/29/single-most-telling-sentence-betsy-devos-said-congress-this-week/

Teasley, M. L. (2017). The dynamics of education reform and school choice. *Children & Schools*, *39*(3), 131–135.

Vondracek, C. (2020). Betsy DeVos says 'education freedom is inevitable' ahead of State of Union. *The Washington Times.* https://www.washingtontimes.com/news/2020/jan/31/betsy-devos-says-education-freedom-inevitable-ahea/

Wang, J. (Ed.). (2019). America's top 50 givers: Meet the philanthropists who gave away the most money in 2018. *Forbes.* https://www.forbes.com/top-givers/#53678c9666ff

Wilkerson, M. (2017). Betsy DeVos and the segregation of school choice. *The Education Digest*, *82*(8), 19-24.

Young America's Foundation. (n.d.). History of Young America's Foundation. https://www.yaf.org/about/history/

Chapter Five

TRACKING CATHOLIC SCHOOL FUNDING FROM K–12 THROUGH HIGHER EDUCATION

Kevin J. Burke, *University of Georgia*

In this chapter, I chart the contours of a decline in Catholic K–12 enrollment over the last half of the 20th and the first half of the 21st centuries. Rather than a tour of the gallows, this chapter provides an (admittedly limited) accounting of this system and the rationale behind a decades-long movement within sectors of the Catholic educational establishment that sought to save itself and its schools by leveraging ties to conservative activist think tanks and funders through a full embrace of neoliberal educational reform. This analysis was done through a case study of a single organization that can be made synecdoche for the most troubling instincts of a system flailing as it founders. There is danger in the threat that it might pull public education at the state and national levels down with it. My sense is that, generally speaking, most scholars in the educational research and policy establishment pay little, if any, attention to Catholic education. Thus, a body of critical work about and around this system of schooling has remained largely unconstructed over the years. This chapter is an attempt to partially remedy that inattention. It is important to note, of course, that the story told here is partial; it is self-evidently true that there are people in, and involved with, Catholic schools doing yeoman's work in the service not only of students but also of their highest religious ideals. Also, there are people within institutions dedicated to Catholic education who have not drunk from the well of neoliberal education reform as savior-for-all-things educationally parochial. My strong assertion is that these people and the teachers they prepare, as well as the students they teach, are being done an active disservice by Catholic educational organizations that have wholeheartedly embraced marketized reform over the last 30 or so years. This is to say nothing of the collateral damage done to public schooling and public school students and teachers as a result of Catholic education's outsized public policy influence. There has been, in short, an abandonment of the catholic (the universal) in pursuit of nostalgia over the particularized version of the Catholic that limps on in schools across the country.

Comprising some 6,300 schools and serving nearly 2 million students (McDonald & Schultz, 2019), the American Catholic educational system remains the largest network of private schooling in the world, accounting for fully a third of private school enrollment in the United States in 2019. Still, that network is shrinking and has been since the latter half of the 1960s. Although total student enrollment in public schools in the United States rose 7% from 2000 to 2016 (National Center for Educational Statistics, 2019), Catholic school enrollment fell by 19% over a roughly congruent set of years (National Center for Educational Statistics, 2019). Although some new schools have opened in the last decade, the story of Catholic schooling, vis-à-vis enrollment, has been grim.

The contraction has aligned closely with a cratering of religious vocations (Schuth, 2011)—there were, for example, 19,000 more priests and 118,000 more religious sisters in 1967 than there were in 2010—and an exodus from the church by the laity—Catholicism experienced the largest net loss of adherents of any religious denomination in the United States between 2007 and 2014 (Masci & Smith, 2018). These catastrophic numbers have been blamed variously on the doctrinal and liturgical reforms of the Second Vatican Council, the rise of feminism and a progressive secularization of the culture, and a surge in distrust of institutions, in general, after the Vietnam War and of the church, specifically, in the wake of near-constant revelations of systemic sexual abuse of minors. The decline in enrollment coincided with a significant movement away from so-called national parishes—those organized specifically for Polish or Irish or German immigrant populations, for example—and toward a territorial model that marked a shift in perceptions of foreignness of Catholic populations in the United States (Dolan, 2002). The exception to the rule was maintenance of racially segregated churches on the national model for Black Catholic populations in places like Chicago (Johnson, 2018) into the mid-20th century and beyond; this was an extension of European immigrant "races" becoming White as they sought, with tacit if not explicit support of the Catholic hierarchy, to distance themselves from their Black co-religionists.

Whatever the proximal causes, Catholic schools are slowly dying. From a logistical standpoint, much of this has to do (in addition to the previously mentioned) with the cost of attendance as well as massive White flight from industrial inner cities, which served as the lifeblood of the parish system that sustained the growth of the church in the United States from the 19th century on. Much of this White flight, it should be said, was facilitated by in the most generous reading possible, an ambivalent religious bureaucracy that often sided with "recent [European] immigrants" who saw "living in an all-white area like most other white Americans" as a mark "of their decency" (Johnson, 2018, p. 133). Failing to deploy all the religious tools of unity across races available to them through the clear theologies of Catholic doctrine,[1] (arch)bishops, parish priests, and religious sisters on balance (although with happy exceptions; see, for instance, Flinn, 1970), through racially segregative policies at the parish and parish school level, seeded the demise of their own institutions. A push against the racist narratives of Black inferiority that fed real estate practices and drove racial violence might have staunched the outflow of Whites to the suburbs and attracted a more racially diverse laity into parishes. It might have eased transitions when neighborhoods "changed" had parish schools integrated through outreach to Black Protestants and Catholics both. But this never really happened on any significant scale, and Catholic schools have been reaping what was sown in the mid-20th century ever since. African Americans, distrustful of a church that failed to advocate for racial unity in its loudest voice, converted to Catholicism in minuscule numbers and generally only found themselves welcome in parish and religious-order high schools after enough White parishioners, facilitated in their racial paranoia by a mostly uninterested hierarchy, had moved to the suburbs. There is, of course, a different story that might be told about the explosion of American Latine Catholic populations, but it ends the same way: in segregated neighborhoods with segregated and largely under-resourced schools for people of color.

Robust parishes feeding sufficient weekly tithes into school coffers could, in the past, sustain schools at least up to the point when they were staffed by a captive—and, functionally speaking, "free"—workforce of religious sisters, brothers, and priests. Shifting to a lay faculty has added a major fiscal burden on schools as they must now account for family benefits, retirement funds, and the general need to at least gesture toward competing on salary with nearby public schools. Consequently, as parishes have emptied out, this fiscal burden has been shifted to tuition-paying families. As tuition has increased, inner-city Catholic schools have, generally speaking, been put out of reach for poorer kids—who now tend to be non-Catholic in places such as the south and west sides of Chicago or the inner corridors of Philadelphia. Suburban and more affluent White Catholics have come to accept public schools, for which they often pay significant taxes as the price for sustaining, among other things, segregated schooling as sufficient alternatives to private education. What remains is a roughly tripartite system of prestigious academies, often run by religious orders (think the Salesians); recent "reform"-era networks of schools for the poor that either require corporate and nonprofit largesse to provide shared labor opportunities to students as a way to offset tuition (e.g., the Cristo Rey model; see Kearney, 2008)or work young teachers at burnout levels in a take on the no-excuses charter model (e.g., Nativity Prep Model); and shoestring inner-city diocesan schools are hanging on, in many places, due to tax credits and vouchers. It is to tax credits and vouchers, and their elevated place in the vision of Catholic schools, that I wish to attend in this chapter.

The preceding is largely prologue to a political shift I trace from the early 2000s where drivers in Catholic school policy—the National Catholic Educational Association, the United States Conference of Catholic Bishops (USCCB), and the prominent Teach for America (TFA) replica programs at Catholic universities—mirrored (or precipitated, depending on how you choose to approach it) a culture-wars turn to the right by the bishopric. In other words, as local diocesan and parishonal funding for education failed and schools floundered, the church increasingly turned to the economic justifications of marketization, choice, and conservative funders and foundations to make a case for robust public funding for Catholic schools.[2] And they did so, at first, under the auspices of a relatively stable, if small, body of research that suggested Catholic schools added something unique, admittedly valuable, and easily measurable to the educational landscape.

Catholic Educational Research, A Précis

Couched in the language of the common good, taken from Bryk et al. (1993) and rooted, originally, in work by Andrew Greeley (2002; Hoffer, Greeley & Coleman, 1985) that asserted a Catholic School advantage, the church has made common cause with conservative funders and drove through public pronouncement, religious blandishment, and the laundering of ideas through university centers and conservative think tanks a great deal of public education policy, especially at the level of the states, over the course of the last 20-odd years. In a conscious and coordinated move, the Catholic educational system set itself up in direct contrast to public schooling as a successful alternative to a massive failing bureaucracy. As it saw its share of Catholic students bleed away to the suburbs, some Catholic education policy drivers turned to market logic as a way to stave off closure. This is, in some ways, bred into the system. Created initially as an escape from the (perceived and real) Protestant biases of early common schools, the Catholic education system has always embraced its role as a remnant set apart (DelFattore, 2004; Dolan, 2002).[3] And although it was at one time a bulwark, although an imperfect one, against religious and racist persecution, it came to harbor outposts of these exact discourses at its height and into its decline (e.g., Burke & Gilbert, 2015; Neville, 2019).

Broadly speaking, very little attention is paid to Catholic education in the United States in the educational research literature except when it is attended to by advocates in, for instance, methodologically troubling, if not outright misleading, ways (e.g., Brinig & Garnett, 2014; Smarick & Robson, 2015).[4] This inattention is a mistake, as there is outsized political power and money behind the system and in seeking to save it. Indeed, in the relatively rare cases when nonadvocates have attended to Catholic education in the research, whatever Catholic school advantage might have existed in the 1980s and 1990s seems either to have slipped away or to never have existed in the first place (e.g., Hallinan & Kubitschek, 2012; Reardon et al., 2009; Wenglinsky, 2007). To the former point, theories are often connected to the increased professional development requirements hung over the heads of public schooling in an age of accountability (e.g., Lubienski et al., 2008; Lubienski & Lubienski, 2014), and although we might rightly argue with the metrics used to measure "success" in these cases, the point still stands that whatever advantage might have once appeared in these kinds of data no longer does. And the long-held argument that Catholic schools serve the common good and thus should be provided for out of the commons ought to be at least put into question, certainly if the idea is to best serve students most in need. At the very least, it might be an opportunity for reconsideration of the orientation between the Catholic school sector and its public (and other private) peers, especially if we are to take into account, as we should, the ongoing practice of firing Catholic school teachers for engaging in their constitutionally protected right to marriage (Herron, 2019) or getting pregnant out of wedlock (M. Williams, 2019). That, unfortunately, has not happened. There are implications, in other words, related to public funding to be considered here: If the public purse is being used to support certain versions of institutionalized discrimination, in schools whose academic benefit is, in many ways, mixed, then what ought best be done from a policy perspective? The answer, as yet, is essentially "Well, we don't know," mostly because of a lack of critical study of the Catholic sector and its inflection on the public educational system.

This chapter examines ways in which private foundation money has been harnessed by Catholic universities and conservative Catholic bishops to drive educational policy toward school choice and push public money into Catholic schools, regardless (and often because of) the consequences for public schools and their students. We begin, in the tradition of Gallop (2002), with an exorbitant moment of the anecdotal.

Attending to Catholic Influence

Prior to attending to the funding routes through which Catholic education is often benefiting from, if not driving educational policy at the level of the states and in the current administration, federally, it is worth recounting an episode from 2017. On March 3, President Donald J. Trump made his first visit to a U.S. school while in office. Fitting with the privatization agenda of his fellow visitor, education secretary Betsy DeVos, Trump spent a day at St. Andrew Catholic School in Orlando, Florida. Of the many controversies surrounding the visit—including the demographics of the school, of which the number of students of color hovers at about three quarters; ought we have exposed kids of Latine descent to a man who opened his presidential campaign calling Mexicans "rapists" for instance?—there were subtexts made text clearly throughout the visit. Something on the order of 300 of the 350 students at the school attended under the auspices of Florida tax-credit scholarships (Jones, 2017) most prominently those run by Step Up for Students, an organization that began, as most waves of neoliberal reforms have over the years, with a venture capitalist, in this case John Kirtley, leveraging his access to a state legislature.[5] Indeed, fully a quarter of students enrolled in Catholic schools in the dioceses of Orlando receive "Step Up" tax-credit scholarships (Jones, 2017). As the day continued through classroom visits, the president; the secretary; Rick Scott, then governor of Florida; and Florida senator Marco Rubio were joined by Kirtley, whom Step Up (n.d.) cites as the prime mover behind the explosion of tax-credit funding for private schooling in Florida. The day became, by the time a press conference panel was organized, an extended advertisement for the virtues of school choice. Less well advertised, however, was a more obscure connection: that to the University of Notre Dame. For, in fact, St. Andrew is what is called a Notre Dame ACE Academy. ACE Academies are run through the Alliance for Catholic Education (ACE), under the auspices of the Institute for Educational Initiatives (IEI) at the university and modeled after Knowledge Is Power Program (KIPP) schools. Missing from all the pictures of the day are representatives of ACE, who were, in fact, present. This was no accident; the press conference praising school choice with a supportive secretary of education and a malignant, although in this case wholly ignorant, president (at least with regard to educational policy) was the culmination of some 20-odd years of policy machinations driven out of the IEI. But the publicity tied to the president's racism was unwelcome, and so, although the Catholic school connection was made public, the Notre Dame ties to the space were backgrounded, only picked up by some certain news agencies (see, for instance, Catholic News Service, 2017).

Begun in the late 1990s, in answer to the burgeoning crisis in Catholic school staffing as religious vocations fell off, ACE was, initially, something of a TFA replicant. It rose in prominence, at the University of Notre Dame, alongside the IEI, under whose penumbra a number of endeavors regarding K–12 education came to be housed. There were, and remain, significant differences between TFA and ACE related to cohort size, religious mission (all new teachers are placed in Catholic schools for instance), and ongoing academic support (ACE teachers earn an MEd from the University of Notre Dame upon completion of their two-year commitment; see Alliance for Catholic Education, n.d.-a).[6] In the intervening years, and mirroring many of the moves of the public education reform movement, ACE has expanded its portfolio to include, among other things, KIPP-replica Catholic schools (see Alliance for Catholic Education, n.d.-b),[7] as well as a voucher and tax-credit advocacy "policy" arm (see Alliance for Catholic Education, n.d.-c). There are, it should be said, praiseworthy programs within the IEI structure, but the larger driving ethos has always been about "saving" Catholic schools, and that focus has run very specifically on the pursuit of conservative money through right-wing educational policy priorities. Indeed, as of 2017, ACE and the IEI, in some combination, had received seven-figure donations from the Annenberg, Conrad Hilton, Charles Koch, and Walton Family Foundations, as well as six-figure donations from the Douglass and Maria DeVos Family Foundation.

That the undermining of public schooling in America might occur as a result of saving Catholic schooling through school choice is not, sadly, incidental to this work, although, generally speaking, the line of argumentation is first about saving private schooling—whose benefits are seen to be embedded in their privateness—regardless. Nicole Garnett, a law professor at Notre Dame—former clerk for Clarence Thomas—and former head of the voucher initiative at the university made this very explicit in a speech celebrating Indiana's new voucher law in 2011, noting that she felt bad for a public school parent she saw each morning as she sent her children off to Catholic school in South Bend because "he knows that school is not going to serve them well" (Fosmoe, 2011, para. 9) She continued asserting that "Catholic schools, as we all know, are the central case for school choice," because "Catholic schools succeed where . . . public schools fail. And particularly, they succeed at educating the kids that society has given up on, who society thinks can't learn," (para. 15) adding, "I want public schools to get better," she said, "but I don't think we should base the case for school choice on whether or not they do" (para. 18).[8] That the research does not necessarily support the claim that Catholic schools succeed where public schools fail is, in some sense, immaterial (see, for instance, the many studies of vouchers in Indiana to emerge out of Notre Dame these past few years; e.g., Waddington & Berends, 2018); they fail by their public nature, by and large, in an ideology that sees the private as the only viable solution to educational issues.

An attentive reader will be wondering why I am singling out a single institute at one university in this work; the question is fair enough. One answer is that it is a beginning point for constructing a larger map of conservative funding behind Catholic educational policy; another is that Notre Dame has constructed itself as a hub of this work. Indeed, in other spaces, Smarick (2014) and others have made explicit the road map for transferring charter school expansion techniques to the private and, specifically, Catholic sectors. They further account for the ways in which Notre Dame and ACE have come to drive the American Catholic bishopric's thinking about Catholic school policy in the direction of conservative funding priorities, noting that

> since 2009, Notre Dame's Alliance for Catholic Education has hosted a series of meetings among bishops to discuss the revitalization of Catholic K-12 schooling. . . . ACE's John Schoenig sees 'growing receptivity among bishops to new models. The paradigm has shifted fundamentally in these six years' . . . [indeed] by insisting on updated structures and helping to pay for them, donors can have a powerful influence on this crucial transition. (Smarick & Robson, 2015, p. 38)

The ACE program was founded by two Holy Cross priests. ACE and the IEI, however, remain tied most prominently to one of them, a political scientist named Tim Scully. The university shuttered its Department of Education in 1977, and in the creation of the ACE program and its attendant MEd, leaders at Notre Dame were tasked with creating a program, whole cloth, with few scholars in the field of education (e.g., aside from disparate members of the faculty housed in psychology) present at the university. This was not seen as a significant problem by academic leaders in the space, particularly Scully, who, when interviewed about the former department and his role in heading up the alternative certification program that emerged after its demise, noted,

> The charitable interpretation was that schools of education are not known for their academic rigor, nor are they known for their entrepreneurial spirit, nor are they particularly famous for independent thinking or reform in education. I believe, and this may offend you, that it was a providential decision that they closed the department of education, because departments of education are full of mediocre scholars, not all of them, but many of them. (Mooney, 2016, pp. 20–21)

We need not spend too much time on the inside politics of a particular university as it relates to the closing or reopening of given departments except to say that the preceding is more or less standard reform-speak palaver rooted in, it should be said, no actual evidence. The point in singling out Scully is not to hold him out as exceptional in any way—he is very much of a kind with fellow neoliberal reformists in that he sees very little value in actual educational expertise. He is a massive fundraiser and is well connected to conservative donor networks; those last two are often predicated on the first one as has often been demonstrated. More on the donor networks in a moment, but for now, we might note that the point is perhaps evidenced best by his receipt of the William E. Simon Prize from the Manhattan Institute for Lifetime Achievement in Social Entrepreneurship in 2013 for his creation of ACE and stewardship of the IEI that houses it at Notre Dame (Garvey, 2013). It is important to note, too, that prominent support for vouchers has run deep in the blood of the university for some time now (Winters, 2010).

Alongside those conversations among bishops aimed at shifting attitudes toward funders' priorities, ACE has hosted a number of educational fora over the years, the most prominent of which was a university-sponsored, yearlong "conversation" about education reform in the United States in 2011. As was very much in the zeitgeist in certain sectors, the main event featured screenings on campus of *Waiting for Superman (*Strickland, B. et al., 2011) as well as a "discussion" between Michelle Rhee, John Diulio, Sara Martinez Tucker, and Howard Fuller. Rhee is well known to those who think about the worst excesses of the recent reform era. Fuller as well is fairly prominent, having run the Black Alliance for Educational Options, a pro-voucher organization in Milwaukee. Martinez Tucker was an undersecretary of education under George W. Bush and Diulio and a professor of political science at the University of Pennsylvania perhaps best known for his creation and promulgation of the superpredator myth from the mid-1990s (C. Williams, 2011). Other, smaller events featured a who's who of education reform including Jeb Bush, Terry Moe, and Chris Christie. Beyond that were lesser lights, such as Juan Rangel, who, as head of the United Neighborhood Organization (UNO) charter network in Chicago, was indicted on securities fraud charges; Tony Bennett, then superintendent of schools in Indiana, who was forced to resign for changing state evaluation grades for some charter schools; and Bob McDonnell, who, as governor of Virginia, was indicted, although later acquitted, on wire fraud, bribery, and obstruction charges.

Beyond the preceding, the IEI runs an annual school choice symposium featuring well-known figures in the larger neoliberal reform movement as a way to aid Catholic school superintendents, principals, parents, and teachers in pushing for expanded public funds (Schmitt, 2013). The organization is well connected to conservative think tanks beyond the Manhattan Institute. ACE administration gets invitations to events sponsored by the American Enterprise Institute (Makin, 2008), the Heritage Foundation (Willis, 2012), and the Aspen Institute (n.d.; see Christian Dallavis) and funnels graduates consistently into the right-leaning Department of Education Reform at the University of Arkansas (see Chapter Four on the Walton Family Foundation funding). Indeed, ACE graduates are prominent in right-wing policy shops, including

EdChoice (n.d.) and Empower Illinois (n.d.; see John Schoenig). The entanglements are too multifarious to list here, as they often are with interested think-tank policy networks, in general, and in right-wing circles, broadly. But the larger point is that the leaders in prominent school choice advocacy organizations are heavily influenced by individuals connected to Catholic education, generally, and the ACE program, specifically, and vice versa. This does not have to be a sinister thing necessarily, as these individuals might well have the best interests of students in mind in their work. It should be said, however, that this may not necessarily extend to the best interests of students in public schooling.

The point is twofold here. First, by failing to attend to the religious roots of some of the school choice movement, particularly as it emerges from Catholic circles, we forget the nature of a missionary endeavor. Missionaries are not merely bloodless policy advocates; rather, they are religiously convicted in their pursuit of a godly solution. Faith, in this case, then, justifies means (saving Catholic schools and souls in the process), often regardless of their collateral effects. Second, although ACE is singular in its work, it is not necessarily exceptional. It is part of a network of conservative activist school-choice funding nodes and ought to be examined as such alongside other organizations pushing these policies. Notre Dame holds a hallowed place in the American Catholic establishment. Other Catholic organizations often follow the way in which it moves, whether they want to or not, in large part, because of the resources available to the South Bend institution. Over the years, ACE pushed the American Catholic bishops in the direction of a particular version of conservative school choice policy that we ended up with the USCCB (n.d.) putting school choice as a public policy priority and linking directly to the American Federation for Children and EdChoice to justify its stances. The bishops have neither the expertise nor the time, or they have chosen not to devote time, to attend fully to the larger educational policy issues facing the country. In the absence of considered scholarship, they have turned to ACE for solutions; ACE has turned to the organizations funded by the donor network that keeps it afloat.

By way of conclusion, it is important to put forward that I am a graduate of the ACE program's MEd. As a member of ACE at Notre Dame, I taught in a small Catholic high school in Phoenix, Arizona, and, as often happens—and is well documented—with these alternative certification programs, parlayed that brief experience in the classroom into other things to my professional benefit. Indeed, after finishing my PhD, I was employed as a faculty member in the ACE program for 5 years before leaving and taking up my current position. This particularized history can be read, of course, as providing me with many reasons for writing this chapter—a kind of protracted revenge, a Freudian response to the place that made me—most of which will be true, in part. What I have found, however, is that because so little critical scholarship on Catholic education and, in particular, its policy choices exists, those who attend to such things will inevitably be interested parties. It is, however, important to note that my time as a faculty member with the ACE program colored my sense of the underlying intentionality of policy drivers in ways that are vital for understanding how educational policy is pushed by a not-so-shadow network not only of conservative Christian donors in the DeVos mold but also of conservative Catholic ones whose mold we have not well attended to.

The more important point is that things could be different. There are Catholic educational scholars who are rooted in and think about Catholic schooling who would, given the opportunity, do different work thinking about how Catholic schools might thrive without acquiescing to the neoliberal narrative of scarcity of funding amid competition. There are Catholic colleges of education with critical scholars who do legitimate policy work rooted in deep expertise who might better advise the bishops, parents, superintendents, and other advocates for Catholic schools and who are not beholden to the constrained narratives that come with the strings bound up in seven-figure donations. In the end, this chapter is meant as a goad to the broader educational establishment to pay attention to Catholic education as more than a niche and as part of the policy ecosystem in American education not only because funding matters but also because there are likely messages that could be taken from these schools for the improvement of the educational system as a whole. Furthermore, it is vital, if Catholic schools are to survive, for their leadership to shift their arguments from pushing for funds at the expense of public schools to a prophetic indictment (Kaveny, 2018) of the notion of scarcity in education at all. Catholic schools would do well to think about how their relationship to the regulatory regime that accompanies public funding might be altered in a different fiscal landscape, but they would do even better by a broader and deeper public if they started thinking of themselves as allied with public schooling rather than in competition with it. That only happens with a break from conservative funding and radical right-wing narratives about what school is about and how we have to think of it as economic in argument first; that only happens, as well, when critical scholarship about the relationship between prominent movers in the field and donor networks is made available and examined for what it might be doing to the schools, the students, the parents, their communities, and the church as a whole.

References

Alliance for Catholic Education. (2016, October 5). *Kopp, Barth honored with 2016 Notre Dame Award for Outstanding Contributions to Catholic Education*. https://ace.nd.edu/news/kopp-barth-honored-with-2016-notre-dame-award-for-outstanding-contributions-to-catholic-education

Alliance for Catholic Education. (n.d.-a). *ACE teaching fellows*. https://ace.nd.edu/teach/

Alliance for Catholic Education. (n.d.-b). *Notre Dame ACE academies*. https://ace.nd.edu/academies/

Alliance for Catholic Education. (n.d.-c). *Program for education access*. https://ace.nd.edu/pea/

Aspen Institute, Pahara Fellows: Christian Dallavis. Retrieved from https://agln.aspeninstitute.org/profile/4359

Aspen Global Leadership Network. (n.d.). *ALGN directory*. https://agln.aspeninstitute.org/directory/pahara

Brinig, M. F., & Garnett, N. S. (2014). *Lost classroom, lost community: Catholic schools' importance in urban America*. University of Chicago Press.

Bryk, A., Lee, V., & Holland, P. (1993). *Catholic schools and the common good*. Harvard University Press.

Burke, K. J., & Gilbert, B. R. (2015). Racing tradition: Catholic schooling and the maintenance of boundaries. *Race Ethnicity and Education, 19*(3), 524–545.

Catholic News Service. (2017). Trump visits Catholic school to show support for school choice. *Catholic Herald*. https://catholicherald.co.uk/trump-visits-catholic-school-to-show-support-for-school-choice/

DelFattore, J. (2004). *The fourth R: Conflicts over religion in America's public schools*. Yale University Press.

Dolan, J. (2002). *In search of an American Catholicism: A history of religion and culture in tension*. Oxford University Press.

EdChoice. (n.d.). *Michael McShane*. Retreived from https://www.edchoice.org/our-team/michael-mcshane/

Empower Illinois. John Schoenig. Retrieved from https://empowerillinois.org/about/leadership/#:~:text=John%20Schoenig%20is%20Director%20of,and%20Empower%20Illinois%20Board%20Secretary.,

Empower Illinois. (n.d.). *Leadership*. https://empowerillinois.org/about/leadership/

Everson v. Board of Education, 330 U.S. 1 (1947).

Flinn, P. (1970, September 26). I teach in a racist school. *America*, pp. 201–203.

Fosmoe, M. (2011, July 9). Law professor lauds Catholic schooling. *South Bend Tribune*. https://infoweb.newsbank.com/resources/doc/nb/news/13D2EA9704983560?p=AMNEWS

Gallop, J. (2002). *Anecdotal theory*. Duke University Press.

Garvey, M. O. (2013). *Rev. Tim Scully, founder of Notre Dame's ACE program, to receive Manhattan Institute's William E. Simon Prize* [Press release]. https://news.nd.edu/news/father-tim-scully-founder-of-notre-dames-ace-program-to-receive-manhattan-institutes-william-e-simon-prize/

Gordon, S. B. (2007). "Free" religion and "captive" schools: Protestants, Catholics, and education, 1945–1965. *DePaul Law Review, 56*(4), 1177–1220.

Greeley, A. (2002). *Catholic high schools and minority students*. Transaction.

Green, P. (2011). African Americans in urban Catholic schools: Faith, leadership and persistence in pursuit of educational opportunity. *Urban Review, 43*(3), 436–464.

Hallinan, M. T., & Kubitschek, W. N. (2013). School sector, school poverty, and the Catholic school advantage. *Catholic Education, 14*(2), 143-172.

Herron, A. (2019, July 9). Indianapolis Catholic school controversy: Cathedral settles with teacher over gay marriage. *Indianapolis Star.* https://www.indystar.com/story/news/education/2019/07/09/indianapolis-cathedral-high-school-gay-teacher-archdiocese-settlement/1686671001/

Hoffer, T., Greeley, A., & Coleman, J. (1985). Achievement and growth in public and catholic schools. *Sociology of Education, 58*, 74-97.

Johnson, K. J. (2018). *One in Christ: Chicago Catholics and the quest for interracial justice.* Oxford University Press.

Jones, K. (2017). President Trump visits Catholic school, praises education for both mind and soul. National Catholic Register. Retrieved from https://www.ncregister.com/daily-news/president-trump-visits-catholic-school-praises-education-for-both-mind-and-soul

Kaveny, C. (2016). *Prophesy without contempt: Religious discourse in the public square.* Harvard University Press.

Kearney, G. R. (2008). *More than a dream: How one school's vision is changing the world.* Loyola University Press.

Lubienski, C. A., & Lubienski, S. T. (2014). *The public school advantage: Why public schools outperform private schools.* University of Chicago Press.

Lubienski, S. T., Lubienski, C., & Crane, C. C. (2008). Achievement differences and school type: The role of school climate, teacher certification, and instruction. *American Journal of Education, 115*(1), 97–138.

Makin, J. H. (2008, December 1). *Print money and cut back the payroll tax.* American Enterprise Institute. https://www.aei.org/publication/school-choice-encouraging-new-and-better-schools/print/

Masci, D., & Smith, G. A. (2018). *7 facts about American Catholics.* Pew Research Center. https://www.pewresearch.org/fact-tank/2018/10/10/7-facts-about-american-catholics/

McDonald, D., & Schultz, M. (2019). *United States Catholic elementary and secondary schools 2018–2019: The annual statistical report on schools, enrollment and staffing.* https://ncea.org/NCEA/Proclaim/Catholic_School_Data/NCEA/Proclaim/Catholic_School_Data/Catholic_School_Data.aspx?hkey=8e90e6aa-b9c4-456b-a488-6397f3640f05

Mooney, B. A. (2016). *The Department of Education at the University of Notre Dame in retrospect and prospect* (Undergraduate Thesis). University of Notre Dame, Notre Dame, IN.

National Center for Educational Statistics. (2019). *Back to school statistics.* https://nces.ed.gov/fastfacts/display.asp?id=372#PK12_enrollment

Neville, M. L. (2019). "Racism is a God-damned thing": The implications of historical and contemporary Catholic racism in ELA classrooms. In M. M. Juzwik, J. C. Stone, K. J. Burke, & D. Davila (Eds.), *Legacies of Christian languaging and literacies in American education: Perspectives on English language arts curriculum, teaching, and learning* (pp. 82-95): Routledge.

Philpott, T. L. (1991). *The slum and the ghetto: Immigrants, Blacks, and reformers in Chicago 1880–1930.* Wadsworth Publishing Company.

Reardon, S. F., Cheadle, J. E., & Robinson, J. P. (2009). The effect of Catholic schooling on math and reading development in kindergarten through fifth grade. *Journal of Research on Educational Effectiveness*, *2*(1), 45–87.

Schuth, K. (2011). Training grounds: Are U.S. Catholics entering a post-seminary world? *Boston College Magazine*, *71*(3), 30–32.

Smarick, A. (2014). *The chartered course: Can private school choice proponents learn from the charter school sector?* Friedman Foundation for Educational Choice.

Smarick, A., & Robson, K. (Eds.). (2015). *Catholic school renaissance: A wise giver's guide to strengthening a national asset.* The Philanthropy Roundtable.

Schmitt, W. (2012, January 30). *ND launches new partnership program in St. Petersburg, FL, area.* Alliance for Catholic Education. https://ace.nd.edu/news/nd-launches-new-partnership-program-in-st-petersburg-fla-area

Schmitt, W. (2013, July 2). *Symposium prepares leaders to advocate for equal educational options.* Alliance for Catholic Education. https://ace.nd.edu/news/symposium-prepares-leaders-to-advocate-for-equal-educational-options

Step Up for Students. (n.d.). *History.* https://www.stepupforstudents.org/about-us/history/

Strickland, B., Canada, G., Guggenheim, D., & Paramount Home Entertainment (Firm). (2011). *Waiting for "Superman."*. Hollywood, Calif: Paramount Home Entertainment.

United States Conference of Catholic Bishops (1963). *On Racial Harmony.* http://www.usccb.org/issues-and-action/cultural-diversity/african-american/resources/upload/On-Racial-Harmony.pdf

United States Conference of Catholic Bishops. (n.d.). *Public policy.* http://www.usccb.org/beliefs-and-teachings/how-we-teach/catholic-education/public-policy/index.cfm

Waddington, R. J., & Berends, M. (2018). Impact of Indiana choice scholarship program: Achievement effects for students in upper elementary and middle school. *Journal of Policy Analysis and Management, 37*(4), 783–808.

Wenglinsky, H. (2007). *Are private high schools better academically than public high schools?* Center on Education Policy.

Williams, C. (2011, April 12). *Professor Nicole Stelle Garnett moderates sold-out program on K–12 education reform.* https://law.nd.edu/news-events/news/professor-nicole-stelle-garnett-moderates-sold-out-program-on-k-12-education-reform/

Williams, M. R. (2019, August 19). Former KC Catholic school teacher says she was fired for being pregnant and unmarried. *Kansas City Star.* https://www.kansascity.com/news/local/article234156097.html

Willis, Y. (2012, September 28). Two-night conference to discuss issues of poverty. *Bethel.* https://magazine.betheluniversity.edu/2012/09/28/3411/

Winters, M. S. (2010, February 19). Notre Dame leaders back DC scholarship program. *National Catholic Reporter.* https://www.ncronline.org/blogs/ncr-today/notre-dame-leaders-back-dc-scholarship-program

Endnotes

1 See the statement from the United States Council of Catholic Bishops from 1963 titled "On Racial Harmony" which asserts that "discrimination based on the accidental fact of race or color, and as such injurious to human rights . . . cannot be reconciled with the truth that God has created all men with equal rights and equal dignity" (p. 1). Contrast that statement with Philpott's (1991) account of a Black Catholic

attempting to receive communion at all-White St. Bride's, where he was told by the priest, "There are churches for your kind to go to. Don't come here making trouble. Go away, you, Go!" (p. xii) or more contemporaneous accounts of ongoing racist attitudes toward Black students in Catholic schools (e.g., Burke & Gilbert, 2015).

2 It is important to note that Catholic schools have long received *some* public funding primarily through federal title funds. This began with a leaking of strict separation after the *Everson v. Board of Education* (1947) ruling and expanded manifestly through increased access to tax and voucher mechanisms, mostly at the level of the states, from the 1980s onward. And truthfully strict separation is much complicated by creative cooperative relationships maintained between public districts and Catholic dioceses from the mid-20th century on (see Gordon, 2007). It is often pointed out, as well, by advocates for public funding for Catholic schools that the United States is one of the very few countries that does not provide robust public funding for religious schools. These same groups that advocate for public monies, however, are often the most vehement in resisting federal and state oversight of these funds when they get to the schools. Whereas, for instance, Canadian Catholic schools are publicly funded, they are also subject to strict regulation as regards their adherence to the Canadian Charter for Rights and Freedoms, which prohibits discrimination based on, among other things, sexual orientation. U.S. Catholic school advocates have long resisted the application of civil rights law to their schools.

3 One need only look to still-extant Blaine Amendment laws—as well as the Bennett law from Wisconsin, for instance—on the books in some states to get a flavor for the ways in which past religious bias has, to a real, although often exaggerated, degree, been carried forward into the present. Although certainly with the constitution of the current Roberts Supreme Court, religious actors have seen a distinct shift toward favoring the Exercise Clause at the expense of the Establishment Clause.

4 For a happy exception, see Green's (2011) work on the ambivalent question of race and benefits in Catholic schooling for African Americans.

5 Between 2003 and 2017, Step Up for Students has received seven-figure total donations from the Conrad Hilton Foundation and the Walton Family Foundation as well as six-figure donations from many other conservative foundations including, in various iterations, the DeVos family trust(s). To say nothing of the volume of public funding that has been funneled through them to students and into private schooling.

6 Indeed in 2017, ACE would grant Wendy Kopp, the founder of TFA, a "Notre Dame Award for Outstanding Contributions to Catholic Education." What Kopp had done for Catholic education specifically except opening the door for public funding and the destabilizing of public schooling through the deprofessionalization of teachers in her linking of private conservative (and neoliberal) philanthropies to educational policy strings remains something of a mystery (Alliance for Catholic Education, 2016). The founder of KIPP was honored as well. His contributions to Catholic schooling remain mysterious, too.

7 These were funded prominently by the Walton Family Foundation (Schmitt, 2012).

8 Professor Garnett is married to Rick Garnett, a law professor at Notre Dame who is said to advise Vice President Mike Pence on education policy issues, a perhaps not incidental detail here.

Chapter Six

THE CITY FUND TAKES IT TO "THE PEOPLE": HOW TOP-DOWN SCHOOL REFORMS IMPOSED ON NEW ORLEANS WILL BE BANKROLLED AS BOTTOM-UP INITIATIVES IN CITIES

KRISTEN BURAS, *Georgia State University*

> Failing to inform and engage communities can hobble the citywide effort to scale charters. . . . [E]arly community engagement, including parent education, can build an environment in which they can thrive. . . . The early stages of reform in New Orleans were not—to the city's detriment—driven by grassroots efforts.
>
> —Neerav Kingsland, former chief executive officer and chief strategy officer of New Schools for New Orleans, with co-authors in *New Orleans-Style Education Reform: A Guide for Cities* (Brinson et al., 2012, pp. 33–34)

> The most important thing for [the City Fund] is to identify a small group of cities that already have local leadership aspiring to drive change aligned with *our* [emphasis added] core beliefs. We want to see if we can help them make their public education systems much better [through charter school advocacy].
>
> —Kameelah Shaheed-Diallo, Partner at the City Fund (in Snyder, 2018, p. 17)

In this chapter, I chart the newly emerging face of privatization in education. Specifically, I examine a strategic approach, represented by the City Fund, that bankrolls top-down school reforms imposed on New Orleans as bottom-up initiatives by seeding localized pro-charter groups in target cities across the nation. For the past 15 years, post–Hurricane Katrina New Orleans has been subjected to mass charter school expansion. This has included the replacement of experienced teachers with new recruits through New Schools for New Orleans (NSNO), an outfit for charter school and human capital development serving as a conduit for philanthropic monies (Buras, 2011b, 2015; Buras & Urban South Grassroots Research Collective, 2013). Notably, New Orleans' transformation into the nation's first all-charter-school district was supported by federal grants and private philanthropic investment that advanced reforms with little to no input from affected communities (Buras, 2012; Buras et al., 2010; Sanders, 2018). Despite the gross failure of this experiment, it has been touted as a national model by the Heritage Foundation (Meese et al., 2005), Thomas B. Fordham Institute (Smith, 2012), and other conservative think tanks. The Mind Trust (2011), an Indianapolis-based charter school incubator, for example, issued a "bold plan" to transform its public schools following the New Orleans model.

Drawing on sustained research in New Orleans, I chart the path from NSNO, the city's leading charter school incubator, where Neerav Kingsland was formerly the chief executive officer (CEO), to his leadership as managing partner of the City Fund. The City Fund was established through a $200 million initiative anchored by funding from the Laura and John Arnold Foundation and Hastings Fund as well as contributions from the Dell, Gates, Walton, and Ballmer Foundations (Snyder, 2018). The purpose of the City Fund, Kingsland explains, is to scale up school reform efforts that he claims have been successful in New Orleans. According to Kingsland, the City Fund should "support other cities who are interested in using similar strategies" (Snyder, 2018, p. 5). However, reforms in New Orleans have had disastrous consequences and drawn heavy criticism as antidemocratic and top-down in their implementation (Buras, 2015; Buras et al., 2010, 2013; Buras & Sanders, 2018; Saltman, 2007). Sanders (2018) refers to what happened in New Orleans as a coup d'état of public schools.

I analyze the ways in which the City Fund aims to engage "local" actors in mobilizing around school privatization. Kameelah Shaheed-Diallo was a former senior vice president of strategy and community engagement for the Indianapolis-based Mind Trust, a predecessor of the City Fund. Now Kingsland's partner at the City Fund, Shaheed-Diallo reflects on the Mind Trust's citywide efforts, stating, "We didn't do enough to understand the perspectives of the people the proposed changes would affect the most. That experience taught us . . . that those closest to the problems are often best positioned to voice and design solutions" (Snyder, 2018, p. 7). Looking ahead, Shaheed-Diallo shares that "over the next decade, [the City Fund would] love to see 10 or so cities show that there might be a better way to deliver public education" (Snyder, 2018, p. 17). Targeting 10 cities in the next 10 years is another bold plan to expand the New Orleans model despite its destructive effects. This time, it may be accomplished by *soft rule*, the provision of funds conditioned on adherence to a particular political objective. The political objective in this case entails charter school advocacy by traditionally marginalized and/or community-based groups carefully selected and formatively engaged by the City Fund. Some have referred to this strategy as astroturfing (the creation of "fake grassroots" groups; e.g., see Strauss, 2014). However, I believe a more complex analysis that accounts for conservative ideology and strategy and examines ways that members of traditionally marginalized groups sometimes develop fragile alliances with elite groups is required (Apple & Buras, 2006; Buras, 2008; deMarrais et al., 2019; Pedroni, 2007). In this chapter, I examine shifts in conservative ideology and strategy around public school privatization; as the City Fund's work takes shape, it will be equally important to analyze relationships with groups at the community level.

The City Fund is the outgrowth of the combined work of NSNO, the Mind Trust in Indianapolis, and Cities for Education Entrepreneurship, also known as the CEE-Trust (later renamed Education Cities). The brainchild of the Mind Trust, Education Cities connects and consults with local organizations working to privatize urban education in their respective cities. The City Fund is a next-gen strategy in an ever-evolving urban school profiteering project. In this chapter, I trace its lineage and strategic vision.

With increasing criticism of top-down education reforms, including a long history of White philanthropic control over Black education (Watkins, 2001), the City Fund seeks to mediate such criticism by supporting local groups in major cities, thereby recasting imposed reforms as grassroots mobilizations. To understand the roots of this renovated strategy and the significance of the City Fund and allied philanthropic efforts, I argue that one must understand what has transpired in New Orleans and how key actors with a history there are now deeply involved in exporting the model to cities nationwide. In charting this history, I expose the elite racial and economic commitments undergirding conservative philanthropic efforts, misleadingly presented as "community engagement."

Individuals engaged in elite network analysis must do more than follow the money. They must carefully examine the strategic decisions, moves, concessions, and recalibrations that occur in the effort to privatize public schools in urban communities. The exercise of power is not always a linear or straightforward process (Apple & Buras, 2006; Buras, 2008, 2010). Philanthropists cannot only *pay* their way; they must also *pave* their way. Sometimes this is accomplished through attempts to generate consent and shape demands that partly align with their own. For example, philanthropists may nurture relationships with select community actors who share confluent understandings and act on those understandings in ways that advance elite entrepreneurial efforts to convert public schools into profit centers.

In what follows, I chart the history of the state takeover, philanthropic investment, and mass charter school expansion in New Orleans, situating NSNO as part of a top-down project in which communities of color targeted by education reform had little say in the matter, even though such reform intimately affected families, their schools, and neighborhoods. I reveal how powerbrokers positioned New Orleans as a guide for cities across the nation. With this background in mind, I trace the links among NSNO, the Mind Trust, and, ultimately, the City Fund (see Figure 6.1) and increasing concern about community criticism that charter schools have been imposed from above rather than representing the "choices" of affected groups. Finally, I critically examine the City Fund's narrow conception of community engagement, the discursive attempt to frame privately managed charter schools as simply new and improved public schools, and the aggressive 10-year plan to bankroll local pro-charter efforts in major cities nationwide. I conclude that the terrain has become more complicated as those at the top seek to strategically "engage" community actors in charter school advocacy at the ground level.

Figure 6.1
The City Fund Lineage—Partial Chronology of Elite Entrepreneurial Network Development

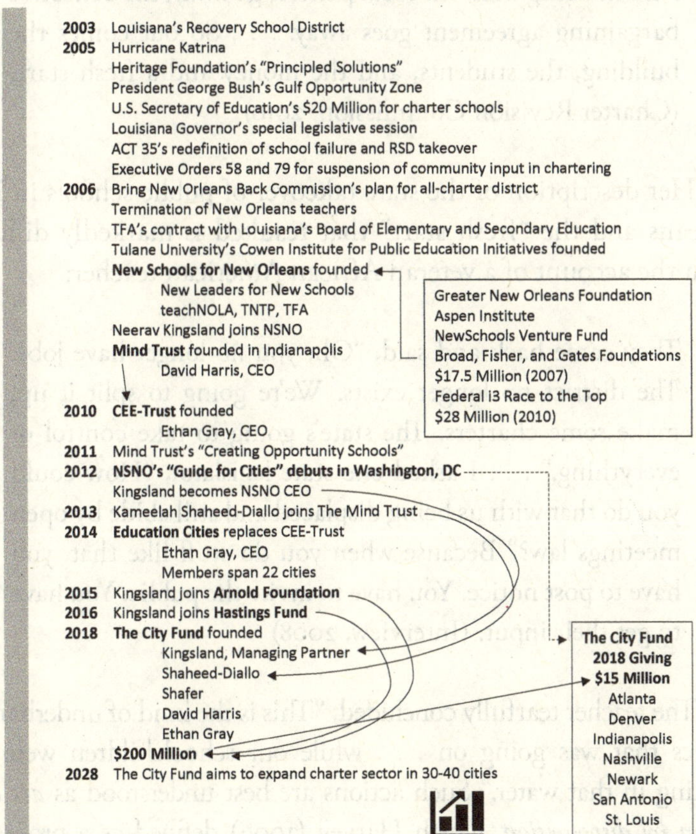

RSD = Recovery School District; TFA = Teach for America; NSNO = New Schools for New Orleans; CEO = chief executive officer; CEE-Trust = Cities for Education Entrepreneurship; i3 = Investing in Innovation.

The Assault by Education Entrepreneurs: How Destruction Happened From The Top Down In New Orleans

Leslie Jacobs, a member of New Orleans' business elite, former Orleans Parish School Board member, and architect of Louisiana's state-run Recovery School District (RSD) had this to say about post-Katrina education reform:

> We did a different model [in New Orleans]. We decided to take the failing schools away from the school district. . . . And in doing that, the local policies go away, the collective bargaining agreement goes away. . . . So out comes the building, the students, and the money and a fresh start. (Charter Revision Commission, 2010)

Her description of the state takeover of public schools in New Orleans and the "fresh start" that resulted is markedly different from the account of a veteran African American teacher:

> They came back and said, "Oh, you no longer have jobs. The district no longer exists. We're going to split it up, make some charters. The state's going to take control of everything." . . . I asked one state legislator, "How could you do that with us being displaced and still abide by open meetings law?" Because when you do stuff like that, you have to post notice. You have to invite the public. You have to get their input. (Interview, 2008)

The teacher tearfully concluded, "This is the kind of underhanded tactics that was going on . . . while our schoolchildren were still floating in that water." Such actions are best understood as *accumulation by dispossession*, which Harvey (2006) defined as a process in which assets previously belonging to one group are put in circulation as capital for another group. In New Orleans, this has included the commodification of Black schools for White exploitation and profit (Buras, 2015, in preparation; see also Harris, 1995).

NSNO played a leading role in dismantling the city's school district by incubating "new schools" and recruiting "new talent" to grow a privately managed charter sector. To fully understand NSNO's role, it must be situated in the wider network of federal, state, and local actors that shaped New Orleans as the nation's first all-charter-school district—the same model the City Fund now aims to export to other cities. Early on, takeover and mass chartering involved federal and state intervention as well as allies in city government and the actions of local education entrepreneurs supported by national philanthropies.

Within days of Hurricane Katrina's strike on August 29, 2005, the conservative Heritage Foundation issued a report on "principled solutions for rebuilding lives and communities" on the Gulf Coast (Meese et al., 2005, p. 1). Infused with the language of choice, entrepreneurialism, and markets, the Heritage Foundation offered the following education guidelines:

> New approaches to public policy issues such as enhanced choice in public school education should be the norm. . . . The critical need now is to encourage investors and entrepreneurs to seek new opportunities within these cities. . . . The key is to encourage private-sector creativity—for example, by declaring New Orleans and other severely damaged areas "Opportunity Zones." (p. 1)

Three days after the Heritage report, President George W. Bush (2005) delivered a national address from New Orleans and urged Congress to create a Gulf Opportunity Zone in Louisiana, Mississippi, and Alabama where the government "will take the side of entrepreneurs as they lead the economic revival" (para. 20). The next day, the Heritage Foundation followed up with "how to turn the president's Gulf Coast pledge into reality," stressing that "Congress should use existing federal charter school funding to encourage the development of charter schools" (Butler et al., 2005, para. 24). Such reconstruction was a federal mandate for state leaders—one soon to be bolstered by strategic funding.

Within two weeks of the storm, on September 14, U.S. Secretary of Education Margaret Spellings (2005) issued a letter to state leaders:

> Because charter schools are exempt from many State and local education rules, they may be uniquely equipped to serve [storm affected] students. Accordingly, the [U.S.] Department [of Education] is prepared to consider requests for statutory and regulatory waivers of various requirements under the CSP [Charter School Program] and other federal statutes and regulations over which the Secretary of Education exercises administrative authority. (para. 2)

Additionally, Spellings' letter stated that $20 million was available "to assist States and charter schools to meet the immediate needs of students" (para. 3). Written requests for federal charter school funds were to be submitted by September 23—just nine days later—or they would expire.

In November 2005, Louisiana governor Kathleen Blanco called a special legislative session in Baton Rouge. It became the occasion for passing Act 35, which redefined what constituted a "failing" school so that most of the New Orleans public schools could be deemed failing and placed in the state-run RSD. Act 35 enabled 107 of the 128 schools to be folded into the RSD, whereas only 13 schools could have been assumed before the legislation was passed (United Teachers of New Orleans [UTNO] et al., 2006). On the floor of the state legislature where the bill was circulating, a Louisiana Federation of Teachers (LFT) representative asked why all of a sudden the denotation of failure had shifted upward, with the School Performance Score (SPS) cut point now just below the state average (i.e., shifting from 60 to 87.4), and what exactly a "failing school" was. A White suburban senator responded, "A failing school is whatever we say it is" (Interview, 2009). The LFT representative reflected on the meaning of the senator's statement: "The powers now had a very clear charge.

And the charge was these schools are going to be taken over . . . and going to be sold out, they're going to be chartered" (Interview, 2009).

Around this same period, Blanco signed Executive Orders 58 and 79 suspending certain provisions of charter school law, such as the need to consult and obtain the votes of affected faculty, staff, and parents before converting an existing public school into a charter school (Louisiana Federation of Teachers, 2005; Louisiana Federation of Teachers & American Federation of Teachers [AFT], 2007). In short, neighborhood public schools were to be shuttered and/or replaced with privately managed charter schools without community input.

On November 30, 2005, the announcement went out: 7,500 New Orleans teachers and school employees were informed that they would be fired and lose health insurance on January 31, 2006 (Louisiana Federation of Teachers & American Federation of Teachers, 2007; United Teachers of New Orleans et al., 2007); they constituted a substantial portion of the city's Black middle class. In a piece titled *Go Southeast, Young Man*, Isaacson (2006) lauded unfolding education reforms as a "civic revival," writing, "A system of competing charter schools has sprung up, nurtured by the state and fostered in Washington" (para. 11). It did not feel like a revival to veteran teachers. They had been fired en masse without due process and without any regard for either their contributions as educators or the protections and entitlements of UTNO's collective bargaining agreement. Meanwhile, the Louisiana Department of Education advertised nationwide for teacher positions with the RSD and the state Board of Elementary and Secondary Education approved a contract with Teach for America (TFA; Buras, 2015, 2016; Civil District Court, 2012).

Locally, New Orleans mayor Ray Nagin established the Bring New Orleans Back Commission (BNOB) in October 2005, with the BNOB's leaders drawn from the business elite (Buras, 2005). Among appointees was James Reiss, chair of New Orleans Business Council, who declared, "Those who want to see this city rebuilt want to see it done in a completely different way: demographically, politically, and economically" (Cooper, 2005, p. A1). The BNOB formed various subcommittees, among them city planning, economic development, culture, and education, and each was tasked with formulating a component of the larger reconstruction plan. Headed by Tulane University president Scott Cowen, the BNOB's education committee issued its plan in January 2006, advocating a "world-class public education" in the form of an all-charter-school district (Bring New Orleans Back Again, 2006). Significantly, the committee noted its consultation of "top education experts" such as Wendy Kopp, founder of TFA; Mike Feinberg, founder of the Knowledge Is Power Program (KIPP); and Sarah Usdin, founder of the soon-to-form NSNO.

Federal, state, and local government created an opportunistic space for education entrepreneurs, including a powerful and predominantly White entrepreneurial university and an array of locally situated, but nationally funded, charter school and human capital development groups. Enter the Cowen Institute for Public Education Initiatives at Tulane University, which described itself as an "action-oriented think tank that informs and advances solutions . . . to eliminate the challenges impeding the success of K–12 education" (Cowen Institute, 2010, p. 1). As a Cowen representative explained, education reformers recognized that Tulane could "move something along," particularly because it is "the largest employer in the city—we have more political capital in the state and DC than any other entity" (Interview, 2009). The need was pressing as "new nonprofits were arising," such as NSNO, "yet [without] a lot of coordination between anybody" (Interview, 2009). The Cowen Institute opened its doors in March 2007. Just beyond the main desk was an incubation room for charter schools supported by NSNO. From the beginning, Cowen Institute provided free room and board to the city's most aggressive pro-charter groups, including NSNO; an alternative teacher recruitment triad composed of teachNOLA, the New Teacher Project, and TFA; and New Leaders for New Schools (NLNS), a recruitment and professional development project for principals and charter school board members.

New Schools for New Orleans

In March 2006—just six months after the storm—Sarah Usdin founded NSNO. Usdin earlier taught as a TFA teacher, worked as TFA's executive director in Louisiana, and acted as a founding partner for The New Teacher Project (Usdin, 2012). NSNO initially received $500,000 in seed money from the Greater New Orleans Foundation, which connects philanthropic donors with local organizations (Childress et al., 2010, p. 386). As Usdin's affiliations suggest, NSNO's founding and funding were made possible by her and others' involvement in an elite network that stretched far beyond New Orleans. Within weeks of the storm, Usdin rode in a National Guard helicopter alongside Walter Isaacson—native New Orleanian, president of the Aspen Institute (an entrepreneurial think tank), and chair of TFA's board at the time—to survey the city's destruction. Not only would the Aspen Institute become a hub for actors in a wider policy network supporting NSNO, but related philanthropies would also provide financial resources, including NewSchools Venture Fund (Isaacson, 2007). Isaacson reported that at the July 2006 convening, "the attendees decided that they needed a 'harbor master' in New Orleans, someone who could coordinate the various organizations, funders and school operators" (para. 6). NSNO assumed the role.

By December 2007, Usdin and staff "fielded countless congratulatory phone calls from education reform leaders around the country" (Childress et al., 2010, p. 384). The Eli and Edythe Broad, Bill and Melinda Gates, and Doris and Donald Fisher Foundations had awarded $17.5 million jointly to NSNO, TFA, and NLNS to recruit new teachers and principals and open new charter schools in New Orleans (Maxwell, 2007). These national foundations—financed by wealthy White philanthropists—clearly grasped that New Orleans was an opportune place for implementing the market-based reforms they hoped to spread. Additionally, in 2010, NSNO received $28 million from the federal Investing in Innovation program (i3), a component of Race to the Top (Brinson et al., 2012).

NSNO is committed to charter school and human capital development. Its strategy is fivefold as it seeks founders to *start* charter schools, principals to *lead* charter schools, teachers to *teach* in charter schools, members to *serve* on charter school boards, and investors and philanthropists to *contribute* to these efforts (see New Schools for New Orleans 2008a, 2008b, 2008c). For example, its Incubation Program provides "resources to new school founders in the year before opening" and announces that "if you are an experienced, dynamic, entrepreneurial educator . . . then this is your chance" (New Schools for New Orleans, n.d., p. 7). From 2007 to 2010, the organization launched 10 charter schools, seeded three local charter management organizations (CMOs), and provided 21 start-up grants that supported more than 90% of newly approved charter schools (New Schools for New Orleans, 2010).

NSNO partnered with the national organization NLNS to recruit, train, and place principals and other school leaders in the public schools of New Orleans (New Schools for New Orleans, 2008a). In its early years, NSNO (2010) boasted the training of 36 charter school boards for more than 90% of charter schools in the city. In this way, those who possess forms of capital closely linked to class and race status benefit from and exercise disproportionate power over public schools attended by African American students.

An additional "human capital" initiative was teachNOLA, a teacher recruitment collaboration with the New Teacher Project, a national organization that "works with clients on a fee-for-service basis" to place "alternate route teachers" in "high-needs schools" (New Teacher Project, 2010). TeachNOLA claims to have "eliminated the city's teaching shortage" (New Schools for New Orleans, 2010). Skirting the fact that the shortage was engineered through state policy, teachNOLA placed new teachers in 96% of the city's charter schools between 2007 and 2010 (New Schools for New Orleans, 2010).

Before 2005, only 10% of the city's teachers were in their first or second year of teaching; in 2008, 33% were (Nelson, 2010; United Teachers of New Orleans, 2010). Nelson (2010) explained: "New Orleans' low-achieving poor and minority students attend schools with the least experienced teachers" (p. 12), and "charter school governance is associated with a disproportionately white teacher population" (p. 19). In 2004–2005, approximately 75% of the city's teachers were Black. By 2009–2010, less than 50% of the teachers were Black (Nelson, 2010, pp. 18–19; Zubrzycki, 2013). In 2010–2011, nearly 40% of the city's teachers had been teaching for three years or less, and the percentage of White teachers had nearly doubled since the storm from 24% to 46% (Zubrzycki, 2013).

A veteran Black teacher reflected on the rapid charter school expansion and mass firing of educators:

> I explain the dismissal as a hostile takeover, a power struggle [by] those who wanted the control of the millions of dollars that was involved in education in Orleans Parish. . . . This was primarily controlled by African Americans who were able to allot contracts and do all the necessary things that they needed to do to control their own destiny. The powers that be [were] not pleased with that. They were looking for years to find ways to wrest control back from the district because the district served a majority African American population. (Interview, 2008)

For NSNO, the takeover model was a guide for other cities.

A Guide for Cities

In 2012, Louisiana senator Mary Landrieu, co-chair of the Senate Public Charter School Caucus with Tennessee senator Lamar Alexander, hosted a forum for education policy makers in Washington, D.C. The forum centered on *New Orleans-Style Education Reform: A Guide for Cities (Lessons Learned, 2004–2010)* (Brinson et al., 2012), a report published by NSNO. Landrieu (2012) proclaimed:

> With its *Guide for Cities*, New Schools for New Orleans is doing the important work of sharing lessons learned throughout the transformation of New Orleans' public

> schools. Through relentless focus on accountability, human capital, and charter school development, New Orleans has become a national leader in education reform. . . . I hope that this story and the *Guide for Cities* will inspire and equip other cities to follow New Orleans' lead. (para. 2)

Next to Landrieu was Neerav Kingsland, NSNO's chief strategy officer at the time. Kingsland echoed Landrieu's (2012) remarks and added, "The New Orleans story is really one of transferring power back to educators and parents—to date, this had led to incredible gains in student learning" (para. 4).

The *Guide* provides a partial map of the elite network that has shaped human capital and charter school development in New Orleans and makes clear whose voice NSNO values. In its opening pages, the authors "thank the following people for sharing their time and insights," listing CMO leaders in New Orleans and elsewhere, national pro-charter entities, such as the American Enterprise Institute and NewSchools Venture Fund, and Louisiana's RSD, among others (Brinson et al., 2012, p. 3). In the foreword, Kingsland and Usdin write, "Tens of thousands of students, families, teachers, and leaders make up the New Orleans system, and we are in no position to speak for all of them," yet they indicate they have "worked to glean the real lessons from this collective effort" (Brinson et al., 2012, p. 11). It is unclear how a top-down takeover could be considered "collective" in any democratic sense. They also declare in the foreword: "If numerous cities undertook this course, our urban education landscape could be transformed over the next decade" (Brinson et al., 2012, p. 11).

The *Guide* concludes by emphasizing the need to "build community support for dramatic reforms" (Brinson et al., 2012, p. 33). It warns that:

> failing to inform and engage communities can hobble the citywide effort to scale charters. . . . [E]arly community engagement, including parent education, can build an environment

> in which they can thrive. . . . The early stages of reform in New Orleans were not—to the city's detriment—driven by grassroots efforts. . . . In response to legitimate concerns about a lack of community voice, the RSD, numerous community groups, and NSNO are testing a new community engagement process for charter openings. . . . NSNO, working with community facilitators, is coordinating meetings, tours of high-performing [charter] schools, and trainings for stakeholders to develop a vision for what a successful school will look like in their neighborhood. (pp. 33–34)

NSNO tested a new community engagement process for charter openings. Notably, community members would not be asked whether they desired charters—this had already been decided by NSNO and its philanthropic donors. Community engagement is equated with "parent education" and "stakeholder trainings," which is to say that community members do not educate NSNO; NSNO "educates" them about what a successful school (read: charter) will look like in their neighborhood.

The *Guide* suggests various "community engagement practices," such as meeting with community groups before charter school openings; establishing transparent procedures for how, when, and why a traditional school will be closed; involving the community and parents in the closing procedures; supporting families in finding new placements when a traditional school closes; and mobilizing charter school parents in support of broader charter school reforms (Brinson et al., 2012, p. 34). This is not grassroots reform. Charter schools *will* open; traditional schools *will* close; families *will* be placed in new charter schools. Nowhere is there a commitment to supporting the community's educational vision. Rather, the community is invited to participate marginally in a process already set in motion by NSNO and its narrow circle of partners.

In an interview, Kingsland explained the significance of this entrepreneurial network to NSNO:

> At the end of the day, we are morally accountable to the students of New Orleans and that's what motivates our staff. More practically speaking, we're accountable to where we get money from. That's the only reason we operate, is because other folks invest in us. . . . So, just like anybody else we have to prove our worth and every couple of years we have to go back to the folks who have invested in us and show them results for them to continue investing. (Hess, 2012, p. 3)

When it comes to competing loyalties—one moral and the other monetary—the danger is that financiers win out, especially when they are the "only reason" for NSNO's ongoing operation.

Around the time the *Guide* was published, Usdin stepped down as NSNO's CEO in order to run for a seat on Orleans Parish School Board. The financing of Usdin's campaign in November 2012 reflected network relationships (Vanacore, 2012). Not surprisingly, Neerav Kingsland stepped up as CEO. Prior to this, he served as NSNO's director of human capital (2006–2008), vice president of school development and human capital (2008–2010), and chief strategy officer (2010–2012). He worked as NSNO's CEO from 2012 to 2014 and then served as senior education fellow over education giving for the Arnold Foundation from 2015 to 2018 and as CEO of education giving for the Hastings Fund from 2016 to 2018. These foundations are the lead financiers of the City Fund, which Kingsland joined as managing partner in July 2018 (Kingsland, 2019).

Despite Kingsland's claims about "incredible gains in student learning," the performance of charter schools in New Orleans has been dismal. Drawing on SPS and letter grades provided by the RSD in 2011–2012—the same period the *Guide* was issued—Research on Reforms (Hatsfield, 2012) offered the following summary: 100% of the 15 state-run schools assigned a letter grade received a D or F, and 79% of the 42 charter RSD schools assigned a letter grade received a D or F. Most striking is the fact that these letter grades were earned *after* the state altered the SPS cut point for failure following

Katrina, subjecting charter schools to less stringent standards than pre-Katrina public schools (see Buras, 2015, pp. 176–178). In 2019, after 15 years of innovation by NSNO, nearly half of New Orleans' all-charter-district schools received a letter grade of D or F by the state (Hasselle, 2019). Nonetheless, the City Fund, whose exemplars are NSNO and the Mind Trust, wants to replicate the New Orleans model in no less than 10 new cities over the next decade.

Aside from poor achievement, charter school reform has been damaging on many levels. The mass firing of Black veteran teachers and the closure of historic Black schools, as well as their replacement by inexperienced White recruits and charter operators from beyond the city, have been culturally and economically destructive. Additionally, charter schools have been part of a larger plan to racially and spatially reconstruct New Orleans, with Black neighborhoods gutted of essential infrastructure during the rebuilding process, including neighborhood public schools. Moreover, the state-run RSD disenfranchised Black parents, with governance over local schools no longer controlled by a locally elected school board. The recent return of RSD charter schools to local board governance has not proved better, as the legislation that defined the terms of their return disempowered the local board—not to mention that the board was stacked with charter advocates in the intervening years. Civil rights complaints and lawsuits have been filed to challenge such inequities, alongside student and community protests. However, the entrepreneurial venture has proceeded full force, altering its public relations (PR) strategies rather than engaging the substance of community demands for racial equity and self-determination (Buras, 2011a, 2012, 2015, in prepartion; Buras & Sanders, 2018; Calhoun et al., 2014; Ferguson, n.d.; Henry, 2016; Rethink New Orleans, 2018; Sanders, 2018; Southern Poverty Law Center, 2014).

New Schools For New Orleans, The Mind Trust, And The City Fund: Tracing The Lineage

Around the same time that NSNO's *Guide for Cities* (Brinson et al., 2011) was published, the Mind Trust (2011) issued a 160-page report titled *Creating Opportunity Schools: A Bold Plan to Transform Indianapolis Public Schools.* It opens by asking,

> WHAT IF. . .
>
> - About $188 million now controlled by Indianapolis Public Schools [IPS] central office was reallocated to school leaders to accelerate student learning and operate the school?
> - The city became a national magnet for the most talented teachers, principals, education entrepreneurs, and operators of top school models? (Mind Trust, 2011, p. 3)

David Harris, founder and CEO of the Mind Trust, asserts that the plan "would replace business as usual with innovative approaches drawn from the best research, ideas, and practices from around the country" (Mind Trust, 2011, p. 4). Harris founded the Mind Trust in 2006—the same year NSNO developed—with the hope of expanding the Indianapolis charter sector. He previously directed the mayor's charter school office.

The Mind Trust's (2011) bold plan references New Orleans 99 times and NSNO 21 times. Indeed, the report laments that

> IPS has no concerted, ongoing, and well-funded effort to invite the city's or country's top talent to incubate new schools in the district or recruit successful national models. This is a stark contrast from cities such as New York and New Orleans, which have both engaged in intensive, well-funded efforts to incubate new schools . . . through partnerships with external organizations. (p. 32)

In developing the plan, the Mind Trust traveled to New Orleans "to learn more about their reforms" (p. 99). Appendix E of the report focuses singularly on NSNO and its efforts to build the charter sector, while Appendix F provides a more general overview of the charter experiment in New Orleans. The citation of Cowen Institute reports and NSNO's *Guide for Cities*, which had not been publicly released, reveals the tight-knit relationship among these groups (Mind Trust, 2011). The report notes that "in the haste to re-establish schooling in the devastated city [of New Orleans], some community members felt excluded from the process of transforming schools" (Mind Trust, 2011, p. 143). To address this, it referenced NSNO's community engagement process that "notif[ies] families and other affected community members nine months before a school was transformed" (Mind Trust, 2011, p. 143). Notifying community members of a decision made in their absence—even if advance notice is given—hardly constitutes authentic engagement, yet this is embraced as a core operating principle.

In 2010, the Mind Trust spawned the Cities for Education Entrepreneurship Trust (CEE-Trust), "a national network of city-based non-profits, foundations, and mayor's offices dedicated to accelerating the pace of education innovation and reform" (CEE-Trust, 2011, p. 2). One CEE-Trust video emphasizes the three Cs of the trust—a convener, a collaborator, and a consultant in sharing lessons and moving charter reform forward on a national scale (CEE-Trust, 2013). NSNO's Kingsland appears in the video. For its first convening in 2011, CEE-Trust gathered almost 30 members in New Orleans to share strategies around charter school incubation. "Participants heard presentations from some of the nation's leading charter school incubation experts," including Kingsland–NSNO and Harris–Mind Trust (CEE-Trust, 2011, p. 3). A follow-up report chronicled the lessons learned during the convening and warned that "moving into a new geography poses ground-level challenges too, including attracting highly-effective teachers and school leaders who understand and agree with the CMOs model, and dealing with local and district leadership that may be hostile to charters"

(CEE-Trust, 2011, p. 5). Overcoming so-called ground-level challenges was recognized as crucial, without any sense that resistance to the imposition of top-down reform and an educational vision not of the community's own making might be legitimate. Foreshadowing the creation of the City Fund, attendees at the CEE-Trust meeting also "suggested that [members] could pool resources to fund an incubator whose sole focus would be to support the launch of new charters/CMOs in member cities" (CEE-Trust, 2011, p. 11).

Not long after the convening, CEE-Trust published *Kick-Starting Reform* (Gray et al., 2012), a three-city report on transforming public education; it focused on Indianapolis, New Orleans, and Detroit. Kingsland and Usdin appear in the acknowledgments. Ethan Gray, director of CEE-Trust at the time, explains that the report "tells the stories of [three] organizations, exploring their organizational models, strategies, and long-term theories of change" (p. 5). NSNO's profile reads:

> When NSNO started . . . some organizations closely aligned with the previous system expressed skepticism or labeled NSNO as an organization of "outsiders" because it sought counsel from national leaders and worked with national groups and because some of its leaders had not earned stripes in the city's traditional public schools. (p. 16)

Over time, NSNO says it has tried to "widen the tent" to partners beyond business and philanthropy, creating "more of a formal strategy" around developing relationships (Gray et al., 2012, p. 16). It should be emphasized that wider partnerships are built to "expand reach" and "increase impact," not to work in solidarity with communities that may have their own vision of what is best for their children. Kingsland boasts of NSNO's increasing power: "Now we're at the table five months before decisions get made, which is very different from advocating while decisions are being made or after they have been made" (p. 16). Significantly, NSNO values a seat at the decision-making table, but the communities that NSNO "engages" are simply informed of decisions already made. There is no evidence that NSNO or other network actors place substantial weight on engaging the wider community, except to bring on board those receptive to their education and training efforts. Part of kick-starting reform requires developing community resources and "other public relations materials that increase the community's understanding of great schools" (Gray et al., 2012, p. 29). There is a vast difference between PR and community engagement, but NSNO and CEE-Trust make no distinction.

By 2014, CEE-Trust had morphed into Education Cities, a network of leaders for great "public" schools. Education Cities (2014) spanned 22 cities with local organizations committed to the common goal of charter school expansion. Kingsland and Harris provided editorial support on the report that unveiled the newly branded or "relaunched" entity: "While we have a new name, we will continue our core convening, consulting, and writing," explained Gray, current CEO of Education Cities (Education Cities, 2014, p. 5). He also affirmed the ongoing commitment to "a rapid increase in the number of high-quality public schools in member cities" (p. 5). The report is "an introduction to the harbormaster approach" (Education Cities, 2014, p. 6). Of course, the harbormaster approach—that is, appointing a city-based organization to coordinate and lead the broader charter expansion process—was identified as important during NSNO's founding almost 10 years earlier.

Among the strategies that effective harbormasters employ is "community engagement" (Education Cities, 2014). In language stronger than that associated with earlier reform efforts, Education Cities declares, "Many recent reform efforts have been done *to* rather than *with* communities" (Education Cities, 2014, p. 22; italics in the original). It goes on:

> Effective harbormasters recognize that constant and authentic engagement with families, business owners, civic leaders and others is necessary to ensure that schools reflect the priorities of the community. We would note, however,

> that this is the area of work where harbormasters have struggled the most. Often, education leaders are more adept at navigating conversations with grasstops leaders than they are at listening to, learning from and engaging with grassroots constituents. Given the issues of race, class, and power embedded in public education, it is critical that harbormasters deepen their commitment to community engagement and elevate the leadership and voices of those not typically heard. (Education Cities, 2014, p. 22)

One strategy recommended is investing in an external organization that specializes in community engagement, such as Stand for Children, itself funded by big money (e.g., Gates, Walton). Other suggestions include the Mind Trust's "bus tours for families and community leaders to visit high-performing [charter] schools and organizing events with noted local and national education experts to build the community's understanding of different pressing issues" (Education Cities, 2014, p. 26). Furthermore, the Mind Trust's new education program for community leaders in Indianapolis, "with a special emphasis on leaders of color," is highlighted (p. 26). Education Cities concludes by warning that neglecting such strategies means "risking the impression of imposing change on communities rather than building locally owned movements" (p. 34).

The "impression" of imposition seems more like the ongoing reality. The discourse on community engagement, however, has become noticeably more explicit and strident in recent years. Education Cities' call for elevating grassroots leaders not typically heard, especially considering the race and class dynamics of reform, is precisely the mission that the City Fund would embrace and bankroll.

The City Fund—A Shift In Strategy, Not Agenda: How Destruction Will Happen From The Top Down Going Forward

The City Fund was unveiled in 2018, and its connections with NSNO, the Mind Trust, and Education Cities are clear. As mentioned earlier, Kingsland, managing partner of the City Fund, is a former NSNO CEO. Shaheed-Diallo, also a City Fund partner, formerly led the Mind Trust's community engagement work. Fellow City Fund partner Kevin Shafer acted as chief innovation officer for Camden City School District in New Jersey—another site of charter expansion (Snyder, 2018). Two of the three founding partners acting as lead spokespeople for the City Fund are people of color—Kingsland and Shaheed-Diallo. The City Fund gets its money, however, from wealthy White philanthropists—namely, the Arnold Foundation and Hastings Fund, both of which formerly charged Kingsland with education giving. Moreover, all lead City Fund partners have links to lineal organizations such as NSNO, the Mind Trust, or urban partners affiliated with Education Cities.

On July 31, 2018, a series of nearly identical announcements were made, often with exact wording shared across missives. On his blog, Kingsland (2018) declared that over the past 15 years, New Orleans, Washington, D.C., and Denver "have made their entire public education systems better." Indianapolis and Camden, he says, "have taken these breakthroughs" and "seen promising early results." The City Fund, he explained, is meant to expand such work. The Arnold Foundation and Hastings Fund will continue as "anchor funders" as the new team helps "provide better support to local leaders" who can "test these breakthroughs at a little larger scale." The post is "signed" by team members, including not only Kingsland, Shaheed-Diallo, and Shafter, but also Harris, Gray, and others (Kingsland, 2018). The very same day, Arnold Ventures (2018) issued a press release, *New Nonprofit Will Lead Education Reform Efforts for the Foundation*, explaining that the City Fund will partner with a subset of cities that wish to try the approaches proved successful in New Orleans and elsewhere. Education

Cities (2018) also issued its own release, declaring, "Education Cities is undergoing an evolution that we think will better support local education leaders." Although the City Fund continues "core activities" once undertaken by Education Cities, Education Cities will "shift" its focus to support two new initiatives—Community Engagement Partners to build capacity of education organizations to partner with local communities to create "great public schools" and School Board Partners to advise a network of elected school board members in supporting "conditions for quality public school growth in their districts."

A few months after the City Fund launched, Kingsland, Shaheed-Diallo, and Shafer did a debut interview together and shared the fund's goals (Snyder, 2018). Kingsland's words echoed his July 2018 blog, evidence of the well-oiled PR machine. The interview proceeds: The City Fund has $200 million, possibly more, to support its initial efforts. The fund will expand successful education reform models to additional cities while sharpening the model in existing cities. During these exchanges, Shaheed-Diallo concedes that the Mind Trust "didn't do enough to understand the perspective of the people the proposed changes would affect the most" (Snyder, 2018, p. 7). She says that the City Fund aims to "invest in the types of educators, leaders, and community members I saw making change in Indianapolis" and hopes "parents and families" will be "at the center of this change" (Snyder, 2018, p. 8). But which *types* exactly is she talking about? She makes this clear during the interview, stating, "The most important thing for us is to identify a small group of cities that already have local leadership aspiring to drive change aligned with *our* [italics added] core beliefs. We want to see if we can help them make their public education systems much better" through charter advocacy (Snyder, 2018, p. 17).

The crux of the matter is this: Criticism has come from many quarters, with communities at the center of privatization efforts articulating grave concerns about the hostile takeover and its destructive effects (e.g., see Alliance to Reclaim Our Schools, 2015; Buras, 2015; Ewing, 2018; Rethink New Orleans, 2018). It is bad press—bad business—so the powers that be must calibrate their approach. They need a grassroots voice, some person or some group in the community that will take their side and proclaim that school choice is the answer to inequities that plague urban schools, even if on-the-ground evidence demonstrates otherwise. They pay well—$200 million well—from a hefty City Fund to bankroll allies locally. However, no amount of money can generate real community support for something that has been dreamed up and pushed down by elites who do not know or value the culture and history of the community or have any sense of what a truly public neighborhood school is (Buras, in prepartion). The powerful rarely consider how much neighborhood public schools would benefit from resources they have been systematically denied since the state began financing public education for African Americans and other racially marginalized groups over a century ago (DeVore & Logsdon, 1991). The root cause of educational inequities will not be addressed by school choice because placing the interests of Whites over communities of color is what set the problems in motion from the start. Treating Black and Brown people as a form of capital for White exploitation has a long and ugly history; it happened "back then," and it continues to happen. Only now we are asked to believe this is the result of choice and community engagement.

Another strategy the City Fund employs to depoliticize its political agenda and quell resistance is ironing out the language used by charter school proponents. Ironically, the most vehement advocates of charter school expansion are now evacuating the language of choice. Here again, the City Fund debut interview provides a glimpse into this discursive shift. A few examples make the point. In the debut interview, Shafer introduced himself through his work as chief innovation officer for Camden, where he created "new public school models" and supported "talented educators" (Snyder, 2018, p. 5). Charter schools are referred to as new public school models and inexperienced recruits supplied by human capital providers are called talented educators. "Giving more power to educators" is a proxy for Shafer's desire to weaken teacher unions (Snyder, 2018, p. 6). Likewise, "partnerships with proven nonprofit organizations" stands in for CMOs and charter networks (Snyder, 2018, p. 6). Shaheed-Diallo says her time at the Mind Trust taught her the importance of engaging communities in conversations about "how to best deliver public education," thus charter school incubation is packaged as simply another way to deliver a public good (Snyder, 2018, p. 7). For her, charter schools are "innovative public schools" (p. 9) or simply "high-quality schools" (p. 10). She at one point acknowledges, "When we talk about empowering educators to create new schools, in many cases these schools are charters" (Snyder, 2018, p. 10). But for the most part, she and others consciously avoid such vocabulary.

Talking in circles, Kingsland explains that while monies come from philanthropy, "our strategy doesn't come from them" (Snyder, 2018, p. 16). Rather, "it comes from the cities that have made public education better" (p. 16). Yet the two are indisputably connected. Cities that received money from national philanthropies for the sole purpose of subjecting public schools to management by private CMOs is what supposedly made them "better" (Snyder, 2018, p. 16). How, then, does strategy not originate with philanthropies and the priorities that undergird their investment? Reforms may happen at the city level, but the direction of change starts at the top.

In the next decade, Shaheed-Diallo wants to see 10 cities "show that there might be a better way to deliver public education" (Snyder, 2018, p. 17), that is, to expand the charter sector. Although she indicated in the City Fund debut interview that she hoped to reach 10 in 10, a leaked City Fund presentation used to solicit funding from donors prior to launch revealed otherwise. Between 2018 and 2021, the fund hopes to have success in at least 20 cities and then, from 2022 on, to influence "every major city in America" (Barnum, 2018a, para. 14). In 7 to 10 years, it hopes to reach 30 to 40 cities (Barnum, 2018a, para. 15). The ultimate goal is to expand the urban charter sector, "often scaling to serve 30–50 percent of students" (Barnum, 2018a, para. 9). Clearly, private language portrays one set of goals while public language portrays a softer version.

It is perhaps too soon to know the exact shape of things to come, but Kingsland specifies that initial grants were given to local groups in various cities, including "some combination of local nonprofits, community and parent advocacy organizations, and high-performing schools" (Snyder, 2018, p. 15). More specifically, Kingsland stated that $15 million had been spent by December 2018, going to the Mind Trust in Indianapolis, RootEd in Denver, City Education Partners in San Antonio, the Newark Charter School Fund and New Jersey's Children's Foundation, the Opportunity Trust in St. Louis, and RedefinED in Atlanta. Nashville charter schools received direct funds (Barnum, 2018b).

Hegemony: Paving The Way, Not Just Paying

The City Fund represents a new way of organizing the efforts of philanthropic donors committed to charter school expansion and privatization. Rather than raw top-down imposition of the charter school takeover model, "local" leaders and groups that share the City Fund's "core beliefs" will be bankrolled as grassroots organizers and community-based spokespeople for what ultimately is the City Fund's agenda: to privatize urban public schools far beyond New Orleans.

NSNO developed a new community engagement process for charter openings. Notably, community members would not be asked whether they desired charters—NSNO and its philanthropic donors made that determination. Community engagement is enacted as a unidirectional process of "parent education" and "stakeholder trainings." Now, the City Fund seeks to support "local" leaders, specifically those whose vision aligns with "our" agenda. Imposition mediated by carefully selected community allies is not community-driven reform; it is not organic or grassroots; it is an elite strategy to counter criticism of top-down efforts by giving those efforts a "community" face—and, in doing so, possibly grow a base of support.

Yet new developments in conservative educational strategy underscore something important: grassroots resistance matters. In New

Orleans and elsewhere, community pushback against public school privatization has exposed the elite racial and economic interests at play. In a packed 2010 public hearing on state takeover and charter school expansion in New Orleans, one community activist declared:

> What we're talking about here tonight is a simple question of democracy. We want in Orleans Parish what every other parish has in this state and that's the right to control our own schools. High crimes and misdemeanors have been carried out against the people of New Orleans . . . by the RSD and the people who run these charter operations. We don't believe that these schools have served the best interests of the majority of our African American students. (Buras, 2012, p. 171)

Youth affiliated with Rethink New Orleans (2018), a grassroots racial justice organization, have likewise protested school privatization as a form of violence, asserting, "We demand substantive youth and community input and veto power on all decisions regarding school openings, school closings, school leadership and school locations" (p. 8). Philanthropic efforts to pave a way around such resistance present new challenges. Harris, Mind Trust founder and City Fund partner, has made clear that the purpose of initiatives like the fund is to "help cities around the country build the right conditions for education change" (McCoy, 2018, para. 5). As the "right conditions" are built, those committed to fighting accumulation by dispossession must also develop new strategies. This means closely following philanthropic investments at the grassroots level and the alliances formed as a result; it also necessitates exposing the deeply flawed notion of community engagement at the heart of such investments. The City Fund will not support the substantive input and power demanded by community groups committed to real equity, self-determination, and democratic educational transformation; rather, the fund will engage those who are responsive to the fund's input and power. It is difficult to know who exactly is doing the City Fund's bidding; almost two years after its founding, the City Fund still has no website. Hegemony, particularly rule by consent as opposed to coercion, is a complicated project, but the lines that separate these are not always so clear. The terrain is getting increasingly complicated and opaque as the top seeds the bottom, builds reform with "the people," and mediates long-standing criticism that the wealthy White few are dictating education policy for the poor Black and Brown many. [1]

References

Alliance to Reclaim Our Schools. (2015, August). *Out of control: The systemic disenfranchisement of African American and Latino communities through school takeovers.* http://www.reclaimourschools.org/sites/default/files/out-of-control-takeover-report.pdf

Apple, M. W., & Buras, K. L. (Eds.). (2006). *The subaltern speak: Curriculum, power, and educational struggles.* Routledge.

Arnold Ventures. (2018, July 31). *New non-profit will lead education reform efforts for the foundation* [Press release]. https://www.arnoldventures.org/newsroom/new-non-profit-will-lead-education-reform-efforts-for-the-foundation/

Barnum, M. (2018a, August 21). *40 cities in 10 years: Leaked presentation offers more details on new group's goals to spread charter (and charter-like) schools.* Chalkbeat. https://chalkbeat.org/posts/us/2018/08/21/city-fund-presentation/

Barnum, M. (2018b, December 9). *The City Fund's next steps: These 7 cities are the focus of the biggest new education player.* Chalkbeat. https://chalkbeat.org/posts/us/2018/12/09/city-fund-seven-cities-atlanta-indianapolis-newark-denver-san-antonio-st-louis-nashville/

Bring New Orleans Back Commission. (2006, January 17). *Rebuilding and transforming: A plan for world-class public education in New Orleans.*

Brinson, D., Boast, L., Hassel, B. C., & Kingsland, N. (2012). *New Orleans-style education reform: A guide for cities (Lessons learned, 2004-2010).* New Schools for New Orleans.

Buras, K. L. (2005). Katrina's early landfall: Exclusionary politics behind the restoration of New Orleans. *Z Magazine, 18*(12), 26–31.

Buras, K. L. (2008). *Rightist multiculturalism: Core lessons on neoconservative school reform*. Routledge.
Buras, K. L. (2010). Education, cultural politics, and the new hegemony: How multiculturalism became a neoconservative weapon. In Z. Leonardo (Ed.), *Handbook of cultural politics and education* (pp. 341–371). Sense Publishers.
Buras, K. L. (2011a). Challenging the master's plan for the Lower Ninth Ward of New Orleans. *Z Magazine*, *24*(5), 19–22.
Buras, K. L. (2011b). Race, charter schools, and conscious capitalism: On the spatial politics of whiteness as property (and the unconscionable assault on black New Orleans). *Harvard Educational Review*, *81*(2), 296–330.
Buras, K. L. (2012). "It's all about the dollars": Charter schools, educational policy, and the racial market in New Orleans. In W. H. Watkins (Ed.), *The assault on public education: Confronting the politics of corporate school reform* (pp. 160–188). Teachers College Press.
Buras, K. L. (2015). *Charter schools, race, and urban space: Where the market meets grassroots resistance*. Routledge.
Buras, K. L. (2016). The mass termination of Black veteran teachers in New Orleans: Cultural politics, the education market, and its consequences. *The Educational Forum*, *80*(2), 154–170.
Buras, K. L. (in preparation). *What we stand to lose: The legacy of Carver High School and the threat of school closures* [Book].
Buras, K. L., Randels, J., Salaam, K. Y., & Students at the Center. (2010). *Pedagogy, policy, and the privatized city: Stories of dispossession and defiance from New Orleans*. Teachers College Press.
Buras, K. L., & Urban South Grassroots Research Collective. (2013). New Orleans education reform: A guide for cities or a warning for communities? (Grassroots lessons learned, 2005–2012). *Berkeley Review of Education*, *4*(1), 123–157.
Buras, K. L., & Sanders, R. (2018). History rewritten: Masking the failure of the Recovery School District. *New Orleans Tribune*, *34*(6), 8–10.
Bush, G. W. (2005, September 15). *Text of Bush speech*. www.cbsnews.com
Butler, S. M., Carafano, J. J., Fraser, A. A., Lips, D., Moffit, R. M., & Utt, R. D. (2005, September 16). *How to turn the president's Gulf Coast pledge into reality* (Webmemo 848). Heritage Foundation. http://www.heritage.org/research/reports/2005/09/how-to-turn-the-presidents-gulf-coast-pledge-into-reality

Calhoun, W., Lellelid, A., & Quigley, W. P. (2014). *Civil rights complaint.* Better Education Support Team and Loyola University New Orleans College of Law.

Charter Revision Commission. (2010, January 28). *Proceedings* [Transcript]. Jacksonville, FL.

Childress, S. M., Bensen, S., & Tudryn, S. (2010). New Schools for New Orleans. In S. M. Childress (Ed.), *Transforming public education: Cases in education entrepreneurship* (pp. 384–410). Harvard Education Press.

Cities for Education Entrepreneurship-Trust. (2011). *Charter school incubation: A recap of the CEE-Trust conversation held in New Orleans, January 27–28, 2011.* www.cee-trust.org

Cities for Education Entrepreneurship-Trust. (2013). *CEE-Trust introduction* [Video]. https://vimeo.com/42408467

Civil District Court for the Parish of Orleans. (2012, June 20). *Eddy Oliver et al. v. Orleans Parish School Board et al.* [Reasons for judgment].

Cooper, C. (2005, September 8). In Katrina's wake—Old-line families escape worst of floods and plot the future. *Wall Street Journal*, p. A1.

Cowen Institute. (2010). *The state of public education in New Orleans.*

deMarrais, K., Brewer, T. J., Herron, B., Atkinson, J. C., & Lewis, J. B. (2019). *Philanthropy, hidden strategy, and collective resistance.* Myers Education Press.

DeVore, D. E., & Logsdon, J. (1991). *Crescent City schools: Public education in New Orleans, 1841–1991.* Center for Louisiana Studies at the University of Southwestern Louisiana.

Education Cities. (2014, December). *Building education cities.* Education Cities. http://www.education-cities.org

Education Cities. (2018, July 31). *Press release.*

Ewing, E. L. (2018). *Ghosts in the schoolyard: Racism and school closings on Chicago's South Side.* University of Chicago Press.

Ferguson, P. (Director). (n.d.). *A perfect storm* [Series]. Bayou and Me Productions. https://www.aperfectstormthemovie.com/

Gray, E., Ableidinger, J., & Barrett, S. K. (2012, August). *Kick-starting reform: Three city-based organizations showing how to transform public education.* Cities for Education Entrepreneurship-Trust. https://publicimpact.com/wp-content/uploads/2018/11/Kick-Starting-Reform.pdf

Harris, C. I. (1995). Whiteness as property. In K. Crenshaw, N. Gotanda, G. Peller, & K. Thomas (Eds.), *Critical race theory: The key writings that formed the movement* (pp. 276–291). New Press.

Hasselle, D. (2019, November 23). Nearly half of New Orleans' all-charter district schools got D or F grades; what happens next? *Times-Picayune.* www.nola.com

Hatsfield, C. J. (2012, November 5). *National model for reform or district in academic crisis?* [Brief]. Research on Reforms.

Harvey, D. (2006). *Spaces of global capitalism: Towards a theory of uneven geographical development.* Verso.

Henry, K. L. (2016). Discursive violence and economic retrenchment: Chartering the sacrifice of Black educators in post-Katrina New Orleans. In J. K. Donnor & T. L. Affolter (Eds.), *The charter school solution: Distinguishing fact from rhetoric* (pp. 80–98). Routledge.

Hess, R. (2012, May 21). Straight up conversation: New NSNO CEO Neerav Kingsland. *Education Week.* http://blogs.edweek.org/edweek/rick_hess_straight_up/2012/05/straight_up_conversation_new_nsno_ceo_neerav_kingsland.html

Isaacson, W. (2006, June 8). *Go southeast, young man.* Aspen Institute. www.aspeninstitute.org/node/2953

Isaacson, W. (2007, September 6). The greatest education lab. *Time.* www.time.com/time/magazine/0,9171,1659767,00.html

Kingsland, N. (2018, July 31). *The City Fund* [Relinquishment blog]. https://relinquishment.org/2018/07/31/the-city-fund/

Kingsland, N. (2019, January 26). *Neerav Kingsland.* LinkedIn. https://www.linkedin.com/in/neerav-kingsland-4991a828

Landrieu, M. L. (2012, March 1). *Landrieu hosts education panel and launches New Orleans style education reform: A guide for cities* [Press release].

Louisiana Federation of Teachers. (2005, November 2). *Letter to Blanco regarding Executive Orders 58 and 79.*

Louisiana Federation of Teachers & American Federation of Teachers. (2007, January). *The chronology: Scenario of a nightmare.*

Maxwell, L. A. (2007, December 13). Foundations donate millions to help New Orleans schools' recovery. *Education Week.* https://www.edweek.org

McCoy, D. P. (2018, March 15). *The Mind Trust shaped Indy's charter scene. Now founder David Harris is going national.* Chalkbeat. https://chalkbeat.org/posts/in/2018/03/15/david-harris-leaves-the-mind-trust-to-start-new-national-education-organization/

Meese, E., Butler, S. M., & Holmes, K. R. (2005, September 12). *From tragedy to triumph: Principled solutions for rebuilding lives and communities.* Heritage Foundation.

Mind Trust. (2011, December). *Creating opportunity schools: A bold plan to transform Indianapolis Public Schools* (Report prepared by Public Impact). https://www.themindtrust.org/wp-content/uploads/2016/02/opp-schools-full-report.pdf

Nelson, F. H. (2010, September). *Teacher quality and distribution in post-Katrina New Orleans.* American Federation of Teachers.

New Schools for New Orleans. (2008a). *Lead.* Retrieved from http://newschoolsforneworleans.org/

New Schools for New Orleans. (2008b). *Serve.* Retrieved from http://newschoolsforneworleans.org/

New Schools for New Orleans. (2008c). *Start.* Retrieved from http://newschoolsforneworleans.org/

New Schools for New Orleans. (2010). *Our impact.* Retrieved from http://newschoolsforneworleans.org/

New Schools for New Orleans. (n.d.). *Transformations* [Informational folder].

New Teacher Project. (2010). *About us: Our business model.* www.tntp.org

Pedroni, T. C. (2007). *Market movements: African American involvement in school voucher reform.* Routledge.

Rethink New Orleans. (2018). *End school violence: Privatizing our schools is violent.*

Saltman, K. J. (2007). *Capitalizing on disaster: Taking and breaking public schools.* Paradigm Publishers.

Sanders, R. (2018). *The coup d'état of the New Orleans Public Schools: Money, power, and the illegal takeover of a public school system.* Peter Lang.

Smith, N. (2012, January). *The Louisiana Recovery School District: Lessons for the Buckeye state.* Thomas B. Fordham Institute. www.edexcellence.net/publications/the-louisiana-recovery-school-district.html

Snyder, S. (2018, December 9). *74 Interview: "The City Fund" founders talk about their new campaign to identify America's most innovative public school systems and the first metro areas where they'll be investing.* https://www.the74million.org/article/74-interview-the-city-fund-founders-talk-about-their-new-campaign-to-identify-americas-most-innovative-public-school-systems-and-the-first-metro-areas-where-theyll/

Southern Poverty Law Center. (2014). *SPLC negotiates landmark settlement to help New Orleans students with disabilities* [Press release]. https://www.splcenter.org/news/2014/12/19/splc-negotiates-landmark-settlement-help-new-orleans-students-disabilities

Spellings, M. (2005, September 14). *Letter from the secretary of education to states affected by Hurricane Katrina.* U.S. Department of Education.

Strauss, V. (2014, October 12). How to spot a fake "grassroots" education reform group. *The Washington Post.* https://www.washingtonpost.com/news/answer-sheet/wp/2014/10/12/how-to-spot-a-fake-grassroots-education-reform-group/

United Teachers of New Orleans, Louisiana Federation of Teachers, & American Federation of Teachers. (2006, November). *"National model" or flawed approach? The post-Katrina New Orleans Public Schools.*

United Teachers of New Orleans, Louisiana Federation of Teachers, & American Federation of Teachers. (2007, June). *No experience necessary: How the New Orleans school takeover experiment devalues experienced teachers.*

United Teachers of New Orleans. (2010, March). *The New Orleans model: Shortchanging poor and minority students by over-relying on new teachers* (Brief).

Usdin, S. N. (2012). *Meet Sarah.* www.sarahusdin.com/meetsarah/

Vanacore, A. (2012, October 9). Sarah Usdin draws $110,000 haul in Orleans Parish School Board race. *Times-Picayune.* www.nola.com

Watkins, W. H. (2001). *The White architects of Black education: Ideology and power in America, 1865–1954.* Teachers College Press.

Zubrzycki, J. (2013, April 19). TFA alumni aid new teachers in New Orleans. *Education Week.* www.edweek.org

Endnotes

1 In this chapter, I cite interview data from my early research in New Orleans, indicating the year that testimony was collected.

Chapter Seven

THE WALTON FAMILY FOUNDATION: KEY PLAYERS, INITIATIVES, AND ITS GROWING INFLUENCE ON COLLEGES AND UNIVERSITIES

KATHLEEN DEMARRAIS, *University of Georgia*
BRIGETTE HERRON, *University of Georgia*
JANIE COPPLE, *University of Georgia*

Funding from the Walton Family Foundation (WFF) has significantly benefited the K–12 privatization movement by funding charter schools, supporting high-stakes accountability measures for schools and educators, and supporting school voucher programs. More recently, the foundation was identified as one of the largest "green philanthropies" in the United States, shifting one stream of funding toward giving to protect the environment, rivers, and waterways (Callahan, 2017). Currently, the WFF's descriptions of giving strategies and 990s forms reveal how they strategically focus funding on three areas: (1) the arts through art museums and art education, (2) special projects related to their home region of Arkansas, and (3) support for K–12 and higher education institutions. At first glance, these disparate funding streams may seem odd, as they do not fall into typical categories of "conservative" or "progressive" projects for funding. However, the WFF has a history of funding projects in line with the particular interests of the heirs of Sam Walton, founder of Walmart and namesake of the WFF.

Most scholarly literature on the subject covers Walton's funding of K–12 initiatives, with less attention to the foundation's funding for colleges and universities or the connections between kindergarten and 12th grade, the arts, and the environment. The WFF has enormous power in its ability to facilitate change through giving to particular initiatives. It has resources to orchestrate large networks of strategic giving, aided by the benefits it receives as a tax-exempt organization. We argue that the purpose and influence of WFF funding, particularly its growing influence on colleges and universities, must be carefully unpacked along with the interests of key players who have the select privilege to decide what gets funded. Through an analysis of the WFF's publicly available tax filings over the last 16 years, as well as relevant websites and literature, we examine the WFF's philanthropy over time, followed by a specific analysis of its recent giving to institutions of higher education. We highlight the impact of Walton dollars on higher education as well as the ways this funding connects to other key funding interests including K–12 schooling and the environment. The following research questions guided this study:

1. What is the history of the WFF, and how do the Walton family members work within the foundation on particular philanthropic causes?
2. What are the key funding initiatives of the WFF between 2003 and 2017?
3. More specifically, how has the WFF funded higher education institutions during this time?
4. What is the impact of the WFF on higher education?

We begin with a brief review of the literature related to the WFF. Next, we discuss research methods, the history, and context of the WFF and explore how the WFF's philanthropic investment in higher education supports programs and initiatives shaping the arts, K–12 education, and the environment. By making this philanthropy's impact and intentions visible, we address the overall question: Is the WFF good for higher education?

Literature Review

Recent academic scholarship and journalistic accounts have addressed what Callahan (2017) calls the rise of the "New Philanthropic Power Elite," a group of extremely well-connected and ultra-wealthy family dynasties who use philanthropy as a tool to promote their own personal interests in ways beyond the reach of everyday citizens. MacLean (2017) described the long history of the radical right's ties and influence over this process, outlining how libertarian billionaires like the Koch family have been using their wealth and power to undermine democratic systems in the United States for decades. Jane Mayer (2016) explored how the philanthropy of the radical right has employed the strategy of concealing their philanthropic investments to influence the American political process, with particular focus on the Koch brothers, the Scaife family, and many others. Academic works have explored how these elite philanthropic dynasties exert considerable influence in promoting particular neoliberal and conservative ideologies in the realm of P–12 and higher education (deMarrais et al., 2019). However, few accounts focus on the impact of the WFF, a similar philanthropic dynasty, and the ideologies that guide its giving.

Callahan (2017) identified the Walton family as a member of the New Philanthropic Power Elite, for their use of their combined power and wealth to exert influence over public institutions while maintaining a low profile about the purposes of their giving. The Walton family operates somewhat differently from philanthropic dynasties like the Kochs in that they have more players who hold a diverse set of interests and projects. Most of the key stakeholders in the WFF are not the original family members but the children and grandchildren (and the children's and grandchildren's spouses) who gained control of the WFF after the patriarch and founder of Walmart, Sam Walton, passed away in 1992. Because Sam Walton did not utilize the services of donor-advised funds, which allow funders to determine and limit what kinds of funding will take place after their death, Walton's extended family have been able to focus their philanthropic giving on their own particular areas of interest. Because of the unique nature of the WFF, more academic research is needed to explore the foundation's myriad interests and influences, especially in higher education.

The limited academic literature on the WFF trends situates the philanthropy in a triad with the Gates Foundation and the Broad Foundation, identifying the WFF as one of the "venture philanthropies" pursuing particular causes related to the American K–12 education system (Saltman, 2010; Scott, 2009). Academic literature about the WFF has focused primarily on the funding of K–12 initiatives, primarily the charter school movement and privatization efforts. Funding charter advocacy has been a primary activity by the WFF, which joined Gates and Broad in giving large amounts to charter advocacy groups. Specifically, Walton increased its giving to think tanks and advocacy groups to more than $200 million a year by 2014 (Callahan, 2017, p. 175). Callahan described how the foundation has strategically linked advocacy to creating new educational institutions, arguing, "Walton has spent the bulk of its education dollars on actually building charter schools, but it has also worked to create a policy climate where charters are embraced," (p. 175). Although its profile has changed over time, the WFF has managed to give sizable amounts of money toward specific causes, while maintaining the public profile of a smaller organization (Preston, 2011a).

The WFF is open about its strategies to support charter schools. According to Preston (2011b), no other philanthropy has done more financially to help make charter schools a permanent feature of the American K–12 education. An evaluation report commissioned by the WFF reported the foundation's investment strategies of supporting charter schools had been successful in "supporting the creation of high-quality seats for low income students" (p. 6). The report identified WFF's strategy as investing in charter schools where test scores had shown greater improvements than in local district schools or charter schools that were not receiving foundation funds (Carr & Holley, 2014). Because the foundation's strategy was to invest in schools that were already improving their test scores, it is difficult to determine the impact this giving had on improving the quality of the schools or on access to high-quality schools for low-income students. Not all investments in charter school funding and high-stakes accountability paid off. Jaffe (2016) points to the WFF's failed attempts to promote charter efforts in Chicago because of resistance from Chicago's teacher's union.

In contrast, Gross and Shapiro (2014) argued that venture philanthropies like the WFF, place public schools in jeopardy by increasing turbulence and strong-arming schools into an ethical dilemma: Accept the money and abide by Walton's terms of influence, or reject the money and allow the school to fail from a lack of resources. According to Gross and Shapiro the philanthropic strategies of foundations like WFF, with their emphasis on high stakes accountability and privatizing public schools through the creation of charters do more harm than good, with less public accountability. Rogers (2015) warned that the WFF has already fundamentally restructured the American K–12 education system, and the economic elite only gain further power to shape our social infrastructures by giving. Philanthropy in education influences policy making without any of the checks and balances that existed previously (Rogers, 2015).

Although identifying a model to help educators escape the influence of venture philanthropists through democratic ethical educational leadership, Gross and Shapiro (2014) warn that venture philanthropic strategies are quickly becoming a global phenomenon as they spread to countries beyond the United States. In terms of their influence on teacher education, the Waltons are the single largest funders of Teach For America, with grants totaling more than $100 million (Callahan, 2017, p. 233). The WFF's sizable donations toward particular causes can be incredibly influential, as Callahan noted in his description of WFF's financial support fueling charter school growth in Washington, D.C.:

> The nation's capital became a top battleground for education funders in 2007, after Mayor Adrian Fenty appointed Michelle Rhee chancellor of the D.C. Public Schools. Rhee

> didn't just push charters, she rammed through a new teacher evaluation system that gave big bonuses to top teachers and penalized or fired ineffective ones. A group of foundations led by Walton and Broad helped shoulder the costs of the system to the tune of nearly 65 million. (p. 163)

Our review of extant literature points to a popular critique of WFF funding strategies promoting school choice, charter schools, and privatization in kindergarten through 12th grade with less attention focused on WFF's purposes and motivations for philanthropic giving to higher education. Although research into the WFF's giving in higher education is quite limited, news and institutional reports have tracked recent WFF giving to the following higher education institutions:

- $64 million for doctoral fellowships at the University of Arkansas (Black Issues, 2003)
- A $300 million matching grant at the University of Arkansas, the largest ever at the time to a public institution (Strout, 2005)
- A $10 million matching grant for high-need and first-generation students at Colorado College (Diverse Issues in Higher Education, 2010)
- $27.5 million to Arizona State University's Global Institute of Sustainability supporting training and program development for environmental sustainability (ASU Now, 2012)

These examples raise questions about the WFF's intentions and influence over higher education, with the enormous gifts they bestow and the power they wield due to their considerable wealth. In the next section, we describe our research methods and then turn to exploring the history and context of the WFF and its key players and how their personal interests and projects influence their strategic philanthropic giving in higher education.

Research Methods

We used two approaches to understanding the WFF's funding and philanthropic efforts. The first approach relied on the Foundation Directory Online (FDO) database (now called Candid), a source providing information about individual and nonprofit philanthropic giving, with a mission to "strengthen the social sector by advancing knowledge about philanthropy in the United States and around the world" with efforts to "increase transparency and knowledge about philanthropy aid nonprofits" (Candid, 2020). We began with a search of the WFF from 2005 to 2017, the most recent date with complete 990 tax filings information. We then searched philanthropic giving for individual living members of the WFF, primarily the children of founder Sam Walton (Alice Walton, Jim Walton, and Rob and Melani Walton). After an initial data sort of "support strategies" for donations, we identified three primary targets for charitable donations: the arts, the environment, and education (K–12/higher education). Within the education category, we distinguished between funding for K–12 and higher education to provide clarity around giving patterns directed toward higher education as aligned with our overarching research questions. For each target area, we identified the largest single donations and ranked grant recipients of more than $1 million total by amount received to track organizations/causes receiving the most sizable funding. We further summarized donations by state to compare spending geographically.

The second approach to our research was a careful review of relevant publicly available website information, starting with the WFF and branching out to related institutions, organizations, people, and so on. We examined the FDO database information on WFF giving, searching recipient websites, boards of directors, and donor-funded projects to gain a better understanding of the causes the WFF supports. We focused special attention on the top 10 recipients of arts, education, and environmental funding from 2003 to 2017. Notable WFF donations following these years were self-reported on the WFF website or obtained through institutional and press releases. For 2009 to 2017, 990 tax filings are available on the WFF's website. However, there are no 990s for the Walton Family Charitable Support Foundation (WFCSF) reported. In the following section, we present the findings from our research around the WFF's philanthropic investments: education, the arts, and the environment.

History And Context Of The WFF

In an "explosion of new wealth in the old economy" (Callahan, 2017, p. 33), American families with large sums of preexisting wealth, such as the Kochs and Waltons, have witnessed their wealth inflate. For instance, the Waltons' wealth has grown by $70 billion since 2005, which is attributed to a rise in Walmart's stock. This rise in dynastic wealth led the WFF to greatly expand its giving for charter schools, contribute significantly to the development of art museums and art education programming, and fund an expansive new environmental program. As seen in the earlier charter school example, the WFF's significant contributions (many channeled through higher education) in the arts and the environment have the potential to wield significant impact. According to a recent article published in the *Arkansas Times*, the WFF's $120 million gift to establish the School of Art at the University of Arkansas is "the largest ever given to a U.S. university in support of or to establish a school of art" (Brantley, 2019, para. 7). Regarding the WFF's philanthropic investment in the environment, the Waltons rank among the largest "green philanthropists" in the United States with a focus on preserving rivers and waterways (Callahan, 2017).

As context for understanding the WFF, an organization Callahan (2017) refers to as "right-of-center" (p. 8), we start with a brief overview of the history of the Walton family and the business that enabled its vast wealth. Samuel M. Walton (1918–1992) and Helen Alice Walton (1919–2007), founders of the multinational retail corporation Walmart and, subsequently, the WFF, raised a family of four children, Samuel Robson (Rob) Walton (1944–), John Thomas Walton (1946–2005),

Jim Carr Walton (1948–), and Alice Louise (1949–). Rob's children are Ben, Sam R., and Carrie, all living. In 2018, *Forbes* named the Walton children, Jim ($44.6 billion), Alice ($44.4 billion), and Rob ($44.3 billion), respectively, as the 16th, 17th, and 18th richest people in the world (Forbes, 2019). The WFF continues to be run by the Walton family as described on its website:

> The Walton Family Foundation, is, at its core, a family-led foundation. Three generations of the descendants of our founders, Sam and Helen Walton, and their spouses, work together to lead the foundation and create access to opportunity for people and communities. (Walton Family Foundation, n.d.-a)

The board is chaired by Carrie Walton Penner (granddaughter) and includes Alice Walton, James Walton (grandson), Lukas Walton (grandson), and Rob Walton (son). The descriptions of the "Strategic Learning Questions" on the WWF website include three main areas: the Home Region, the K–12 Education Program, and the Environment Program (Walton Family Foundation, n.d.-b). Interestingly, there is no mention of strategic learning questions in higher education. However, Jim Walton, quoted in a press release on the University of Arkansas's (2013) website, stated, "universities are powerful engines for driving regional and national economics" (Adame, 2018). In the sections that follow, we examine key players in the WFF's philanthropic giving, causes they support, and ways their giving is channeled through higher education.

Rob Walton and the Environment

Unpacking the motivations behind the WFF's environmental giving requires an in-depth look at Rob Walton's interests in environmental philanthropy. Rob Walton, oldest of the first generation of Walton children, attended the College of Wooster and graduated from the University of Arkansas in 1966 with a degree in business administration, followed by a degree from Columbia Law School in 1969. After Sam Walton's death in 1992, Rob moved from vice chair to chair of the WFF board of directors. Rob and his third wife, Melani Lowman-Walton, established the Rob and Melani Walton Foundation whose mission is to "elevate people, planet, and purpose by changing what people feel is possible and know is doable" (Rob and Melani Walton Foundation, n.d.). The Rob and Melani Walton Foundation funds projects independently and in partnership with the WFF ranging from music wellness and the performing arts to urban farming and environmental sustainability. Since 2011, the WFF in partnership with the Rob and Melani Walton Foundation has donated more than $28 million to Sustainability Solutions Services at Arizona State University (ASU), an environmental program founded and sponsored by Rob and Melani Walton within the Walton-supported Global Institute of Sustainability. The establishment of Sustainability Solutions Services and support for ASU's Global Institute provides an avenue for the Rob and Melani Walton Foundation and the WFF to invest in research and leadership influencing environmental policy and programming through higher education.

Guided by Rob and Melani Walton's personal interest in environmental sustainability, research, and leadership, the WFF donated more than $600 million dollars to over 240 recipients towards environmental causes in the United States, Canada, and Mexico between 2005 and 2016. Of the 18 organizations receiving single donations over $1 million, the top five recipients included Conservation International ($198,265,648); Environmental Defense Fund ($125,532,127); National Wildlife Federation ($44,312,198); Nature Conservancies of Little Rock, Arkansas, and Arlington, Virginia ($43,808,451 collectively); and Ocean Conservancy ($31,419,847). The WFF awarded environment-related grants totaling $830,445,893 to 511 organizations between 2003 and 2017. The four largest recipients were natural resources ($590,466,209), biodiversity ($358,241,135), environment ($160,693,060), and environmental education ($35,660,312). The top natural resource grant recipients included Conservation International

($199,285,648), the Nature Conservancy ($31,134,369), National Wildlife Federation ($22,156,099), and the Nature Conservancy Arkansas ($12,809,393). Guided by Rob and Melani Walton's vision and in partnership with their foundation, the WFF became one of the nation's leading philanthropies giving to "green" causes through its support of organizations and higher education institutions steering environmental research and development.

Although the WFF contributed substantial funding to conservation organizations as illustrated above, these efforts are not without their critics. In 2012, the *New York Times* reported the Environmental Defense Fund (EDF) had been working closely with Walmart since 2005 on sustainability issues (Clifford, 2012). Although the *New York Times* initially reported that EDF received no funds from Walmart, others clarified that EDF received significant funds from the WFF (Mitchell, 2012b). Stacy Mitchell (2012a) noted that since 2004, the WFF gave the EDF more than $53 million, including a $13.7 million grant in 2011 that made up 15% of the EDF's budget. The difference between Walmart and WFF, Mitchell (2012a) reminds us, is that the Waltons own 50% of Walmart's stock; a single family owns half of a corporation whose revenues exceed the gross domestic product of many countries in the world.

Although there is no doubt the WFF is engaged in giving toward environmental organizations, closer inspection reveals Walmart as a corporation receives some benefit from the WFF's giving, and it often gives the largest grants to organizations open to collaboration around key initiatives. Mitchell (2012a) reported:

> In addition to EDF, top recipients included Conservation International, which has a corporate partnership with Walmart, and the Marine Stewardship Council, which began receiving foundation support the same year it agreed to certify and provide an eco-label for some of the seafood Walmart sells. These three organizations accounted for 46 percent of the foundation's environmental funding last year. (para. 10)

This level of support illustrates the potential for a quid pro quo relationship among the WFF, certain environmental organizations, and Walmart. Mitchell (2011a) tracked Walmart's sustainability campaign, noting that although the company's public image may have improved, the resulting growth led to an increase in the retailer's environmental footprint, calling the project a "greenwash." Walmart's history of donating to prominent climate-change-denying governors and political candidates friendly to natural gas and fracking industries calls its motivations toward environmental organizations into question (Mitchell, 2011b). As Mitchell (2012a) wrote,

> what does it mean for the environmental movement that the Walton Family Foundation is now one of the largest environmental grantmakers in the nation? For one thing, it means that Walmart's money is exerting significant influence in setting the agenda, defining the problems, and elevating certain kinds of approaches—notably those that reinforce, rather than challenge, the power of large corporations in our economy and society. That's a worrisome trend given how far this company's tentacles already reach into our economy and government. (para. 12)

One potential agenda setting opportunity involves the WFF's interest in water privatization. In an article concerning the expansion of Gross Dam in Denver, Colorado, *Boulder Weekly* (Cortina, 2017) discussed how environmental groups have signed off on environmentally harmful projects, in exchange for small concessions from powerful entities. For instance, the Colorado chapter of Trout Unlimited (a river conservation group) argued that the Gross Dam expansion was the best of a bad situation and would not pursue a lawsuit against Denver Water. Denver Water and the WFF (both proponents of water privatization) were financial sponsors of Trout Unlimited. Additional Walton funding in the area has gone to American Rivers, the Colorado River Trust, Conservation Colorado, the Environmental Defense Fund, and the Nature Conservancy. According to *Boulder Weekly*, "in total, the Waltons have invested tens of millions of dollars into the Colorado River, while simultaneously promoting private water markets as a way to conservation" (Cortina, 2017, para. 31). The potential long-term power that the WFF may hold in determining the agenda for environmental conservation and how this might benefit the interests of the Walmart corporation have already begun to take shape in the form of "impact investing."

Writing for the *Boulder Weekly*, Joel Dyer (2018) argued that current efforts to "save" the Colorado River via impact investing, actually poses a big threat to the river's health. Simply put, the Colorado River's health is in danger because there is not enough water in it. Impact investing (investments made with the intent of generating environmental impact and financial return), such as the kinds of environmental conservation projects that the WFF supports, is interested primarily in saving the future economic growth that can be derived from the Colorado River. However, the WFF's actions have not always been transparent, as Dyer points out:

> Trying to keep up with the Walton Family Foundation when it comes to water has given me whiplash. They constantly proclaim their commitment to saving the all-important Colorado River, yet they also seem to have their tentacles in every environmentally harmful diversion of Colorado River water you can find. (para. 22)

Rather than keeping water in the river, snatching up land investment opportunities downstream and other river infrastructure projects has opened the door to investment and development that can benefit supporting foundations such as the WFF and its associated corporate entities like Walmart. As Dyer explained, the WFF's strategy was multifaceted and well planned:

> The Waltons and their pals are impact investing in our water and they are a lot smarter than those who came before them. They understood from the beginning that there

> were only four possible areas of oversight into their water activities: government, journalists, environmental groups and academics. And they have poured millions of dollars into all of these areas. (para. 42)

Strategic funding to academia was an important part of the plan to secure access to the Colorado River's resources, and Dyer highlighted Walton-funded research concerning water taking place at Colorado State, Colorado University Boulder's Law School, Stanford, and the University of California, Santa Barbara. This case example brings the potential impact and motivations of WFF funding to colleges and universities into focus.

Alice Walton and the Arts

Alice Walton, Sam Walton's only daughter, worth more than $30 billion, built the Crystal Bridges Museum of American Art in her hometown of Bentonville, Arkansas, at a cost of approximately $1.6 billion. With hundreds of millions in Walton money for its acquisitions, the Museum holds famous works by Andy Warhol, Georgia O'Keeffe, and Norman Rockwell. (Callahan, 2017, p. 238). Alice Walton's commitment to philanthropy in the arts has been nationally recognized: She is a previous recipient of the Smithsonian Institution's Archive for American Art medal, was recognized in 2012 by *Time* magazine as one of the world's most influential women, and, in 2018, was inducted into the International Women Forum's Hall of Fame. Her commitment to philanthropy in the arts earned her the Leonore and Walter Annenberg Award for Diplomacy through the Arts (Alice Walton, n.d.).

Alice Walton's commitment to philanthropy in the arts can be seen in the WFF's contributions to art museums, community arts councils and art programming in K–12 and higher education. Between 2003 and 2017, the WFF gave 240 grants to 108 organizations toward the arts totaling $1,432,395,167. The largest recipients are art museums (total $1,384,132,076), which awarded 183 grants to 50 recipients. Grants of more than $1 million went to six museums, with the largest amount providing 14 grants to the Crystal Bridges Museum of American Art, the art museum in Arkansas Alice Walton founded, totaling $1,349,187,151.

The WFF channels the majority of arts funding through the Walton Arts Center Council, Inc. (over $22 million). This organization, formed in 1986, strives to "bring great performing artists and entertainers from around the world to Northwest Arkansas, connecting and engaging people through inspiring arts experiences" (Walton Arts Center, n.d.). The Walton Arts Center showcases exhibits by local artists, supports an education initiative that provides stage performance field trips for local schools, and workshops for community members. The Walton Arts Center Council complex also encompasses the Walmart Amp (Arkansas Music Pavilion), which provides a large-scale venue for nationally acclaimed musicians, bands, and performing artists.

The WFF's philanthropic investment in the arts has recent ties to higher education in their home state of Arkansas. In 2017, the WFF, through the WFCSF, made a single $120 million gift toward the establishment of the University of Arkansas School of Art. Although not much is known about the WFCSF, it appears to have been established to support higher education initiatives in Arkansas (Callahan, 2017). According to a news release issued by the University of Arkansas the Walton gift—"the largest ever given to a U.S. university to support or establish a school of art"—supports the following goals:

- Providing unprecedented levels of financial support for students in the form of scholarships, travel grants and internship opportunities.
- Engaging the region in outreach and public service through partnerships with Crystal Bridges Museum of American Art and a variety of community arts organizations.

- Expanding graduate programs and degree offerings in art history, art education and graphic design. (University of Arkansas, 2017)

The WFF donated over $36 million to arts programming between 2005 and 2016. Most single and recurring donations target community museums and local performing arts centers; however, of the 102 recipient organizations listed, 35 recipients are arts-based academies and charter schools. This composed 34% of grant recipients of arts-based WFF funding during these years. As funding for arts initiatives in K–12 public schools diminishes, it is important to note the presence of alternative arts education programs supported by Walton money and its ties to charter schools. We now look specifically at the WFF's long-term philanthropic investment in charter schools and the Walton family members driving K–12 charter school funding.

Carrie Walton Penner, Greg Penner, and K–12 Charter School Funding

Carrie Walton Penner, a third-generation Walton, is a major player in K–12 education, giving as a funder and an activist in the school choice movement. Georgetown and Stanford educated, Carrie Walton Penner holds a master's degree in education policy and program evaluation. She serves on the board of the Knowledge Is Power Program Foundation, the largest charter school foundation in the United States (including at least 125 schools), which received $60 million in funding from the WFF. She served on the board for the Alliance for School Choice, an advocacy group supporting charter schools and backing vouchers, the largest source of funding ($20 million) coming from the WFF. She is on the board of the Charter School Growth Fund (recipient of more than $100 million from the WFF), and she is active in several education organizations based in California, where she lives. This includes organizations such as the California Charter Schools Association (recipient of

$40 million in support from the WFF). Serving in the dual roles of philanthropist and campaign donor, Carrie Walton Penner donated more than $1 million in local school board races, in collaboration with her uncle Jim Walton (Callahan, 2017).

Another key player is Carrie Walton Penner's husband, Greg Penner, who is on the chair of Walmart's board and involved in education. Greg Penner served as co-chair for the Charter School Growth Fund and is a board member for Teach For America, the latter receiving grants totaling more than $100 million from the WFF. According to the editor of *Inside Philanthropy* and the author of *The Givers*, David Callahan (2017) explained: "The Penners are one of the top power couples in education reform right now, with huge resources and clout" (p. 233). Theirs are the most recent efforts in the WFF's 20-year history promoting K–12 charter schools and education reform.

Between 2005 and 2016, the WFF donated over $870 million to more than 850 charter schools, public schools, and charter supporting organizations with the Charter Fund (also known as the Charter School Growth Fund, located in Broomfield, Colorado) receiving the most sizable donations totaling more than $130 million between 2007 and 2016. The Charter Fund supports "education entrepreneurs who are building networks of great charter schools" (Sundbom, 2018, para. 3) in more than 28 states across the United States. With its focus on entrepreneurship and education, it is not surprising that the chief executive officer of the Charter Fund, Kevin Hall, has previous employment ties to the Broad Foundation, where he served as chief operating officer, overseeing grant investment strategies, as well as previous employment ties with Goldman Sachs. Notably, Hall cofounded Chancellor Beacon Academies (a manager of private and charter schools across the United States) and received an MBA from the Harvard Business School. In addition to their sizable financial donations, the WFF's K–12 Education Program Committee officer, Annie Proietti, currently serves on the board of the Charter Fund. As a result of the WFF's commitment to the expansion of U.S. charter schools, elite philanthropic foundations have forged partnerships to promote charter expansion in their own communities. In 2015, the Broad Foundation partnered with the WFF and others to expand charter schools in Los Angeles with the aim of moving over half of all school-aged children into charter schools within eight years (Blume, 2015).

The WFF's involvement in charter school and school voucher programs has implications for the WFF's philanthropic impact in higher education. A 2018 article released by the Associated Press ties WFF donations to the United Negro College Fund and the Congressional Black Caucus to efforts toward expanding charter schools in Black communities (Ho, 2018). Andre Perry with the Brookings Institution argued that "the Walton foundation's reliance on black faces to make its case for charters suggests that they're exploiting black people for a 'white agenda'" (Ho, 2018, para. 9). FDO records show more than $6 million in donations to the United Negro College Fund between 2009 and 2017 (Candid, 2020). In 2019, the WFF announced a $1.8 million teacher preparation initiative across three colleges and universities (Bank Street College of Education, Marian University, and New York University), with its stated aim to "prepare teachers to serve students with diverse and varied learning needs, including a focus on students with special needs and English language learners" (WFF, 2019, para. 6). Programs at each university use teacher residency programs (praised for their success in retaining teachers of color in the teaching profession) as a component of teacher training including "a year-long clinical residency in high-performing public charter or district schools in New York City" for Bank Street College participants (Walton Family Foundation, 2019, para. 4).

The WFF's most notable influence on K–12 education reform through higher education can be seen in the University of Arkansas College of Education and Health Professions. In 2019, the WFF and its WFCSF were listed as top contributors to the University of Arkansas, with donations totaling more than $25 million supporting research commercialization, K–12 principal training, and an endowed deanship in the College of Education and Health Professions (Adame, 2019). The College of Education and Health Professions is home to the university's Department of Education Reform (EDRE), established in 2005 through a $10 million gift and matching contributions (University of Arkansas, College of Education and Health Professions, n.d.). Among research initiatives supported through the EDRE are Choice Regulation Watch, a publication outlet that produces papers in favor of school choice initiatives around the United States and the School Choice Demonstration Project, a research arm of the EDRE supporting studies promoting school choice and voucher programs. We now turn to a brief discussion of the research methods used to track the WFF's philanthropic giving in the arts, education and the environment through donations to U.S. colleges and universities.

WFF's Higher Education Funding

Financial scarcity has become the norm on the campuses of many colleges and universities. As state budgets allocate fewer resources for higher education funding, colleges and universities have looked elsewhere to supplement faculty and program resources. Philanthropic actors have used this scarcity of public funding in higher education to their advantage. Exploring how philanthropy's hidden strategies impact public policy, deMarrais et al. (2019) examined how the Charles Koch Foundation

> used a consistent focus, strategy, and ideology to fund programs that train faculty and students who possess a particular ideological frame, to support the placement of those faculty within the institutions through faculty lines, distinguished professorships and institutes in a way that serves to further the Kochs' conservative beliefs. (p. 180)

In his discussion of Charles and David Koch, Callahan (2017) points to a shift away from large donations to political candidates toward slow-burn impact giving targeting think tanks and local and state organizations (including colleges and universities). Callahan contrasts this with previously adopted strategies that targeted large funding directed toward political candidates. He argued that funding ideas rather than candidates "offers a reliable and proven way to slowly change policy and culture over time—and without the high-profile controversies that can come with partisan giving, which is often a concern to wealthy donors who also run businesses" (p. 74). Although our examination of the WFF funding reveals similar strategies for charitable giving, we show how the WFF employs a strategy of giving through higher education that targets education, the arts, and the environment. In this section, we explore the field of higher education, specifically the impact of philanthropic donations on college and university programs and resources. We investigate the WFF along with its affiliated philanthropies—the WFCSF and the Windgate Charitable Foundation—detailing philanthropic efforts in higher education and answering the following questions: (1) How has the WFF funded higher education institutions during this period, and (2) What is the impact of WFF on higher education?

According to records available from the FDO, the WFF donated a total of $255,483,407 to U.S. colleges and universities between 2005 and 2017 (Candid, 2020). To date, ASU is the top WFF higher education recipients, with donations totaling more than $28 million between 2011 and 2017. Other top recipients included the University of Arkansas ($26,138,273), Stanford University ($12,630,589), Harvard University ($12,081,211), the University of Notre Dame ($11,178,432), Colorado College ($10,500,000), and Georgetown University ($10,421,718). A breakdown of top higher education recipients by state yielded results in keeping with top institutional recipients. The following states received WFF support totaling more than $10 million dollars from 2005 to 2017: Arkansas ($101,014,963), Arizona ($29,967,383), California ($28,910,022), Massachusetts ($13,732,984), Colorado ($13,294,063), Indiana ($12,648,563), and Washington, D.C. ($11,325,145). (See Figure 7.1.) We now turn our discussion toward WFF-funded higher education projects and programs, with specific attention to large-scale recipients and states.

Figure 7.1
Walton Family Foundation Higher Ed Top Recipients

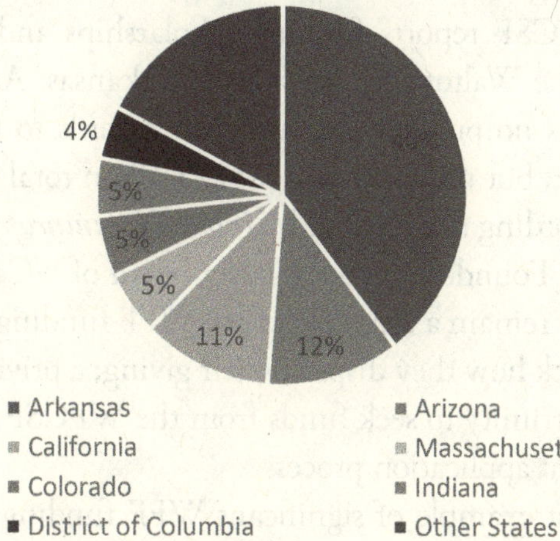

WFF donations to higher education in Walton's home state of Arkansas exceeds higher education spending in any other state, composing 40% of all WFF giving in this category. Top recipients include the University of Arkansas ($26,138,273), the University of the Ozarks ($25,194,935), John Brown University ($13,530,745) and Harding University ($13,085,000). This funding does not reflect Walton donations through its affiliate organization, the WFCS. FDO records show transactions between the WFF and the WFCSF in 2009 ($100,848,750), 2011 ($209,160,000) and 2012 ($100,848,750) supporting the Walton International Scholarship Program (WISP) and "other charitable activities" (Candid, 2020). Sam and Helen Walton founded WISP in 1985 to "expose Central American students to the virtues of democracy and capitalism" (Walton International Scholarship Program, n.d.). The Waltons endowed WISP to fund tuition for recipients attending one of three faith-based Arkansas universities—University of the Ozarks, John Brown University, and Harding University. According to a press release from the University of Arkansas dated November 2018, recent WFCS funding supports a $23.7 million investment to the University of Arkansas's research and economic development program as an integral part of a larger statewide campaign to foster economic growth within the state.

The WFCSF has been a top recipient of funding from the WFF, particularly in grant areas related to higher education and democracy. The WFCSF reports funding scholarships and endowments primarily in the Waltons' home state of Arkansas. As a private institution, it has no publicly available 990 records to track how the money is spent, but they received $419.7 million total between 2003 and 2017. According to an article by *Inside Philanthropy*, the WFCSF is "the Walton Foundation you've never heard of" (Callahan, 2014). Although they remain a top recipient of WFF funding, not only is it difficult to track how they disperse their giving; a privileged few also have the opportunity to seek funds from the WFCSF, which has no website or grant application process.

As a recent example of significant WFF funding to higher education, in a January 7, 2019, press release, ASU announced "the permanent establishment of the Rob and Melani Walton Sustainability Solutions Service, furthering the institution's efforts to become a global leader in sustainability education and applied research" (Franz, 2019, para. 1). The article heralds the Waltons' involvement dating back to 2006, when Rob and Melani Walton joined ASU's Sustainability Board. Since 2011, the WFF, guided by the environmental interests of Rob and Melani Walton, has donated more than $28 million to launch and support the Sustainability Solutions Service (formerly known as the Rob and Melani Walton Sustainability Solutions Initiatives). This program was founded "based around seven cohesive programs designed to co-create solutions, educate future leaders and engage a diverse public" (para. 10). ASU president Michael M. Crow praised Rob and Melani Walton Sustainability Solutions Service as a program that "enables us to create a completely transformed university, one that uses all of its assets, thousands of faculty, tens of thousands of students, all devoted to sustainability solutions as our unifying reason for existence" (para. 7). Sustainability Solutions Service, designed to supplement current Walton-funded programs including the Executive Master of Sustainability Leadership, the Global Sustainability Studies Program, the Rob and Melani Walton National Teachers' Academy, and the Rob and Melani Walton

Sustainability in Science and Technology Museums program. Continued WFF philanthropic giving to ASU through the Rob and Melani Walton Sustainability Solutions ensures WFF influence into environmental sustainability, teacher education, science and technology, and global leadership programming. As of 2019, the Waltons have contributed over $31 million to ASU's Sustainability Solutions.

Windgate Charitable Foundation

The Windgate Charitable Foundation is headquartered in Siloam Springs, Arkansas, and was founded in 1993 by Dorothea Hutcheson with Wal-Mart stock. The Foundation's director John Brown called Windgate "the Walton Family Foundation's little brother" (Peacock, 2014). The Windgate Charitable Foundation currently holds over $350 million in assets (Scutari, 2015) and funds "educational programs in contemporary craft and visual arts . . . k-12 and higher educational institutions for the development and support of the arts, scholarships and effective instructional programs . . . [and] programs for disadvantaged children in Arkansas" (Windgate Foundation, 2020). The organization lists three staff members on its website including John Brown III, former president of John Brown University, an Arkansas-based Christian university and one of three recipients of the WFF-funded Walton International Scholarship Program.

Windgate is a strong supporter of arts education in its home state. Between 2005 and 2017, Windgate donated more than $20 million to the University of Arkansas for arts education, with more than $15.5 million supporting the construction of a visual arts building at the university's Fort Smith campus. Remaining funds (totaling close to $4 million) support the Arkansas Teacher Corps Art Fellows Program, gallery exhibitions, and art department endowments, with 52% supporting "Art Department strategy priorities" (Candid, 2020). Statewide arts education initiatives include a collaborative project with the Crystal Bridges Museum (founded by Alice Walton) sponsoring a distance learning K–12 program for rural Arkansas students (Scutari, 2015).

In addition to Windgate's $20 million contributions to the University of Arkansas visual arts building and programming, Wingate funded an additional $36,326,980 between 2003 and 2017 to the university in support of higher education systems reform and programs support, including over $6 million toward the Department of Education Reform. Housed in the College of Education and Health Professions, the Department of Education Reform was founded in 2005 through a matching contribution program. Its stated aims are to provide "research that will directly inform policy makers at all levels of government, scholars, parents, teachers, administrators, and the public to positively influence the future of Arkansas and the nation's schools" (University of Arkansas, College of Education and Health Professions, n.d., para. 2). Among its programming goals, the department seeks to "obtain additional private, state, and federal funding through the creation of a seed grant program that provides additional funding for promising research and demonstration projects" (University of Arkansas, College of Education and Health Professions, n.d., para. 4).

Although more than 45% of Windgate's philanthropic giving remains in its home state of Arkansas ($204,993,778.00) with interests focused around the arts and educational initiatives, Windgate's philanthropic investments and interests extend into 47 states and the District of Columbia. California ($87,955,600.00), North Carolina ($46,546,309.00), Pennsylvania ($12,229,294.00), and Tennessee ($11,347,588.00) compose the remaining top five Windgate state grant recipients between 2003 and 2017. Although Windgate giving across most of the top five state recipients includes donations to education and the arts, Windgate's giving in California provides an example of Windgate's charitable diversity in recent years.

California is the second-largest state recipient of Windgate grants to date with donations between 2003 and 2017 totaling $87,955,600. Windgate's philanthropic giving in California has increased exponentially since 2014, with 81% of Windgate donations in California occurring between 2014 and 2017. More than $52 million of the $71,390,054 in donations during these three years were granted to the Legacy Foundation Fund (also known as the Resource Legacy Fund). This organization began in 2000 by Lucile and David Packard (co-founder of Hewlett-Packard and founder of the David and Lucile Packard Foundation) with a mission to protect 250,000 acres of land in California. Currently, the Legacy Foundation Fund partners with donors to fund environmental projects primarily in the western United States, Canada, Argentina, and Mexico. According to information in Influence Watch (n.d.), "the fund networks with land trusts in particular areas and acts as a pass-through organization for nonprofits interested in buying and preserving land" (David and Lucile Packard Foundation, n.d., para 31). With its recent interest in environmental philanthropy in California, the Windgate Foundation's philanthropic interests closely mirroring those of its big brother, the WFF, targeting the arts, education, and the environment. The Windgate Charitable Trust appears to be yet another funding arm in the Walton network that enables the Walton family to use philanthropy to their advantage.

Conclusion

For decades, philanthropy's most illustrious donors have wielded ideological influence via large-scale political donations. Although this strategy proved successful in the last decades of the 20th century, such strategies pushed philanthropic giving from the shadows into the spotlight, drawing widespread criticism for high-profile philanthropists such as the Koch brothers. A similar story could be told about the Walton family's philanthropic influence. Callahan (2017) concluded with a chilling analysis and warning about the Walton family's tremendous power and influence through giving: "These private citizens, with such outsized power over public institutions, illustrate the new face of dynastic wealth in America. Get ready for a future with many more philanthropic heirs who operate in the same activist style" (p. 233).

This chapter explored the various ways that the Walton family, through the tax-deductible WFF, used their wealth to influence specific projects related to each family members' interest related to charter schools, the environment, and the arts. Much of this support has been enacted via slow-burn impact through the development of sophisticated networks of giving and influence, of which investment in colleges and universities has played a key role. This prompts concerned citizens to ask, "What power does the Walton family gain through their giving?"

We return to our original question: Is the WFF good for higher education? The WFF operates at a high level of sophistication beyond the reach of everyday citizens. The WFF has the power to exert a slow and steady change. Their gifts appear like a Trojan horse, where deceptive intentions allow the gift maker the upper hand. The consequences are often far-reaching, as the academic literature has argued in terms of WFF's influence on supporting charter schools in K–12 education. The same potential holds true for the WFF's influence on higher education. Associations with higher education institutions provide power through legitimacy and prestige. These associations are positive for the foundation's public image, and the WFF has shown its willingness to adjust its funding to build a more positive image, one that has not been associated with Walmart and the Walton name in the past. They have proved themselves adept at navigating a push–pull between getting what they want ideologically and public critique. Walmart and the WFF owe their wealth to the exploitation of labor across the world and within its stores, enabling its rise into the ultra-wealthy class and pushing the United States further toward a plutocracy. Now the Walton descendants use that money to exert extraordinary influence, and the full extent of these impacts in higher education remains to be seen. In our chapter, we have identified which colleges and universities are receiving the most Walton funding and tracked what sorts of programs and agendas are being supported. We identified a new funding arm in the Walton network—the Windgate Charitable Trust. Future funding initiatives and interventions in the realm of higher education as they impact the fields of K–12 education, the arts, and the environment will require vigilant public attention. The influence of public image and opinion has influenced the initiatives of the WFF in the past or, at the very least, their public relations strategies, as seen in public initiatives surrounding the funding of charter schools and the environment. This demonstrates the need for educators and citizens to not only track the money but also unpack the full relationship of what receiving money actually means. The WFF is a perfect case study for the danger of assuming that "the arts" or "the environment" means that the money is being donated for the greater good or in an apolitical way. There is a fundamental flaw in a system of philanthropic giving when it enables those with more wealth, or a single family, to have a greater say in how we build and maintain our society and educational systems. Through public critique and careful examination, we may still be able to hold these philanthropies accountable and cultivate a necessary skepticism about accepting their gifts. Walmart is not good for higher education because it allows the whims of a few to dictate the possibilities for everyone else, fundamentally challenging our rights to democracy and academic freedom.

References

Adame, J. (2018, November 9). *Walton Family charitable support foundation gives $23.7M to UA*. https://www.arkansasonline.com/news/2018/nov/09/walton-family-charitable-support-foundation-gives-/

Adame, J. (2019, August 7). Walton donations top UA's '19 gift list. *Arkansas Democrat Gazette*. https://www.arkansasonline.com/news/2019/aug/07/walton-donations-top-ua-s-19-gift-list--1/

Alice Walton. (n.d.). Retrieved from http://alicewalton.org/

ASU Now. (2012, March 29). ASU to use $27.5M Walton investment to accelerate sustainability efforts. (2012, March 29). *ASU Now*. https://asunow.asu.edu/content/asu-use-275m-walton-investment-accelerate-sustainability-efforts

Black Issues. (2003, April 24). University of Arkansas earmarks $64 million for doctoral fellowships (noteworthy news). *Diverse Issues in Higher Education*, (5), 14. https://diverseeducation.com/article/2898/

Blume, H. (2015, September 21). Backers want half of LAUSD students in charter schools in eight years, report says. *Los Angeles Times.* https://www.latimes.com/local/lanow/la-me-ln-broad-draft-charter-expansion-plan-20150921-story.html

Brantley, M. (2019, April 24). Waltons give UA $120 million to establish school of art. *Arkansas Times.* https://arktimes.com/arkansas-blog/2017/08/23/waltons-give-ua-120-million-to-establish-school-of-art

Callahan, D. (2014). The Walton Foundation you've never heard of. *Inside Philanthropy.* https://www.insidephilanthropy.com/home/2014/2/28/the-walton-foundation-youve-never-heard-of.html

Callahan, D. (2017). *The givers: Wealth, power, and philanthropy in a new gilded age.* Alfred A. Knopf.

Candid. (2020). About. Candid.org. https://candid.org/about?fcref=pg

Carr, M., & Holley, M. (2014). Maximizing Return: An Evaluation of the Walton Family Foundation's Approach to Investing in New Charter Schools. Foundation Review, 6(4), 6–17. https://doi.org/10.9707/1944-5660.1222

Clifford, S. (2012, April 13). Unexpected ally helps Walmart cut waste. *The New York Times.* https://www.nytimes.com/2012/04/14/business/wal-mart-and-environmental-fund-team-up-to-cut-waste.html?_r=3

Cortina, M. (2017, August 3). Good 'til the last drop: Opponents prepare for final showdown over Gross Dam. *Boulder Weekly.* https://www.boulderweekly.com/news/good-til-the-last-drop/

David and Lucile Packard Foundation. (n.d.). Retrieved from https://www.influencewatch.org/non-profit/david-and-lucile-packard-foundation/

deMarrais, K., Brewer, T. J., Herron, B., Atkinson, J. C., & Lewis, J. B. (2019). *Philanthropy, hidden strategy, and collective resistance: A primer for concerned educators.* Gorham, ME: Myers Education Press.

Diverse Issues in Higher Education. (2010). The Walton Family Foundation has awarded Colorado College a $10 million matching grant for high-need and first- generation students. *Diverse Issues in Higher Education,* (22), 25. Retrieved from http://search.ebscohost.com/login.aspx?direct=true&db=edsgao&AN=edsgcl.257433822&site=eds-live

Dyer, J. (2018, May 31). The new model for saving the Colorado River might just kill it. *Boulder Weekly.* https://www.boulderweekly.com/news/new-model-saving-colorado-river-might-just-kill/

Forbes. (2019, March 5). Billionaires 2019. *Forbes.* https://www.forbes.com/billionaires/#22958420251c

Franz, J. (2019, January 7). Rob and Melani Walton strengthen their commitment to ASU. *ASU Now.* https://asunow.asu.edu/20190104-rob-and-melani-walton-strengthen-their-commitment-asu

Gross, S. J., & Shapiro, J. P. (2014). At the crossroad: Venture philanthropy or a democratic ethical vision for educational leadership? Values and Ethics in Educational Administration, 11(2), 1-8.

Ho, S. (2018, December 25). *Walmart heirs' money influences Black charter schools debate.* AP News. https://apnews.com/8d289b9d35844 11bb23a51cd7e3f597e

Jaffe, S. (2016). Under the Radar. New Labor Forum, 25(3), 8-11.

MacLean, N. (2017). *Democracy in chains: The deep history of the radical right's stealth plan for America.* London: Scribe Publications.

Mayer, J. (2016). *Dark money: The hidden history of the billionaires behind the rise of the Radical Right.* New York: Anchor Books.

Mitchell, S. (2011a, November 7). Walmart by the numbers: Green vs. growth. *Grist.* https://grist.org/business-technology/2011-11-07-walmart-by-the-numbers-green-vs-growth/

Mitchell, S. (2011b, December 7). Walmart spends big to help anti-environment candidates. *Grist.* https://grist.org/business-technology/2011-12-07-walmart-spends-big-to-help-anti-environment-candidates/

Mitchell, S. (2012a, May 10). Walmart heirs quietly fund Walmart's environmental allies. *Grist.* https://grist.org/business-technology/walmart-heirs-quietly-fund-walmarts-environmental-allies/

Mitchell, S. (2012b, May 11). Walmart heirs quietly fund Walmart's environmental allies. *Boulder Weekly.* https://www.boulderweekly.com/news/walmart-heirs-quietly-fund-walmartrsquos-environmental-allies/

Peacock, L. N. (2014, December 4). Philanthropy in Arkansas: Better times, increased giving. *Arkansas Times.* https://arktimes.com/news/cover-stories/2014/12/04/philanthropy-in-arkansas

Preston, C. (2011a). The Quiet Walton Family Fund Creates a Buzz. Chronicle of Philanthropy, (07). Retrieved from http://search.ebscohost.com/login.aspx?direct=true&db=edsgao&AN=edsgcl.249703408&site=eds-live

Preston, C. (2011b). Walton Fund Focuses on Charter Schools. Chronicle of Philanthropy, (07). Retrieved from http://search.ebscohost.com/login.aspx?direct=true&db=edsgao&AN=edsgcl.249703403&site=eds-live

Rob and Melani Walton Foundation. (n.d.). *Home.* Retrieved January 23, 2020, from https://rmwaltonfoundation.org/

Rogers, R. (2015). Making Public Policy: The New Philanthropists and American Education. American Journal of Economics & Sociology, 74(4), 743–774. https://doi.org/10.1111/ajes.12113

Saltman, K. J. (2010). *The gift of education: Public education and venture philanthropy.* New York: Palgrave Macmillan.

Scott, J. (2009). The politics of venture philanthropy in charter school policy and advocacy. *Educational Policy, 23*(1), 106-136.

Scutari, M. (2015, June 24). A closer look at Windgate's big give to Monatana's Archie Bray Foundation. *Inside Philanthropy.* https://www.insidephilanthropy.com/visual-arts/2015/6/24/a-closer-look-at-windgates-big-give-to-montanas-archie-bray.html

Strout, E. (2005). U. of Arkansas Matches Walton Gift, the Largest Ever to a Public Institution. The Chronicle of Higher Education, (36). Retrieved from http://search.ebscohost.com/login.aspx?direct=true&db=edsgao&AN=edsgcl.147070289&site=eds-live

Sundbom, K. (2018, July 11). Walton Family Announces $100 Million for Charter School Investments. Retrieved from https://charterschoolcapital.org/blog/walton-family-announces-100-million-for-charter-school-investments/

University of Arkansas. (2017, August 23). *Visionary gift creates school of art, transforms access to art in Arkansas.* https://news.uark.edu/articles/39335/visionary-gift-creates-school-of-art-transforms-access-to-art-in-arkansas

University of Arkansas, College of Education and Health Professions. (n.d.). *Education reform.* https://edre.uark.edu/index.php

Walton Arts Center. (n.d.). *Mission & history.* https://waltonartscenter.org/about/mission-and-history/

Walton Family Foundation. (2018, June 19). Walton Family announces $100 million for charter school investments. Charterschoolcapital.org. https://charterschoolcapital.org/blog/walton-family-announces-100-million-for-charter-school-investments/

Walton Family Foundation. (2019, April 14). *Walton Family Foundation supports traditional colleges of education, diverse teacher pipelines across the country* [Press release]. https://www.waltonfamilyfoundation.org/about-us/newsroom/walton-family-foundation-supports-traditional-colleges-of-education-diverse-teacher-pipelines-across-the-country

Walton Family Foundation. (n.d.-a). *Board of directors*. https://www.waltonfamilyfoundation.org/about-us/board-of-directors

Walton Family Foundation. (n.d.-b). *Learning*. https://www.waltonfamilyfoundation.org/learning

Walton International Scholarship Program. (n.d.). *History*. http://www.wispweb.org/about.html

Windgate Foundation. (2020). Explore + apply. Windgatefoundation.org. https://www.windgatefoundation.org/explore---apply.html

Chapter Eight

CONSERVATIVE PHILANTHROPY AND HISTORICALLY BLACK COLLEGES AND UNIVERSITIES:

HISTORICAL TRENDS AND THE CURRENT LANDSCAPE

E. Anthony Muhammad, *Georgia Southern University*

On October 4, 2019, President Donald Trump addressed an adoring crowd of more than 400 of his supporters in the East Room of the White House. Greeted with a wave of smartphone cameras and chants of "Four more years," the exuberance was not unlike that of the cheering crowds at any of President Trump's rallies. The resounding applause and cheers were so great in fact, President Trump was forced to proclaim, "That is the loudest I've ever heard anything in this room. You just broke the record. Unbelievable" (Trump, 2019). However, there was something conspicuously different about this crowd of Trump admirers, something surreal. As attendees of this conservative leadership summit, these gleeful, high-spirited Trump supporters were all Black.

These young Black summit-goers were members of the Black Leadership Summit (BLS). Wrapping up their second annual convention last October, the BLS is an outgrowth of Turning Point USA (see Chapter 9). As a prominent conservative organizing and activism network, Turning Point USA's mission is "to identify, educate, train, and organize students to promote freedom" (Turning Point USA, n.d., para. 1) across the nation's high school and college campuses. This strategic, right-wing advocacy group has resulted in not just the BLS but also a Young Women's Leadership Summit, a High School Activist Conference, and a Winter in West Palm

Beach Activist Retreat. The Turning Point USA/BLS alliance is indicative of the ever-increasing nexus between Black organizations and conservative right-wing dollars.

In this chapter, I outline salient features of the relationship between White conservative philanthropy and Black organizations. I focus on the infusion of conservative dollars into historically Black colleges and universities (HBCUs). My discussion highlights the current landscape in HBCU funding and points of tension between HBCUs and their pursuit of funding from philanthropic and political entities that pursue a far-right agenda. In my discussion, I provide a snapshot of the funding practices of prominent right-wing donors and consider the implications of receiving such philanthropic dollars. In the following, a discussion of the history and prevailing landscape of conservative philanthropy in educational funding lays a foundation for understanding current trends in the funding of HBCUs by right-wing entities.

A Short History Of Right-Wing Educational Philanthropy

deMarrais (2019) detailed the genesis of, and turning point in, the right wing's education philanthropy initiative. To recap, the rise of conservative, right-wing funding of higher learning institutions can be traced to the ominous "Powell Memo" of 1971. Appointed to the Supreme Court in 1972 by President Richard Nixon, its author, Lewis F. Powell, titled the memo "Confidential Memorandum: Attack of American Free Enterprise System" (deMarrais et al., 2019, p. 33). Sounding the alarm on what he surmised as an "attack on the free enterprise system" (deMarrais et al., 2019, p. 35), the Powell Memo was meant to galvanize proponents of the free-market system against the looming threat to political and economic systems of America emanating from "the Communists, New Leftists, and other revolutionaries" (deMarrais et al., 2019, p. 33).

According to Powell, the main threats against the political and economic systems came from "the college campus, the pulpit, the media, the intellectual and literary journals, the arts and sciences, and from politicians" (Powell, cited in deMarrais et al., 2019, p. 34). In an effort to nullify and reverse the efforts of these "extremists of the left", Powell called on corporations and the business community in general to engage in collective, long-term organizational efforts. Aimed at the planning and financing of a staff of speakers, scholars, professors, and media personalities, the strategies put forth by Powell called for a flood of college faculty, journals, media outlets, and speakers' bureaus with advocates of the free-market ideology.

Serving as the clarion call of the American business class, Powell's suggestions spurred the creation of the Philanthropy Roundtable (deMarrais et al., 2019). Mobilized as "a consortium of conservative foundations that strategically focuses the funding of these key donors" (deMarrais et al., 2019, p. 37), the Philanthropy Roundtable became instrumental in funding organizations and staff dedicated to the key ideas of "individual gain over public good, deregulation, big tax cuts, and privatization" (Lindsay, cited in deMarrais, 2019, p. 36). The Philanthropy Roundtable and the larger conservative philanthropic community waged this "war of ideas" through

> (1) the development of a cadre of conservative youth on college campus, (2) scholars who can produce ideologically conservative research in clear accessible prose who "graduate" into government service, (3) the development of a network of conservative regional and state policy centers to promote policy supportive of their views, and (4) the development of a conservative media to carry this "knowledge" forward. (deMarrais et al., 2019, p. 52)

After nearly 50 years of dogmatic dedication to the establishment and maintenance of the strategies laid out in the "Powell Memo," today's educational landscape is

> significantly influenced by rightest ideology, ideologues, and other neoliberal and conservative actors who believe that all aspects of education should reflect American exceptionalism, traditional values, norms, and beliefs, while acknowledging fundamental ideas associated with capitalism and free-market nationalism. (deMarrais et al., 2019, p. 17)

Although Powell and the Right have seemingly won the war of ideas waged over the last five decades, their influence has not gained a strong footing on the campus environments of HBCUs. This is not however for a lack of trying. It may be the case that the current proliferation of white, conservative philanthropy to HBCUs, is part of what deMarrais et al. identify as a fifth strategy of the conservative philanthropic community's "war on ideas": "the development of a conservative Black leadership" (p. 54). The remainder of the chapter focuses on this strategy to develop conservative Black leadership in the United States.

The Past As Prologue: Ideological Roots of The Conservative Embrace Of HBCUs

Why exactly are conservative donors interested in giving to HBCUs? One possibility points to the goals of the Philanthropic Roundtable to influence and inspire "free-market" ideology, in this case, on Black college campuses. Attempts by conservative philanthropists to control the direction and content of institutions of higher education are well documented. As Walsh (2019) argued, the Walgreen Foundation, as early as the 1930s, used philanthropic donations to the University of Chicago to establish an educational environment championing American values in an effort to counter the perceived "communist indoctrination by left-wing professors" (p. 2). deMarrais et al. (2019), detailed the prevalence and the particulars of the "strings" that have sometimes accompanied conservative philanthropy, but in the case of donations made to HBCUs, the motivation of conservative donors could also be attributed to shared values.

In supporting HBCUs, conservative donors are not venturing too far from their own ideological comfort zones. As Johnson and Rigueur (2017) point out, "historically Black schools have a tradition of cultural conservatism, respectability politics, and bootstrapping, all of which make them deeply attractive (and viable) targets for Republican outreach" (para. 6). This "conservative" tradition as well as a politics of respectability, can be traced to the social aspirations of those seeking to help the newly freed slaves before and after the Civil War. Many African American leaders of the time "articulated a 'self-help' politics of securing class advancement by espousing the dominant values and behaviors of whites, especially as they pertain to respectability and gender" (Grundy, 2012, p. 46). This quest for respectability continued throughout the 20th century as "Black elites promoted a public discourse that conflated the advancement of the race with adherence to bourgeois morality and emphasized the patriarchal family as the cornerstone of Black progress" (Grundy, 2012, p. 46). This push for conservatism and respectability in newly freed Blacks would inform the motivations of those groups, both Black and White, who would set out to establish the first HBCUs.

When analyzing the modern relationship between HBCUs and their White donors, one soon finds that "what's past is prologue." Although Cheyney University and Lincoln University in Pennsylvania and Wilberforce University in Ohio were established before the Civil War, most of the other 103 HBCUs were established in the years following the Civil War. The founding of many of the nation's HBCUs was the result of philanthropic Whites. For example, the two earliest HBCUs, Cheyney and Lincoln Universities, were started by White missionaries and Quakers, respectively. Established expressly for the purpose of "educating Black citizens" (Gasman, 2013, p. 5), the aim of White missionaries, abolitionists, and philanthropists who established HBCUs was most often to "Christianize Blacks or train them for their industrial enterprises" (Gasman, 2013, p. 5).

From the beginning, there were competing ideologies surrounding the education of formerly enslaved Blacks. Anderson (1988) points to three distinct philanthropic groups primarily responsible for the creation of Black institutes of higher learning between 1865 and 1935. According to Anderson, "Northern white benevolent societies and denominational bodies (missionary philanthropy) and Black religious organizations (Negro philanthropy) established the beginnings of a system of higher education for Black southerners" (p. 239). The third group, White, northern corporate foundations and wealthy individuals (industrial philanthropy), "paralleled the growth of missionary and Black religious philanthropy" and "placed its emphasis almost exclusively on industrial training" (J. Anderson, 1988, p. 245). The focus by industrial philanthropists on industrial training encompassed the critical issue driving the split between the three philanthropic groups.

The dividing line between the three philanthropic groups and of the ante- and postbellum educational landscapes of Black higher education was one of direction. The question was, Should universities educate newly freed slaves in the liberal arts and toward social progress and equality or in the manual and industrial arts toward self-sufficiency? In popular culture, this dichotomy is best known as the choice between educating Blacks in the direction of Du Bois's "talented tenth" or in the direction of Booker T. Washington's tradesmen and -women. Although this pedagogical dilemma predates the W. E. B. Du Bois/Booker T. Washington debates, their arguments best sum up the ideological and pedagogical questions that defined the first 70 years of Black higher education.

The first HBCUs established by White missionary philanthropists and the Black religious groups functioned under the expectation that "the newly emancipated Blacks would move into mainstream national culture, largely free to do and become what they chose, limited only by their own intrinsic worth and effort" (J. Anderson, 1988, p. 240). As a result, in crafting the educational environments of their Black institutions, they opted for a "classical liberal education for Black Americans as a means to achieve racial equality in civil and political life" (J. Anderson, 1988, p. 240). The northern White industrial philanthropists, on the other hand, fostered educational environments in their colleges and universities based on what came to be known as the "Hampton Model" (J. Anderson, 1988). Named for the pedagogical approach implemented at Virginia's Hampton University by its founder, Samuel Chapman Armstrong, the Hampton Model (and later the Hampton–Tuskegee model) was built on the ideology of Armstrong. This ideology included the belief that "freedmen should refrain from participating in southern political life because they were culturally and morally deficient and therefore unfit to vote and hold office in 'civilized' society" (J. Anderson, 1988, p. 38). In an effort to train up Black teachers who would then be charged with the task of educating the Black masses, Armstrong adopted industrial education as the hallmark of Hampton. Thus, the "Hampton Idea" (J. Anderson, 1988, p. 36), with its focus on technical, trade, and manual education, "viewed industrial education primarily as an ideological force that would provide instruction suitable for adjusting Blacks to a subordinate social role in the emergent New South" (J. Anderson, 1988, p. 36). In contrast to the emancipatory and equality-seeking goals of the missionary and Black HBCUs enacting liberal arts pedagogy, the industrial education of the Hampton Idea "essentially called for the effective removal of Black voters and politicians from southern political life, the relegation of Black workers to the lowest forms of labor in the southern economy, and the establishment of a general southern racial hierarchy" (J. Anderson, 1988, p. 36).

Leading the charge in instructing HBCU students in "industrial enterprises" was Booker T. Washington, himself a graduate of Hampton University. As founder of Tuskegee University and referred to as "the most effective and powerful Black conservative in this country's history" (Coates, 2009, para. 1), Washington earned the ire of several of his Black contemporaries. To many, Washington compromised with racist Whites of his day by arguing for the continuation of segregation, the withdrawal of Blacks from the quest for political and social equality, and the training of Blacks in the manual and industrial arts. Focusing on these pursuits rather than on integration and political/social equality for Blacks, Washington's position was a sharp contrast to other Black thinkers of his day, particularly W. E. B. Du Bois.

The promotion of Black self-improvement proved to be a fruitful endeavor for Washington. At Tuskegee University, Washington had crafted a learning environment centered on educating Blacks in agriculture, the manual arts, and various trades. Washington and his financial supporters envisioned limits on the kinds of education Black people should receive. One such financial backer, William Baldwin, a wealthy White businessman from Boston who sat on the board of Tuskegee, insisted that the education of Blacks should promote contentment with their station in life. In his view, Blacks should

> "face the music," avoid social questions, leave politics alone, continue to be patient, live moral lives, live simply, learn to work and to work intelligently, learn to work faithfully learn to work hard, learn that any work, however menial, if well done, is dignified. (Baldwin, 1900, p. 60)

Baldwin described Booker T. as "the Moses" of Black people and Tuskegee as "the hope for the race" (p. 55). The embrace of Washington, and more so his endorsement and implementation of the "proper" kind of education of Blacks, engendered him to many enthusiastic White philanthropists. The acceptance of Washington and his efforts were so gracious among White business elites that Washington himself observed, "In the city of Boston I have rarely called upon an individual for funds [and] not been thanked for calling, usually before I could . . . thank the donor for the money" (Magubane, 2017, p. 3). As a result of his adoption and championing of accommodationist views, Washington was invited to the White House by President Theodore Roosevelt. Seeking to benefit from Washington's influence among many White southerners, Roosevelt consulted with Washington on various political appointments and election strategy, a move bolstering Washington's visibility and subsequent White philanthropic investment in him and his institution (Johnson & Rigueur, 2017).

The pedagogical war between Booker T. Washington's Hampton–Tuskegee Idea and the classical liberal arts education to foster Black leadership waged from the 1860s until the early 1930s. Toward the end of the 19th century, many of the schools opened by the missionary and Black philanthropic groups fell into disarray. A lack of adequate funding, staffing, and resources forced missionary and Black philanthropic schools to look to industrial philanthropists, the champions of the Hampton–Tuskegee Idea, for financial support (J. Anderson, 1988). With a decided advantage in the pedagogical wars, the industrial financiers of Washington's Hampton–Tuskegee model took hold of the opportunity to shape the educational landscape of HBCUs. Although their industrial model of education never fully uprooted the liberal arts models of the missionary and Black philanthropic schools they came to support, the impact of the White industrial philanthropists on the terrain of Black higher education held sway at HBCUs until well into the 1920s.

The support of HBCUs by White conservative forces did not end with Booker T. Washington and his industrial backers. In fact, in some regard, the relationship has continued to be mutually beneficial. Under Republican president Richard Nixon, for example, the urging of Black cabinet members, along with Nixon's political aspirations with Blacks, resulted in the president promising much-needed funding to HBCUs. This funding amounted to nearly $150 million in allocations to HBCUs by Nixon in 1969–1970. This was followed by upwards of $1 billion in funding being directed toward HBCUs over the next decade as a result of the efforts of Black Republicans (Johnson & Rigueur, 2017).

The Republican administrations of Presidents Reagan, and more recently Trump, were also instrumental in realizing some gains for HBCUs. For Reagan, reaching out to HBCUs was clearly a political move meant to pull Black votes away from the Democratic Party. In his efforts, Reagan established meaningful policies impacting HBCUs. He convened luncheons with leaders of Black colleges and universities, he established National Black College Week, he contributed to efforts to save Meharry Medical College, and he increased all-in federal funding of HBCUs by 15% (Johnson & Rigueur, 2017). President Trump has also contributed to the sustenance of HBCUs. Motivated by a quest to outdo President Obama's efforts (Kumar & Douglas, 2017), Trump, like Reagan before him, met with HBCU leaders in a much-publicized Oval Office visit resulting in Trump signing an executive order moving the HBCU initiative into the White House from the Department of Education (Wright, 2017). To his credit, when President Trump signed Executive Order 13779 establishing the White House Initiative to Promote Excellence and Innovation at Historically Black Colleges and Universities, he boosted funding by 17%, giving more money to HBCUs than any other president. In perhaps his most substantial accomplishment, in 2019, Trump signed into law the FUTURE Act, which finally provided guaranteed federal funding for HBCUs in addition to providing a minimum of $255 million annually (Burnett, 2019). For HBCU leaders, their appeals to Trump and congressional Republicans for federal assistance with HBCUs have produced much needed results (Kreighbaum, 2018).

This depiction of the history of right-wing funding of HBCUs is not, however, meant to paint a rosy picture. These historic, targeted efforts of White right-wing philanthropists and government administrations have been far from a panacea to the ongoing issues plaguing HBCUs. In addition, the dubious motivations behind right-wing funding of HBCUs must be considered. Although Republican administrations have often sought to further HBCUs with legislation, philanthropy, and tax dollars, those same administrations have simultaneously pursued policies, legislation, and practices that have undermined, polarized, and even demonized the Black community as a whole. The dire financial dilemmas continuously faced by most HBCUs have indeed made for unlikely bedfellows with Republicans. The turbulent financial realities of HBCUs and subsequent relief efforts on the part of Republicans however, have not resulted in any large influx of Blacks to the conservative Republican ranks.

The historic similarity of shared conservative values between White philanthropists and many HBCUs provides an entry point for mutually beneficial philanthropic donations today. Not unlike the financial needs of the White missionaries and Black philanthropists who appealed to the industrial philanthropists in the early 1900s, the cash-strapped realities of today's HBCUs have resulted in the need to attract funding from a variety of sources, including today's White conservative philanthropic sources. For conservatives, their donations assist in the proliferation of like values while at the same time serve as a buffer against perceptions of racism and antagonism toward the Black community. For HBCUs in dire financial straits, conservative philanthropy offers an influx of vitally important funds. Ironically, the "strange bedfellows" of conservative philanthropy and HBCUs are as conjoined today as they were nearly 150 years ago.

A Snapshot Of Conservative Philanthropic Donations To HBCUs

This chapter closes with a brief look at the current landscape of conservative funding of HBCUs. As discussed, the need for conservative funding can be attributed to the bleak state of financial affairs plaguing many HBCUs. Due to a lack of substantive endowments, decreased state and federal funding, decreased enrollment, crumbling infrastructure and facilities, and the forced closure of several institutions, the financial crises facing many HBCUs are being addressed by seeking funding from all quarters. These financial pitfalls are, in large part, driven by a history of discriminatory funding by state and federal sources that have existed since the establishment of the Second Morrill Act in 1890, an act passed ostensibly to bolster the proliferation of HBCUs (Albritton, 2012, p. 315). This discrepancy in the funding of HBCUs and their

White institutional counterparts has continued up through today. For example, in recent years, 61% of HBCUs have not received the mandated state allotments meant to assure one-to-one parity with funds received by their White statewide counterparts (Lee & Keys, 2013). These discrepancies are on top of the overall drop in federal funding HBCUs experienced between 2003 and 2015, a drop amounting to 42% of funding dollars to private HBCUs (Williams & Davis, 2019, p. 2). The state and federal neglect, accompanied by a lack of alumni support and a historic dearth of fundraising infrastructure, have coalesced to produce the current state of financial affairs for many HBCUs.

To stopgap some of these shortfalls, many HBCUs have resorted to accepting funds from controversial right-wing conservative sources. Recently, Spelman, Morehouse, and Clark Atlanta University received a five-year $5.4 million grant from the Walton Family Foundation to "create an Art History major and elevate its Curatorial Studies program to a minor" (Davis, 2018, para. 5). Other such donations have not been without controversy. Take for instance the Koch brothers' gift in 2014 of $25 million to the United Negro College Fund (UNCF), an organization that provides a range of support to 37 HBCU member institutions. After receiving the funds from the Koch brothers, who some have accused of backing racist policies and practices (Mayer, 2016), the UNCF came under intense fire from some of its supporters. Later, in 2017, Charles Koch made another substantial $25.6 million to the Thurgood Marshall College Fund (TMCF), another HBCU-serving organization. In addition to the outcry associated with receiving donations from persons seen as hostile toward Blacks, another criticism of the gift centered on potential strings attached. Noting the history of Koch donations compromising the independence of universities, one critic remarked that "when they give the donor control, the trade-off is academic freedom" (N. Anderson, 2017, para. 9). Allowing increased donor control at the expense of academic freedom occurred at Harvard University in the 1980s and has been occurring at George Mason University since the 1970s (Walsh, 2019). These examples demonstrate how right-wing philanthropic donations can and have been used as a Trojan Horse for the attraction, grooming, and launching of the next generation of conservative right-wing ideologues and to further establish conservative beachheads on university campuses.

In terms of exploring specific conservative donors and the HBCUs they donate to, a preliminary picture is beginning to emerge. Focusing on donation data as tracked by Candid (2020), Table 8.1 lists the total donations to HBCUs from five prominent conservative donors (Charles Koch Foundation, Walton Family Foundation, the John William Pope Foundation, the Lynde and Harry Bradley Foundation Inc., and the Dick and Betsy DeVos Family Foundation).

Table 8.1
Total Donations of Select Conservative Donors to Historically Black Colleges and Universities, 2005–2017

SOURCE	AMOUNT
Charles Koch Foundation	$13,852,900
Walton Family Foundation	$2,393,077
John William Pope	$150,500
The Lynde and Harry Bradley Foundation Inc.	$135,000
Dick & Betsy DeVos Family Foundation	$32,000

Clearly the largest conservative donors to HBCUs were the Koch brothers and the Walton family. Their donations to the UNCF and the TMCF notwithstanding, the two donors gave gifts of varying sizes to a variety of schools. Although the majority of donations were made between 2013 and 2017, the earliest donation listed for the Walton family was in 2006 and for the Koch brothers, 2003. Donations from the Walton family ranged from $1,000 to Florida A&M University to $540,000 to Morehouse College. The Koch brothers, donations ranged from $10,000 to Alabama A&M University, Mississippi Valley State University, and Xavier University of Louisiana to $166,000 to Wiley

College. The largest financial donations made by the Waltons was $942,450 to the UNCF and $13, 254,500 by the Kochs to the TMCF. Hampton University was the recipient of two donations from the Lynde and Harry Bradley Foundation Inc.; Shaw University and North Carolina Central University were the recipients of donations from John William Pope; and the Dick & Betsy DeVos Family Foundation made three donations exclusively to the UNCF.

The dangers of right-wing activist philanthropy are clear. As detailed by deMarrais et al. (2019), the generous donations given to universities often come with strings attached. The "fifth strategy" of the conservative philanthropic community's takeover of education was the development of a conservative Black leadership. Although there is no direct evidence to date of an explicit conservative agenda being entrenched on Black campuses, financial donations can and have impacted university direction and policy. Noting the impact of philanthropy on the development of Spelman's curriculum over the years, Peeples (2010) noted that "Spelman College's ability to secure philanthropic support, despite its miniscule financial beginnings, largely influenced its curriculum and its development into a leader among HBCUs" (p. 246). After detailing the history of philanthropic donations secured by Spelman's past presidents, Peeples solidified the point by proclaiming "the connection between philanthropy and the curriculum is uncontestable in the history of Spelman College" (2010, p. 258). The financial needs of today's HBCUs, the desire of conservative philanthropists to use HBCU donations to soften charges of conservative anti-Black sentiment, and a shared history of respectability politics between conservatives and HBCUs can eventually lead to inroads being made by conservative activists onto Black campuses. The long-term impact of these inroads on the development of conservative ideology on HBCU campuses is yet to be seen.

Conclusion

An activist wing of conservative philanthropy evolved out of the Powell Memo of the 1970s. Heading the call to arms, right-wing philanthropic organizations banded together to engage in a war of ideas for the hearts and minds of the American public. A major front in their war were the campuses of America's colleges and universities. By establishing conservative centers and grooming waves of up-and-coming conservative ideologues, the conservative philanthropy machine has shifted economic, educational, and political thought in society.

A less successful strategy in this conservative takeover has been the development of cadres of Black conservative leaders. Given the existential issues facing HBCUs and in light of conservative efforts to seek cover from racially antagonistic branding, the stage is set for the conservative advance onto the campuses of America's HBCUs. The affinity for respectability politics at HBCUs is what has attracted conservatives. The history of aid from conservative administrations, including the current Trump administration, is what attracts HBCUs. The question is, How much influence comes with conservative donations to HBCUs? Although the question for now is rhetorical, the lessons of history are clear. There has never been a time when HBCUs were not in need of funding. Additionally, there has never been a time when conservative, "industrial" donors did not seek to control, fashion, and otherwise subjugate the minds of their Black beneficiaries. Is the situation any different today? For now, the answer eludes us, but the realities of funding gaps, universities closing down, lost accreditations, and crumbling infrastructures may render the question moot. In response to a question about taking Koch money, one HBCU president responded, "I can take their money and use it for good" (Washington, 2014, para. 6). The lessons of history may be sidelined by HBCU's Faustian bargain with conservative donors, a bargain that is all too often necessitated by perennial financial hardships.

References

Albritton, T. J. (2012). Educating our own: The historical legacy of HBCUs and their relevance for educating a new generation of leaders. *Urban Review, 44*(3), 311–331.

Anderson, J. D. (1988). *The education of Blacks in the South, 1860–1935*. The University of North Carolina Press.

Anderson, N. (2017, January 11). Charles Koch teams with Black colleges on education and criminal justice research. *The Washington Post*. https://www.washingtonpost.com/local/education/charles-koch-teams-with-Black-colleges-on-education-and-criminal-justice-research/2017/01/11/ab8a8d02-d838-11e6-9f9f-5cdb4b7f8dd7_story.html

Baldwin, W. H. (1900). The present problem of negro education. In F. S. Root (Ed.) *Journal of Social Science Containing the Proceedings of the American Association, 30, Saratoga Papers of 1899* (pp. 52–63). Damrell & Upham and the Boston Book Company.

Burnett, J. (2019, December 14). Senate bill funding historically Black colleges and universities cements Trump's support of HBCUs. *Black Enterprise*. https://www.blackenterprise.com/senate-bill-funding-historically-black-colleges-and-universities-trump-support-hbcus/

Candid. (2020). *About*. Candid.org. https://candid.org/about?fcref=pg

Coates, T. N. (2009, March 31). The tragedy and betrayal of Booker T. Washington. *The Atlantic*. https://www.theatlantic.com/entertainment/archive/2009/03/the-tragedy-and-betrayal-of-booker-t-washington/7092/

Davis, J. E. (2018, September 20). *Spelman College awarded $5.4 million grant from the Walton Family Foundation for Atlanta University Center initiative to increase diversity in museum field*. Spelman College. https://spelman.edu/about-us/news-and-events/news-releases/2018/09/20/spelman-college-awarded-$5.4-million-grant-from-the-walton-family-foundation-for-atlanta-university-center-initiative-to-increase-diversity-in-museum-field

deMarrais, K., Brewer, T. J., Herron, B., Atkinson, J. C., & Lewis, J. B. (2019). *Philanthropy, hidden strategy, and collective resistance: A primer for concerned educators*. Myers Education Press.

Gasman, M. (2013). *The changing face of historically Black colleges and universities.* Penn Center for Minority Serving Institutions. https://www.gse.upenn.edu/pdf/cmsi/Changing_Face_HBCUs.pdf

Grundy, S. (2012). "An air of expectancy": Class, crisis, and the making of manhood at a historically Black college for men. *The Annals of the American Academy of Political and Social Science, 642*(1), 43–60.

Johnson, T. R., & Rigueur, L. W. (2017, February 27). *The GOP's long history with Black colleges.* Politico. https://www.politico.com/magazine/story/2017/02/trump-black-colleges-universities-hbcus-republicans-214834

Kreighbaum, A. (2018, February 28). HBCUs and the Trump administration: Leaders of historically Black colleges say their strategy of working closely with the White House and congressional Republicans is working. *Inside Higher Ed.* https://www.insidehighered.com/news/2018/02/28/hbcu-leaders-meet-say-strategy-under-trump-paying

Kumar, A., & Douglas, W. (2017, February 27). Trump seeks to outdo Obama in backing Black colleges. *McClatchy.* https://www.mcclatchydc.com/article134827019.html

Lee, J. M., & Keys, S. W. (2013, September). *Land-grant but unequal: State one-to-one match funding for 1890 land-grant universities.* (APLU Office for Access and Success, Publication No. 3000-PB1). Association of Public and Land-Grant Universities.

Magubane, Z. (2017, March 9). The cautionary tales and complicated legacies of historically Black colleges and universities. *Cognoscenti.* https://www.wbur.org/cognoscenti/2017/03/09/web-du-bois-booker-t-washington-hbcus-zine-magubane

Mayer, J. (2016, March 15). Who sponsored the hate? *The New Yorker.* https://www.newyorker.com/news/news-desk/who-sponsored-the-hate

Peeples, Y. T. (2010). Philanthropy and the curriculum: The role of philanthropy in the development of curriculum at Spelman College. *International Journal of Educational Advancement, 10*(3), 245–260.

Trump, D. (2019). *Remarks by President Trump at Young Black Leadership Summit 2019* [Transcript]. https://www.whitehouse.gov/briefings-statements/remarks-president-trump-young-Black-leadership-summit-2019/

Turning Point USA (n.d.). About. https://www.tpusa.com/

Walsh, D. A. (2019). *Conservative philanthropy in higher education*. Urban Institute. https://www.urban.org/sites/default/files/conservative_philanthropy_in_higher_education.pdf

Washington, J. (2014). *Black colleges face hard choices on $25M Koch gift*. CBS News. https://www.cbsnews.com/news/Black-colleges-face-hard-choices-on-25-million-gift-from-koch-brothers/

Williams, K. L., & Davis, B. L. (2019, January). *Public and private investments and divestments in historically Black colleges and universities* (Issue brief, Minority-Serving Institutions Series). American Council on Education. https://www.acenet.edu/Documents/Public-and-Private-Investments-and-Divestments-in-HBCUs.pdf

Wright, M. W. (2017). Trump signs executive order on HBCUs, says schools will be priority in his White House. *The Undefeated*. https://theundefeated.com/features/trump-signs-executive-order-on-hbcus/

Chapter Nine

OPERATIONALIZING TOXIC IDEOLOGY:

HOW RADICAL RIGHT-WING CAMPUS ORGANIZATIONS UNDERMINE DEMOCRATIC ENGAGEMENT

T. Jameson Brewer, *University of North Georgia*
Amy Swain, *East Carolina University*

For a number of decades, right-wing foundations and nongovernmental organizations, funded by a small number of interconnected wealthy benefactors, have sought to influence academic and student discourse on college and university campuses. The vehicles they have used can be generalized into two categories: more traditional organizations that recruit and train conservative students to become campus leaders (and later participants in movement conservatism) and, more recently, watchdog agencies that police faculty expression deemed to be radical left in an effort to suppress faculty influence.

Although the more traditional organizations have been College Republicans and Tea Party–oriented groups, the most notable among the latter types of watchdog organizations are Turning Point USA (TPUSA), Campus Reform (CR), and, for much of its history, the Foundation for Individual Rights in Education (FIRE). These organizations have risen in prominence over the past decade as they have received significant funding from venture philanthropists that share their political ideology (e.g., the Koch brothers) in addition to a growing platform on conservative media outlets such as Fox News (deMarrais et al., 2019). Subsequently, organizations such as TPUSA employ specific tactics designed to create viral social-media exposure (*This American Life*, 2018), which, in turn, generates more attention for the organization and helps with fundraising and recruitment.

While we readily acknowledge the benefits of having a diversity of political opinion on college campuses and applaud the well-intentioned efforts of students who engage in civil dialogue from both the political Left and Right, in this chapter, we explore the rise of what is decidedly a new type of student-oriented organization that is less interested in dialogue and more interested in visceral and toxic actions that, contrary to their claims, undermine democratic engagement. Although some have argued that designated free speech locations on campus do present legal hurdles to the First Amendment (Howard, 2019), tactics that involve intentionally goading faculty and students into arguments so that videos can be edited out of context and intentionally "tabling" outside of designated areas on campus for the sole purpose of videotaping a university official informing them they have to move as *proof* that colleges are shutting down conservative students' are not in alignment with an honest quest for open debate. Moreover, and perhaps more insidiously, TPUSA operates the Professor Watchlist (Professor Watchlist, n.d.-a), a website that targets professors that are accused of being "too liberal" and publishes personal information about them in a thinly veiled effort to generate a public backlash against them regardless of the actual professional or personal implications. These types of cyber-harassment practices can, and have, opened the door to actual violent threats on professors (Cuevas, 2018). These threats on professors mark a new phenomenon of public targeted online harassment (Ferber, 2018). As Ferber explains, "the term 'public' suggests that it is out in the open and/or carried out by any member of society" (p. 303) and develops online harassment to reflect a specific, sophisticated, targeted, organized, and publicly legitimated threat to academic freedom. To that end, we explore TPUSA, the organization's founding, corporate structure, funding, shared connections, use of traditional and new forms of media, and explore the impacts these tactics have on democratic engagement and campus culture. We first begin with an overview of the harassment of academic freedom.

Historical Precedents

Educational institutions, from secondary schools to universities and colleges of higher learning, have long been sites of ideological debate and the struggle for power (Apple, 2004). These debates have largely focused on the curriculum and structure of public schooling and were influenced by the voices of teaching faculty, educational administrators, politicians, and elite reformers (Tyack, 1974). During the postwar Red Scare of 1919–1920, the struggle for control took on new dimensions as the average citizen became involved in the identification of potential communists and communist sympathizers. According to Robert Murray (1955), the "unintelligent thinking and intolerant actions" (p. 166) of everyday American citizens led to the widespread fear of all political philosophies and ideologies tangentially related to communism, as well as the proliferation of assumptions that bolshevism and the so-called parlor Reds were everywhere—in positions of power across the United States from the White House to the schools. "Because of its professed desire to foster open-mindedness, the educational system was second only to labor in the amount of criticism which it received and the suspicion which it aroused" (Murray, 1955, pp. 169–170). Colleges and universities were identified as "hotbeds of bolshevism" and "radical institutions" for engaging students in reading and exposure to ideas outside the adherence to free-market capitalism and American democracy.

The assaults on academic freedom and moral panic were not relegated to postsecondary institutions. In New York, public school teachers were required to sign loyalty oaths pledging allegiance to the United States and avowing to promote nationalism and jingoism in their classrooms. Anything outside party-line patriotism was not to be tolerated in schools. When a highly respected Quaker teacher, Mary McDowell, refused to sign the oath, her classroom pedagogy came under intense scrutiny by administration, and employment hearings were held to ascertain whether McDowell should keep her position (Goldstein, 2014). Although her teaching record demonstrated excellence in the classroom, McDowell was fired for holding dissident political beliefs. And scores of other similar firings soon followed; anyone assumed to hold disloyal beliefs—proven or unproven—was removed from his or her positions, as well as those who simply asked students to interrogate political ideologies (Goldstein, 2014; Murray, 1955).

The superintendent of New York City schools, William Ettinger, proclaimed there was "no such thing as '9 to 3 patriotism'" (Murray, 1955, p. 171). Ettinger believed that schools were "no place for any teacher whose 'personal convictions' made it impossible for him to be a 'patriotic example to his students'" (Murray, 1955, p. 171). There was broad public support for this position, with national and local newspapers publishing editorials and feeding the hysteria of the uncritical and fearful masses. The message was direct: Anyone who did not practice educational conformity was not welcome in the classroom.

In subsequent years, the coordination and tools of public assault against those believed to be political dissidents amplified. In 1934, Elizabeth Dilling published a precursor to the contemporary Professor Watchlist, a blacklist exposé titled *The Red Network—A Who's Who and Handbook of Radicalism for Patriots* (1935). This book identified 460 "radical" organizations and their individual members. One of the groups identified in the text was the American Federation of Teachers, of whom Dilling said, "Radical; stands for abolition of ROTC; recognition of Russia; full 'academic freedom' to teach anything, including Socialism, Communism, or Atheism" (Tiede, 2017, para. 3). The following year, William Randolph Hearst, who owned the largest newspaper chain in the country, began publishing articles "attacking public school teachers who explained the Depression as a failure of free markets. Teachers who did not purchase Liberty Bonds, did not display the American flag in their classrooms, or did not salute the flag" (Goldstein, 2014, p. 96) were said to be loyal to the Soviet Union. The vitriol continued well into the 1950s with the rise of McCarthyism, which ignited what has been called "anticommunist purges" (Goldstein, 2014, p. 105) of American schools and universities.

What is important here is that educators who were labeled as communist or anti-American need not actually be communist or anti-American as the simple lack of an over-the-top display of patriotism, much in the way of fascism or nationalism, or raising any question critical of American history or policy. Put simply, educators then and, increasingly now, who do not appear to celebrate the United States as the most exceptional country to ever exist are suspected of being "leftist," "liberal," or "radicals." The issue of American exceptionalism is a point specifically taken up by TPUSA. In one publication, the organization suggests that

> humans have rarely been offered freedom and liberty by their fellow man; it is only a recent phenomenon, and even today is still a treasure to find. In fact, there is no time and no place where liberty was offered as freely as in the present day United States

and goes on to suggest that "your liberal professor, however, will try to tell you that America is an evil nation—that it has blood on its hands and that it is no greater than anywhere else" (Turning Point USA, 2015b, p. 2). And,

> while yes, America has had its faults throughout the years, such as poor treatment of natives, slavery, and unequal rights for women, [but] the mistreatments of these groups were occurring all over the world and was considered as normal treatment during that time period. (Turning Point USA, 2015b, p. 2)

The topic of slavery is an interesting one for TPUSA to explain away given the organization's vast documented history of racism to the point where the Anti-Defamation League (n.d.) classifies the organization under the tags "Extremism, Terrorism & Bigotry."

Scatamburlo-D'Annibale (2019) argued that the rise of conservative organizations such as TPUSA, and, generally speaking, the ascendancy of Donald Trump to the presidency, is the result of a decades-long rhetoric in conservative media and Republican circles decrying the existence and prevalence of "political correctness" in society. According to Scatamburlo-D'Annibale (2019), because, "for rightists, culture and economics are intertwined, since their correlation is necessary for both the efficient functioning of capitalism and the hegemony of White patriarchal ideology" (p. 105) the spread of political correctness and the specter of liberals winning the culture war on colleges campuses represents an existential threat to the family and economic values associated with conservatism and why so much money has been invested into organizations like TPUSA to fight back.

TPUSA

The growth of an organization like TPUSA is best understood within the context of a growing resentment toward higher education from those who are politically conservative. And although this growing resentment finds some of its contemporary roots in the disdain for Obama given his affiliation with higher education and notable academics, the election of Trump, a self-described nationalist, has exacerbated animosity toward colleges and professors as Trump has suggested that conservative students are penalized and silenced on campuses (Quintana, 2019), which has aligned with the broader Fox News narrative directed toward colleges (Fox News, 2018). This cycle of media magnification of conservative narratives suggesting that universities and colleges stifle conservative student viewpoints is the result of an ecosystem of social and mainstream media funded heavily by those pushing for conservative ideologies. Shepard and Culver (2018) noted that

> an examination of common cases invoking conservative outrage [about colleges and universities] yields a map of their predictable path through the current media landscape. Campus Reform posts a story, sometimes with attempts to reach a professor or university for comment, and runs a click-bait headline. The piece then gets picked up by conservative online

> media, from more traditional outlets like National Review to newer players like Heat Street, The Blaze, or the Daily Caller. It then may make its way onto the show lineup for TV personalities such as Tucker Carlson or Sean Hannity on Fox News. Even if the original piece had been fair—which in the case of Campus Reform if often is not—it gets twisted and exaggerated over time. . . . These controversies almost always lead to calls for institutions to discipline professors or diversity ideologies on campus and have, in some cases, led to threats against faculty and security problems on campus. (pp. 102–103)

Additional work by Fucci and Catalano (2019) employed cognitive linguistics (e.g., metonymy and framing) with multimodal critical discourse analysis to explore the ways in which campus interactions with TPUSA representatives and protesting students showed that TPUSA benefits from being able to quickly reframe clashes between TPUSA members and individual students or individual faculty. Specifically, TPUSA members reframe themselves as being students, not as being affiliated with TPUSA while framing individual students or individual faculty members speaking out against TPUSA as representative of the entire university and universities writ large, thus reinforcing their narrative that universities are systematically penalizing conservative students' free speech rights and attempting to silence conservative viewpoints.

Of course, it is worth pointing out that despite the hysteria and fear-mongering, studies show that professors are not penalizing students for holding conservative views, nor are they silencing their voices (Perry, 2019). These facts aside, the majority of Republicans now believe that colleges are a negative influence on America. According to the survey conducted by the Pew Research Center, "roughly eight-in-ten Republicans (79%) say professors bringing their political and social views into the classroom is a major reason why the higher education system is headed in the wrong direction," which was a view held specifically by 96% of Republicans ages 65 and older (Parker, 2019). As a result of this misalignment of facts and irrational fears, organizations such as

TPUSA have become the conservative equivalent of Don Quixote and his fight against windmills. And we do not use that analogy flippantly given that Trump has also argued that windmills, themselves, cause cancer and should be fought (Wolf, 2019).

TPUSA (n.d.), founded in 2012, is a 501(c)(3) nonprofit organization that claims it has a presence on 1,500 high school and college campuses and is, thus, the "largest and fastest-growing youth organization in America" yet no further information or citation is provided—specific to the United States or "America" as is most accurately understood as the entire Western Hemisphere. The home page for TPUSA (n.d.) states that the organization's "mission is to identify, educate, train, and organize students to promote freedom". However, elsewhere on the organization's website, TPUSA (n.d.) states as its explicit mission the same phrase, however, the word *freedom* is replaced with "the principles of freedom, free markets, and limited government." In other words, TPUSA defines *freedom* along myopic libertarian dispositions.

TPUSA organizes its work across four initiatives: (1) National Field Program, (2) Innovative Grassroots Messaging, (3) Educational Resources, and (4) Activist Conferences. TPUSA's (n.d.) National Field Program initiative aims to

- Launch, organize, and support student groups to promote the benefits of limited government, capitalism, and freedom,
- Build and maintain the largest national database of students who believe in capitalism and free markets,
- Re-brand free market values on college campuses through student-driven messaging efforts and face-to-face conversations;
- Effectively fight back against intolerance and bias directed toward conservatives in higher education.

As of the fall of 2019, TPUSA has published the following "educational resources":

- "How to Debate Your Teacher (and Win!): Empowering Students to Have the Confidence to Defend their Beliefs in Classrooms and Universities"
- "The Healthcare Games: When Government Runs Healthcare the Odds are Never in Your Favor"
- "Game of Loans: All Students Must Play"
- "If the Founders had Twitter"
- "5 Reasons Censorship Should Offend You"
- "50 Ways the Government Spends Your Money"
- "Indoctrination Prevention: 10 Ways College Professors Indoctrinate America's Youth and How to Prevent It"
- "How America Broke Its Wings . . ."
- "5 Reasons Big Government is the Real War on Women"
- "10 Ways Fossil Fuels Improve our Daily Lives"
- "The Case Against Gun Control"
- "Urban Failure: How Big Government Policies and Liberal Politicians have Destroyed America's Once Great Cities"
- "10 Reasons America is the Greatest Country in the History of the World!"
- "iCapitalism . . . "
- "10 Ways Big Government Harms You"

Of those educational resources listed, the most notably advertised on the TPUSA (2015a) website is the "How to Debate Your Teacher (and Win!): Empowering Students to Have the Confidence to Defend their Beliefs in Classrooms and Universities." The opening lines argue that "today, teachers and professors all across the country are training young minds to believe that capitalism is immoral. It's up to YOU to stand up for what you believe in." In all, the piece is offered without substantiation and relies heavily on emotional appeal and fearmongering. Accordingly,

> this booklet is designed to empower students to fight back against this progressive aggression in our schools. Turning Point USA has outlined a blueprint to deter the typical strategies used by teachers and professors; we have also provided tips to swing the narrative away from indoctrination toward a balanced classroom environment. Throughout this booklet we highlight real life success stories of students who stood up to their teachers and successfully prevented outward anti free enterprise aggression from occurring in their classrooms. We show you that it is possible to fight back and enlighten your fellow classmates to the truth about history, civics, and economics. (TPUSA, 2015a, "Foreword")

In alignment with the general disposition and belief that professors are radical leftists and an attempt to build on, and elevate, anecdotal experiences, the educational pamphlet argues, as a commonsensical notion that

> everybody has that one crazy liberal professor that drives you absolutely insane. Whether they obsess over wealth distribution, bash capitalism, or try to paint the free market as the most awful economic system to ever exist, they are teaching liberalism rather than fact. (TPUSA, 2015a, p. 1)

These commonsensical claims are seemingly bolstered by a small handful of anecdotal stories shared by high school and college students who present their experiences as evidence of conservative oppression in education. From a student testimonial, "I saw professors using the classroom as a platform for their liberal ideas and being completely biased. It really annoyed me that they were given their opinions instead of the facts" (TPUSA, 2015a, p. 2) while no discussion or evidence is provided to qualify what the professor said that was factually inaccurate outside of the student simply not liking what he heard.

After the literature establishes this belief that there is rampant liberal bias in colleges and K–12 classrooms being facilitated by leftist professors, the educational document turns to offering guidance on debating professors. Among the myriad of suggestions, one strategy suggested is to

> anticipate your teacher's next move. Most teachers use the same arguments over and over again. They are rarely challenged and usually aren't used to having a free-flowing debate in their lecture hall. Therefore, as the old saying goes, "know the enemy." (TPUSA, 2015a, p. 5)

Although the publication of this document precedes the election of Trump, the warlike language of "enemy" has increasingly been adopted by the Trump administration—notably directed at journalists.

Another student testimonial included in the pamphlet is that of TPUSA founder Charlie Kirk, who regales readers with his fight against a perceived liberal bias in his high school economics textbook (Kirk did not attend college). The textbook in question was written by Nobel laureate Paul Krugman (Krugman & Wells, 2009) and, in the expert opinion of high school Charlie, Krugman did not know what he was talking about. Specifically, Kirk cites a passage from Krugman's text, "the Regan tax cuts did not accelerate economic growth" and provides a blurry picture of the passage Kirk underlined from the text reading: "Yet estimates of potential output by the Congressional Budget Office and others show no sign of an acceleration in growth after the Reagan tax cuts" (TPUSA, 2015a, p. 9). Although Kirk failed to mention that the Congressional Budget Office is a nonpartisan scoring group, Kirk notes that

> throughout my high school career, President Reagan was one of my heroes and I knew the history of his Presidency rather extensively. I knew immediately this statement from the textbook was deceitful at best, and factually incorrect at the very worse. (TPUSA, 2015a, p. 9)

Kirk goes on to chronicle that he "realized throughout the book there were left-leaning anti-free market stances scattered on almost every page" (TPUSA, 2015a, p. 10) and the whistleblowing efforts he engaged in found a sympathetic audience at Breitbart—launching Turning Point USA soon thereafter. Toward the goal of debating experts and educators, a recurring suggestion to readers is to not come off as an extremist themselves. Rather, "if you are able to successfully paint your professor as an extremist or someone that is way off base, you are very likely to quickly gain support from your classmates" (TPUSA, 2015a, p. 11). As is evidenced by Kirk's own anecdotal testimony, the typical interaction goes: Professor/expert shares empirical data/facts that does not align with the "beliefs" or icons of the conservative student; therefore, the data/facts are "fake news," biased, and to be dismissed. This, as is suggested, is accomplished by labeling the professor as simply an extremist and, therefore, should be ignored in lieu of false knowledge that better aligns with a preconceived political disposition. For TPUSA, K–12 or college content material that does not fit within their myopic worldview is dismissed as indoctrination. The organization's pamphlet "Indoctrination Prevention: 10 Ways College Professors Indoctrinate America's Youth and How to Prevent It" argues that

> the #1 goal of a leftist professor is to change the way their students view the world. Progressive professors want to make you question your beliefs and then hope that you will abandon them altogether. They want to make you think like they do. They want to brainwash you. (TPUSA, 2015b, p. 1)

In their quest to eschew facts in favor of ideological purity, TPUSA often creates memes that generate their own false context surrounding what appear to be data. Take, for example, a meme originally generated by Donald Trump Jr. then broadcast on TPUSA's Facebook page that compared the Obama administration's "failures" to the Trump administration's "successes" on the economy among other measurements. On the unemployment rate, the meme used data from Obama's first year in office (2009) showing an unemployment rate of 9.4% and an unemployment rate of 3.9% under the Trump administration. Because no dates are provided to provide context, the meme presents the "data" as a summary. That is, under the Obama administration, TPUSA followers are expected to surmise that the average unemployment was 9.4% and Trump, in short order, brought it down to 3.9%. Of course, if these numbers and the numbers reflecting gross domestic product growth were reported at the "end" of the Obama administration (i.e., what was accomplished by the end of his tenure) to the beginning of Trump's the ideological argument would lose ground. Moreover, what is also misleading about the meme is that the data attributed to Trump occurred during the first few months of his presidency—a time during which the federal government was operating under the Obama administration's budget. Despite Snopes and Facebook labeling the meme as misleading, TPUSA's post with the title "The Numbers Speak For Themselves! #BigGovSucks" was shared more than 113,000 times and garnered more than 36,000 likes and 7,700 comments.

Given that the bulk of the effort is not an attempt to explore, debate, or discuss the empirical data or facts with professors, much of the "Debate . . . and Win!" (TPUSA, 2015a) pamphlet concentrates on the goal of converting students rather than professors. In fact, it recommends "planting seeds beforehand" with like-minded students "before class and ask them if they will back you up when you debate the teacher" (TPUSA, 2015a, p. 12) to create the illusion in class that there are more students on the TPUSA side than on the side of the professor who is espousing viewpoints TPUSA feels runs counter to a zealous commitment to capitalism. This aligns with the overall goal of TPUSA to characterize content experts as "extremists" or as people who are "way off base" if they are able to generate enough in-class opposition to create the appearance that it is the professor who is marginalized. TPUSA states repeatedly the goal is not to convert or convince professors but rather students because "chances are good that your professor has held this viewpoint for several years and has probably written *research paper upon research paper* [emphasis added], or maybe even written a book based on his or her chosen ideology" (TPUSA, 2015a, p. 14). Another student shared, "I believe that it is my duty to challenge the ideas that are put forward by teachers and texts in order to teach my classmates an accurate and balanced view of the subject" (TPUSA, 2015a, p. 12).

This sentiment shared by a student fits within the TPUSA disposition that argues that, "misinformation is a plague in school systems all across the country. As students, it is our responsibility to correct the falsehoods that are pushed in classrooms every day" (TPUSA, 2015a, p. 13). These dispositions of TPUSA and its followers fall into the rising mantra of anti-intellectualism and anti-expertise sentiment in which lay opinions are elevated to the same level of expert insights and, in the case of lay opinions, informed by staunch ideological positionings supporting conservative viewpoints, those opinions are to be understood as—and fought and debated as—superior to the expert knowledge conveyed by professors and textbooks (Nichols, 2017). That is, a high school student who heard from their parents that Reagan was amazing should be, and is, in a stronger position with regard to facts and evidence than a Nobel laureate is. According to TPUSA (2015a), "America's youth have the right to know accurate information; unfortunately we can't depend on our education system to deliver that. We have an obligation to stand up for principles like fiscal responsibility, free markets, and capitalism" (p. 22).

Funding and Network

TPUSA, as an organization, is heavily funded and connected to the broader conservative political, venture philanthropic network; Fox News; Breitbart; and the Trump administration (see Figure 9.1). With notable connections to the Heritage Foundation, the Reason Foundation, the National Rifle Association, the Diana D. Spencer Foundation, Prager University, Steve Bannon, Roger Stone, Donald Trump, and Donald Trump Jr., TPUSA is situated within a broad network of organizations, news outlets, and financial backing that has helped bolster its rise over the past few years. And although they are not directly connected, TPUSA shares secondary connections with other notable organizations, such as the Walton Family Foundation, Students for Education Reform, Teach For America, and the National Council for Teacher Quality, as well as sharing connections with the Charles Koch Foundation, Dunn's Foundation for the Advancement of Right Thinking, and Reason Foundation.

Figure 9.1
Turning Point USA Political Network

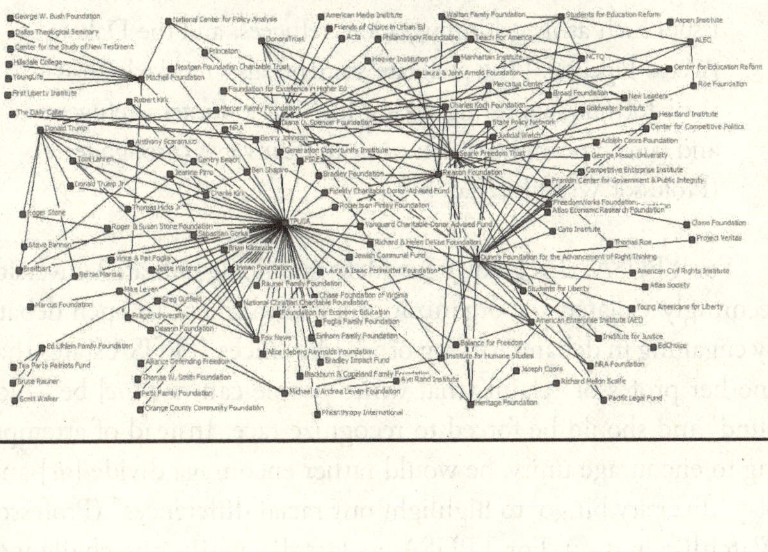

Professor Watchlist

Although the organization focuses on providing talking points and strategies for conservative students to create "gotcha" moments in class and on campus so that selective editing and reporting of the moments can be used as "proof" that colleges are marginalizing the voices of conservative students, TPUSA has also sought to catalogue these professors for public shaming and online targeting. The Professor Watchlist asks students to "expose and document" professors who "discriminate against conservative students, promote anti-American values and advance leftist propaganda in the classroom" (Flaherty, 2016, para. 1) and publishes pictures and contact information of the faculty members. As of October 2019, there were 258 names on the list. A random sampling of the names on the list suggest that what TPUSA takes issue with the most are suggestions that the United States is not a perfect country, that racism exists, that diversity should be celebrated, or anything seen as anti-Trump. For example, a graduate student is on the list because she

> taught students how to argue with conservative relatives about issues such as illegal immigration, refugees, and the Dakota Access Pipeline. [The graduate student] also mocked Christians for not supporting taking in Middle Eastern refugees and said conservatives often come to their views through fear. (Professor Watchlist, n.d.-b)

For TPUSA, this graduate student at Michigan State University seemingly violated the organization's commitment to open debate by engaging in debate. Among other grievances, TPUSA states that another professor "claims that white people can not [*sic*] be 'color blind' and should be forced to recognize race. Instead of attempting to encourage unity, he would rather encourage divide [*sic*] and play 'diversity bingo' to highlight our racial differences" (Professor Watchlist, n.d.-c). For TPUSA, a class discussing the challenges with color-blindness when it comes to race is problematic as, apparently, recognizing race is a liberal disposition. Moreover, TPUSA took issue with the professor's reported activity of diversity bingo. Much of TPUSA's covert racism aligns with the organization's history of racism (as discussed earlier) while it also serves as an artifact of White fragility (DiAngelo, 2018).

Yet, despite the organization's claim that it is interested in highlighting what it considers to be "leftist propaganda" in the classroom, the majority of the additions to the list in the post-Trump era have been professors who are noted not for their comments, activities, or teaching in the classroom but, rather, any perceived slight directed toward Trump using their own social media platforms or media interviews. For example, another entry notes,

> Bob Englehart, adjunct professor at Eastern Connecticut State University and political cartoonist, recently drew media attention for his views opposing the second amendment. In an emotional rant on Facebook, Englehard argued against the second amendment in response to the Las Vegas mass shooting stating the "only way to slow [these attacks] down is to repeal the second amendment'. [*sic*] He goes on to call President Donald Trump a "dumb-f***" for not keeping Americans safe. (Professor Watchlist, n.d.-d).

Another professor, Matthew Boedy, was added for a similar reason as TPUSA did not like an op-ed he authored in the *Atlanta Journal Constitution* expressing his concern about what the state's policy of open-carry gun laws might mean for disgruntled students and faculty safety. Again, in both cases, neither of the professors are accused of expressing these views in the classroom, but rather, TPUSA does not like that they have expressed a view counter to their own in the public sphere. Yet another example is the entry of Simran Jeet Singh. According to Professor Watchlist (n.d.-e), Singh "has made many anti-Trump sentiments, even going as far as posting a picture of himself flipping off New York's Trump Tower. He later went after Trump supporters directly, claiming that they 'tacitly condone racism.'" The problem, aside from the organization targeting the professor for expressing his First Amendment rights outside of the classroom, is that the picture of Singh is not, in fact, the professor but rather his brother (Flaherty, 2017).

Conclusion

When a disastrous wildfire ravages the countryside, burning everything in sight, investigators begin an inquiry into where and how and why the fire began in the first place. Authorities are interested in understanding both the origin and the cause of the blaze. TPUSA's inflammatory rhetoric and baseless fearmongering are lighting up our college campuses. In the case of TPUSA, the origin of the fire is known, publicly legitimated, and deeply funded by an established conservative philanthropic network which fans the flames. We are aware of the cause (or rationale) for such a conflagration: "to identify, educate, train and organize students to promote the principles of freedom, free markets, and limited government" (TPUSA, n.d.), thus presumably protecting an undocumented and unverifiable assault on myopic libertarian dispositions.

As TPUSA continues to proliferate on high school and college campuses, we understand the scope and reach of this wildfire. Given the historical precedence against political and ideological differences in educational spaces, fed by public moral panic and a culture of fear, we are familiar with how long and how high these fires burn. We also know the dangerous potential damage that professors face in this increasingly hostile and contentious political climate. As we witness an increase of hate crimes and hate speech on university campuses and as universities continuously move from public to privately funded changes to their financial structure, there is an increasing animosity toward those academics whose subject matter is considered either politically or ideologically contrary to compliance with established, acceptable (read: nonthreatening) standards (Ferber, 2018). Vulnerable professors, especially those without tenure or in marginalized fields, might silence themselves rather than place themselves on the front lines. But even those who do rush to address and respond to this assault on academic freedom with facts and research (as members of a metaphorical fire brigade), place themselves at risk of being burned and publicly harassed. In some instances, by extension, the professor's family members also face risk and danger of public targeted online harassment (Cuevas, 2018).

What is not readily apparent is the larger damage being done to academic spaces under the guise of TPUSA's "protection" of freedom. Professors are the immediate, easy target, but what of the broader assault on intellectual ideas? Fires that burn freely consume everything in their path, from vegetation to wildlife, and sometimes scorch the earth deep into the root structure undergirding the countryside. When students approach classroom debates as arguments to be won and teachers to be defeated, this undermines democratic engagement and, ultimately, shuts down the exploration of ideas in educative spaces. No one wants to enter an arena to lose, and we risk much when learning and ideas are framed as something to be won or lost rather than supported or evaluated and reshaped. Education is intended to create and enlarge our perspective—to the right and to the left. We must create space to hold new ideas. But we have to seriously consider the growing resentment toward higher education, especially from those who are politically conservative. If students lose faith in higher education, in colleges and universities as sites of open debate and thought, where do we find new growth after the fires have burned out?

References

Anti-Defamation League. (n.d.). *Turning Point USA*. Retrieved January 14, 2020 from https://www.adl.org/resources/backgrounders/turning-point-usa?source=post_page-----d2c75cbc3e02----------------------

Apple, M. (2004). *Ideology and curriculum* (3rd ed.). Routledge.

Cuevas, J. (2018). *A new reality? The far right's use of cyberharassment against academics: A firsthand account by a targeted faculty member*. American

Association of University Professors. https://www.aaup.org/article/new-reality-far-rights-use-cyberharassment-against-academics#.W2metC2ZNTY

deMarrais, K., Brewer, T. J., Atkinson, J. C., Herron, B., & Lewis, J. (2019). *Philanthropy, hidden strategy, and collective resistance: A primer for concerned educators*. Myers Education Press.

DiAngelo, R. (2018). *White fragility: Why it's so hard for White people to talk about racism*. Beacon Press.

Dilling, E. (1935). *Red network: A "who's who" and handbook of radicalism for patriots (anti-movements in America)*. Self-published.

Ferber, A. L. (2018). Are you willing to die for this work?" Public targeted online harassment in higher education. SWS presidential address. *Gender & Society*, *32*(3), 301–320.

Flaherty, C. (2016). Being watched. *Inside Higher Education*. https://www.insidehighered.com/news/2016/11/22/new-website-seeks-register-professors-accused-liberal-bias-and-anti-american-values

Flaherty, C. (2017). Sikh scholar harassed over photo of another man in turban. *Inside Higher Education*. https://www.insidehighered.com/news/2017/07/21/sikh-scholar-harassed-over-photo-another-man-front-trump-tower

Fox News. (2018). *Professor warns liberal colleges are "indoctrinating" kids* [Video]. https://video.foxnews.com/v/5816094387001#sp=show-clips

Fucci, A., & Catalano, T. (2019). Missing the (turning) point: The erosion of democracy at an American university. *Journal of Language and Politics*, *18*(3), 346–370.

Goldstein, D. (2014). *The teacher wars: A history of America's most embattled profession*. Doubleday.

Howard, C. A. (2019). No place for speech zones: How colleges engage in expressive gerrymandering. *Georgia State University Law Review*, *35*(2), 387–431.

Krugman, P., & Wells, R. (2009). *Economics*. New York, NY, Macmillian Publishers.

Murray, R. K. (1955). *Red Scare: A study in national hysteria, 1919–1920*. University of Minnesota Press.

Nichols, T. (2017). *The death of expertise: The campaign against established knowledge and why it matters*. Oxford University Press.

Parker, K. (2019). *The growing partisan divide in views of higher education.* PewResearchCenter. https://www.pewsocialtrends.org/essay/the-growing-partisan-divide-in-views-of-higher-education/

Perry, D. (2019). No, professors aren't discriminating against conservative students. *Pacific Standard.* https://psmag.com/ideas/no-professors-arent-discriminating-against-conservative-students

Professor Watchlist. (n.d.-a). *About us.* https://www.professorwatchlist.org/about-us/

Professor Watchlist. (n.d.-b). *Alba Lamar.* https://professorwatchlist.org/index.php/watch-list-directory/search-by-name/238-alba-lamar

Professor Watchlist. (n.d.-c). *Alvin Lee.* https://professorwatchlist.org/index.php/watch-list-directory/search-by-name/172-alvin-lee

Professor Watchlist. (n.d.-d). *Bob Englehart.* https://professorwatchlist.org/index.php/watch-list-directory/search-by-name/339-bob-englehart

Professor Watchlist. (n.d.-e). *Simran Jeet Singh.* https://professorwatchlist.org/index.php/watch-list-directory/search-by-name/314-simran-jeet-singh

Quintana, C. (2019). 'I am with you': President Trump signs executive order on free speech at college campuses. *USA Today.* https://www.usatoday.com/story/news/politics/2019/03/21/president-donald-trump-executive-order-college-free-speech/3232560002/

Scatamburlo-D'Annibale, V. (2019). The 'culture wars' reloaded: Trump, anti-political correctness and the right's 'free speech' hypocrisy. *Journal for Critical Education Policy Studies, 17*(1), 69–119.

Shepard, J. M., & Culver, K. B. (2018). Culture wars on campus: Academic freedom, the First Amendment, and partisan outrage in polarized times. *San Diego Law Review, 55*(87), 87–158.

This American Life. (2018). My effing First Amendment [Audio file]. https://www.thisamericanlife.org/645/my-effing-first-amendment

Tiede, H.J. (2017). *Exhuming McCarthy (meet me at the book burning).* American Association of University Professors. https://www.aaup.org/article/exhuming-mccarthy-meet-me-book-burning#.XiHzHy3MxTZ

Turning Point USA. (2015a). *How to debate your teacher (and win!): Empowering students to have the confidence to defend their beliefs in classrooms and universities.* https://drive.google.com/file/d/1woJt6VA4RDeccDtAzjUdzDH9NDCpDL3q/view

Turning Point USA. (2015b). *Indoctrination prevention: 10 ways college professors indoctrinate America's youth and how to prevent it.* https://www.scribd.com/document/345168623/Indoctrination-Prevention-10-Ways-College-Professors-Indoctrinate-America-s-Youth-and-How-to-Prevent-It-32

Turning Point USA. (n.d.). *About Turning Point USA.* https://www.tpusa.com/aboutus/

Tyack, D. (1974). *The one best system: A history of American urban education.* Harvard University Press.

Wolf, Z. (2019). *Trump's war on windmills continues.* CNN. https://www.cnn.com/2019/04/03/politics/trumps-war-on-windmills-now-includes-wild-cancer-claim/index.html

Chapter Ten

MISEDUCATING COMMUNITIES:
SINCLAIR BROADCASTING AND THE NATIONALIZATION OF LOCAL NEWS

Janie Copple, *University of Georgia*
Kathleen deMarrais, *University of Georgia*
Brigette Herron, *University of Georgia*

The presence of a free and independent press, and its role supporting a well-informed and educated citizenry, is key to fostering a healthy democratic society. As Hannah Arendt explained in a 1974 interview,

> The moment we no longer have a free press, anything can happen. What makes it possible for a totalitarian or any other dictatorship to rule is that people are not informed; how can you have an opinion if you are not informed? If everyone always lies to you, the consequence is not that you believe the lies, but rather that nobody believes anything any longer. (1978, para. 2)

Given the role media plays in supporting adults to serve as informed participants in our shared democratic society, this chapter explores the existing scholarship around the changing nature of news consumption (both print and media) in the United States in the 21st century. Civic engagement on a national and a local level relies on the people's access to trustworthy information sources that (a) make citizens aware of pertinent issues and (b) provide balanced and transparent coverage. Simply stated, citizens should know where news comes from, who constructs the news, and how network executives intentionally frame news messages for a particular outcome. In this chapter, we chronicle how factors such as increased television channel access and nationalization of print and media outlets have led to a decline in local news consumption. We look specifically at the case of the Sinclair Broadcast Group, a news corporation with ties to familiar conservative causes. We explore Sinclair's consolidation of local broadcast networks and subsequent attempts to nationalize local news broadcasts via must-run news segments with conservative ideological agendas. The research questions driving this chapter include: How did Sinclair Broadcast Group's board of directors wield strategies that expanded its influence into local news markets across the United States? How do the "must-run" segments of Sinclair's Chief Political Analysis, Boris Epshteyn, function as a strategic tool for promoting conservative ideology?[1] and, finally, How does Sinclair's must-run strategy undermine journalist balance to promote a conservative agenda?

Drawing on studies investigating the link between news consumption and civic engagement as a framework for understanding news as an educational tool, we unpack the ideological network behind the Sinclair Broadcast Group. Guided by Fligstein and McAdam's (2012) theory of strategic action fields, we explore Sinclair's involvement as challengers to the principles of free and balanced journalism and show how Sinclair's station consolidation practices and must-run segments dismantle those principles. We examine the rhetoric of Sinclair's chief political analyst, Boris Epshteyn, through a thematic analysis of 61 "Bottom Line with Boris" must-run segments and argue that the presence of must-run segments hinders freedom of the press. This fact is made more pressing by Sinclair's ability and attempts to monopolize a large portion of local news markets. We examine how must-run segments use a particular brand of conservative ideology to influence citizens around national issues using rather than practicing free and independent reporting that adheres to strict journalistic standards.

In the following sections, we describe the larger strategic action field (SAF), which we have defined as a free press, and provide a review of academic literature addressing the nationalization of local news and its impact on civic engagement. We situate our research on Sinclair and local news within Fligstein and McAdam's (2012) theory of SAFs and guide readers through a brief description of this theoretical framework, focusing specifically on actors as incumbents and challengers engaged in a dynamic jockeying for position within the field of local news. We see Sinclair's actors functioning as challengers within the field of the local news, destabilizing news outlets through the acquisition of local news markets. Once stations are acquired, Sinclair's control over station ownership, content, money, and political power challenge news markets, which serve as independent providers of news and commentary specific to a local audience. Next, we explore the history of the Sinclair organization and describe Sinclair's key actors: co-owners, brothers, and board members David, Julian, Frederick, and Duncan Smith. This history illustrates how Sinclair's acquisition history strategically expanded its reach into local broadcast markets and increased its influence over local news content across the United States. Finally, we examine Sinclair's must-run strategy through an in-depth thematic analysis of "Bottom Line with Boris" segments aired on local Sinclair stations during the first quarter of 2019. Despite Sinclair's claims toward balanced journalism, we reveal how actors within this field of challengers intentionally positioned conservative ideology to promote pro-Trump policy.

Media Consumption And Consolidation

In this section, we examine existing scholarship around the changing nature of print and media news consumption in the United States in the 20th and 21st centuries. We chronicle how contributing factors such as increased channel access and nationalization of print and media outlets led to a decline in local news consumption, a phenomenon impacting local civic participation. This historical foundation is essential for understanding how Sinclair employs similar strategies in the production and control of local news. As proponents of conservative ideological slant in local news and political commentary, Sinclair executives and television personalities push against journalistic standards of unbiased reporting and balanced journalism.

Media, communications, and political science scholars have conducted extensive research on the impact of consolidated print media outlets and expansive entertainment options on news consumption in the United States. Prior's 2005 study shows that in the age of increased cable access, more people opted for entertainment over news. Based on Prior's findings, Aalberg, Blekesaune, and Elvestad, (2013) conducted a longitudinal study investigating viewing habits in television markets across Europe. Findings supported a trend toward entertainment over news and indicated a wider gap between "news-seekers" and "news-avoiders" in the United States compared to Europe; the popularity and prevalence of public-service broadcasters in Europe provide one possible explanation (Aalberg et al., 2013). Although a trend toward entertainment viewership may not be surprising in the era of increased channel access, Prior (2005) points to the influence "accidental exposure" has on potential citizen engagement:

> Even broadcast viewers who prefer entertainment programs absorb at least basic political knowledge when they happen to tune in when only news is on. I propose that such accidental exposure should become less likely in a high-choice environment. (p. 579)

Although one might assume increased channel access means more opportunities for citizens to be engaged in politics, the opposite proves true. Those inclined toward political interest will follow the news regardless of choice. Similar research findings after 2013 have been documented (see Archer & Clinton, 2018; Lee & Chy, 2014; Shaker, 2014; Strömbäck et al., 2013).

In a later study on media and political polarization, Prior (2013) showed how declined "accidental exposure" to news—onset by high-choice media environments—accounts for the shift towards partisan elections. "Without their inadvertent news exposure, entertainment fans lacked the occasional push to the polls. The turnout gap between news and entertainment fans widened. And because entertainment fans are less partisan, their dropping turnout rates led to more partisan elections" (Prior, 2013, p. 107). With an increased preference for entertainment over fact and increased partisan elections, the dissolution of trust in journalistic news ultimately manifested a national discourse surrounding so-called fake news. In some cases, "fake news" has increasingly become a rallying cry to discredit any news item that does not align with one's ideological position. Disinformation campaigns on social media sites have run rampant and gone global (Frenkel et al., 2019). Returning to Arendt's (1978) point, if everyone lies to you, how can you believe anything any longer?

In a recent study on the impact of fake news in social media on the outcomes of the 2016 presidential election, Nelson and Taneja (2018) found "Democrats and Republicans are both about 15 percent more likely to believe ideologically aligned headlines, and this ideologically aligned inference is substantially stronger for people with ideologically segregated social media networks" (p. 213). In other words, politically interested individuals tune in to coverage that supports their ideological stance. Lee and Chyi (2014) take a psycho-behavioral approach, proposing a Motivational Consumption Model to explore multiple factors that encourage news consumption including news beliefs, news motivations, and news attitudes. Although our research here focuses on news beliefs rather than electoral outcomes, Lee and Chyi note the salient power of news to motivate public action: "In the context of news consumption, news beliefs are about people's general view of the value of news, which encompasses beliefs about the importance of news in serving as a mobilizing agent that empowers the public" (p. 710). But what happens when people choose local news over competing options and it *is not* local? The following explores the history of dwindling access to local print news and why this is problematic for local civic engagement.

Boulaine's 2011 study on the effects of news media on political interest stated that "television news seems to be the medium of choice for those interested and engaged in politics" (p. 157). Noam (2009) noted that newspapers "have been a stodgy industry for over 70 years" (p. 439), and this is one of multiple factors that account for the decline in local print news. Public response to the mass appeal of broadcast media with its array of entertainment choices is another important factor (Prior, 2005). Noam (2009) credited the collapse of multiple print news outlets with the economic dynamics of "high fixed costs, low marginal costs and commodification" (p. 440). As a result, larger local news outlets in big cities widened their scope, appealing to a national audience. George and Waldfogel (2006) investigated the effects of the 1996–2000 targeted expansion of the *New York Times*, arguing that the national reach of this once-local newspaper decreased the circulation of competing local papers. They argued this move is problematic because "local newspapers are a particularly important source of information about local affairs, hence their circulation provides a good measure of citizens' intake of local information" (George & Waldfogel, 2016, p. 436). Dwindling local news outlets in the late 20th/early 21st centuries exhibited one of the few remaining spaces for information on local politics and civic engagement.

Shaker (2014) examined civic engagement in Denver and Seattle following the closure of local newspapers in 2008 and 2009, respectively. Shaker situated his work alongside Mondak's (1995) previous studies on citizen engagement in Cleveland and Pittsburgh during Pittsburgh's 8-month newspaper strike in the 1990s. Findings indicated a lack of local news readership had no effect on Pittsburgh residents' knowledge of national news and politics but negatively impacted knowledge of local news (Mondak, 1995). Shaker's results showed decreased civic engagement, resulting in low voter turnout and community organizing in Denver and Seattle following the closure of the *Rocky Mountain News* and *Seattle Post-Intelligencer* in 2008 and 2009, respectively. In their recent analysis of local newspaper coverage of 2010 and 2014 midterm elections, Hayes and Lawless (2018) pointed to what they call an "anemic" current within the local news environment (p. 333). The study showed a decline in political coverage during this 4-year period. Their subsequent examination of panel surveys on local candidates in these election years showed voter knowledge was declining.

In this section, we chronicled a brief history of print and broadcast media and explored how the nationalization of print media and increased channel access have contributed to a lack of access to local news and impeded local civic engagement. Building on this historical context, we now turn to a description of our theoretical framework. We explore local news as an SAF, where challengers jockey for corporate consolidation of local stations and control over local content.

Theoretical Framework: SAFs

Fligstein and McAdam (2012) define SAFs as "fundamental units of collective action in society" (p. 9). They assert fields are in a perpetual state of flux, always dynamic and changing as actors within the field jockey to usurp or maintain position. "Fields are constructed on a situational basis, as shifting collections of actors come to define new issues and concerns as salient" (Fligstein & McAdam, 2012, p. 10). As actors define new issues in the field, this can lead to periods of conflict and instability in which incumbents and challengers engage in a struggle over resources and power. In this dynamic, incumbents are actors "defined by their claim on the lion's share of material and status rewards. In addition, the rules of the field tend to favor them" (Fligstein & McAdam, 2012, p. 13). Challengers possess fewer resources and have less authority within the field to wield influence. Challengers "recognize the nature of the field and the dominant logic of incumbent actors [and] can usually articulate an alternative vision of the field and their position in it" (Fligstein & McAdam, 2012, p. 13).

Challengers seek to dismantle preexisting hierarchies within the field that sustain the status quo. Contestation in a field may result in challengers seeking cooperation between social groups within the field to form alliances "rooted in a combination of shared interests and a common collective identity" (Fligstein & McAdam, 2012, p. 15). Social skills of challengers become important as actors appeal to others within the field to "create shared meanings" and provide people "with reasons to cooperate" (Fligstein & McAdam, 2012, p. 46).

Fligstein and McAdam describe systems of embedded fields, where micro-fields exist within larger meso-level structures. "The resulting vertical system looks a lot like a traditional Russian doll: with any number of smaller fields nested inside larger ones" (Fligstein & McAdam, 2012, p. 9). The interconnectedness of fields presents a paradigm in which one field can be impacted by destabilizing forces in another related field. National policy, political instability, or global financial crises can spark an incumbent–challenger contestation in related, "nested" fields creating an SAF. SAFs stabilize over time, presenting new coalitions of incumbents, challengers, and hierarchies.

SAFs provide a framework to explain past and present contested issues and power dynamics in local news. In this context, media owners, content editors, and station personalities jockey for position in a field in which control over station ownership and content, money, and political power are scarce resources. Challengers are corporate station owners, conservative policy makers, and special interests. Historical and contemporary challengers have already shifted the dynamics favoring corporate over local media ownership, consolidating control over profits. Currently, incumbent–challenger dynamics contesting media ownership's control over content presents the tension around which actors jockey for position. Incumbents represent network executives, large national news outlets, and grassroots organizations pushing back against station control over journalist coverage and biased political commentary.

Methods

To explore the Sinclair Network, we used online documents from the Sinclair Broadcasting Corporation and news articles about the network and its founders. We extracted "Bottom Line With Boris" segments aired on Sinclair stations in the first quarter of 2019 to capture the most current production of political commentary from this Sinclair source. All "Bottom Line With Boris" segments can be located on Boris Epshteyn's YouTube channel.[2] We extracted 61 "Bottom Line" transcripts aired between January 31, 2018, and

March 29, 2019, using the transcription tool embedded in YouTube's online platform and pasted transcripts into a Microsoft Word document in chronological order. Autogenerated transcripts were checked for accuracy against the audio recording. Transcripts included the date aired, the segment title, and a verbatim transcript of the segment. Segments ranged between 78 and 127 seconds in length and, with the exception of occasional excerpts from interviews with guests, feature Epshteyn providing his views on current national issues. We employed an inductive approach to coding and categorizing transcript data, noting our initial impressions and potential codes in the margins and writing connections and asking questions of the data through preliminary jottings (Saldaña, 2009). Following an initial reading of the data, we created an Excel database containing entries for each segment including the date aired, segment title, and keywords to describe topics relevant to the segment. This step proved useful to gain an overall understanding of the data. We uploaded transcripts into Atlas.ti (Atlas.ti, 2018, Version 8.4 for second- and third-cycle coding, collapsing initial codes into categories which we reduced to the three themes: (1) Trump as champion of the working class and victim of the left, (2) praise for capitalism and fear of socialism, and (3) protecting the American dream. Before discussing each of these themes in more detail, we provide an overview of the Sinclair Broadcasting Group and Sinclair's organizational structure, with specific attention to the Smith family and its leadership within the organization.

History And Organization of The Sinclair Network

Julian Sinclair Smith created the Sinclair Broadcast Group in 1971. Since that time, the network has grown into a family-run operation, with Smith serving as both a figurative and literal patriarch of the network. Today, Julian's sons occupy chief positions within the company, with son David Smith as the current Sinclair chief executive officer (CEO) and sons Frederick Smith, Robert Smith, and Duncan Smith serving as executive Sinclair board members.

Julian Sinclair Smith believed that the future of broadcasting lay in "the emergence of FM [frequency-modulated] radio and UHF [ultra-high-frequency] television as emerging technologies" (Sinclair Broadcast Group, n.d., "1970's," [sic] para. 1). He began his venture with a single FM radio station in Baltimore, Maryland, and quickly added one of the nation's first UHF television stations (WBFF-TV). In 1986, Julian and his sons merged the operations of three independent UHF stations across Baltimore, Pittsburgh, and Columbus, beginning what would become a long history of station acquisitions. (Sinclair Broadcast Group, n.d.). In the early 1990s, David Smith was elected CEO of Sinclair, just as the company acquired a second station market. By 1994, Sinclair had doubled in size, and in 1995, Sinclair "went public with 13 television stations in eight markets, realizing approximately $111.5 million to fund future acquisitions" (Sinclair Broadcast Group, n.d., "1990's," [sic] para. 4). Deregulation resulting from the Telecommunications Act of 1996 (Telecommunications Act of 1996, 2014) allowed Sinclair to acquire radio station real estate to add to its burgeoning television station acquisitions. Two years later, the company again doubled in size.

Deregulation in the mid-1990s and early 2000s allowed Sinclair to continue its acquisition of local stations across the United States. During this era, the Federal Communications Commission (FCC) media ownership guidelines permitted duopolies under a provision that came to be known as the UHF discount. FCC guidelines typically prohibited ownership of local broadcast stations to exceed 39% in a designated market area (DMA).[3] Under the UHF discount provision, broadcast groups acquiring UHF stations would be discounted by half, allowing more purchase power for groups buying UHF stations in the same DMA. Despite this discount, FCC guidelines still required divestment of single station holdings in the same DMA in excess of 39%. Sinclair's claims that it was appropriately divesting its assets according to FCC guidelines (*Statement of Commissioner Michael J. Copps*, 2001) turned out to be divestment in name only. Sinclair implemented a shell company strategy to maintain content control of its "divested" holdings. One such example of this can be seen through Sinclair's control of Cunningham Broadcasting.

Cunningham Broadcasting, formerly known as Glencairn, Ltd, is headquartered in Baltimore, Maryland, and currently owns 20 television stations in 18 markets (Cunningham Broadcasting About Us, n.d.). A 2001 statement made by then FCC commissioner, Michael J. Copps addressed Sinclair's acquisition of Glencairn, Ltd., arguing Sinclair "has continually pushed against the parameters of ownership structures prohibited by the Commission" (*Statement of Commissioner Michael J. Copp*, 2001, para 1). Next, we look to Sinclair's acquisition of Glencairn, Ltd as an example of how shell strategies operate strategically to expand station ownership/control in a DMA.

Sinclair's 1991 acquisition of a Pittsburgh television station required Sinclair's divestment of another Pittsburgh station to maintain compliance with FCC media ownership guidelines.[4] David Smith's solution to Sinclair's divestment problem came in the answer of Sinclair employee, Edwin Edwards. Sinclair sold its divestment to Edwards but controlled station programming through a local marketing agreement (LMA).[5] Later, when Smith sought acquisition of four additional stations (all located in markets with Sinclair holdings), he turned once again to Edwards. When Edwards was unable to purchase the stations, Smith relied on his mother, Carolyn Cunningham Smith, for financial backing for the divestment. Together with Edwards, Carolyn Smith established Glencairn, Ltd—also controlled via LMAs with Sinclair-owned stations. Throughout the 1990s, Sinclair, under the direction of CEO David Smith, employed divestment practices through LMAs to maintain control of divested stations. Although the FCC fined Sinclair and Glencairn, Ltd. $40,000 each for its involvement in questionable divestment practices (*Statement of Commissioner Michael J. Copp*, 2001), this did little to deflect Sinclair interests in future station acquisition and, more important, control over station content. Content control of divested stations created a scenario in which Sinclair-produced must-run segments influenced more viewers, extending first across a DMA and eventually across the country. In the following section, we examine the individual players in the Sinclair organization, looking to previous press interviews and financial records to illuminate the individual interests and agendas behind the largest corporate owner of local news stations in the United States.

The Smith Family and Sinclair Broadcasting's Organizational Structure

To provide readers with a sense of the Sinclair organization, we examine the Smith family relationships and the roles of the key players in the leadership of the organization and the role philanthropy plays for family members. As mentioned previously, David D. Smith, first son of Julian Sinclair Smith, is the executive chairman of Sinclair and has served as chairman of the board since 1990. David Smith served as the president and CEO of Sinclair for 29 years until 2017. Smith also serves as a board member of Cunningham Communications and Keyser Investment Group, Inc. (which serves as an investment holding for Sinclair). Of the four Smith brothers, David D. Smith is a pivotal actor in the Sinclair Broadcast Group network. Smith's role as the executive chairman of the board positioned him to forge strategies to expand Sinclair's station ownership and control local news content, as we illustrate in subsequent sections.

Frederick Smith, Robert Smith, and J. Duncan Smith serve on Sinclair's executive board. Julian Smith's second son, Frederick Smith, holds an MS, a DDS, and a PA and worked as an oral surgeon in his own practice before assuming the role of vice president of Sinclair in 1990. Frederick Smith serves on the boards of several organizations, including Gerstell Academy, University of Maryland at Baltimore Foundation, and Cunningham Communications, Inc., as well as the development groups in which Sinclair holds investment interests (Sinclair Broadcast Group, n.d.). In 1996, Frederick founded Gerstell Academy, a private P–12 school guided by a faith-based, leadership curriculum model and currently serves as the chairman of the board of trustees. Along with brother, Duncan Smith, Frederick donated $29,000 in 2017 to various Republican congressional candidates (Balcerzak, 2018).

J. Duncan Smith, third son of Julian Smith, has served as vice president, secretary, and director of Sinclair since 1986. Previously, Duncan operated television stations in Pittsburgh, Columbus, Bloomington, and Tampa/St. Petersburg and served on the board of Sinclair's development investment groups.

Robert E. Smith, fourth son of Julian Smith, has served as a director on Sinclair's board since 1986, during which time, he has acted both as secretary and treasurer. Robert holds a private commercial real estate organization RSMK, LLC and serves as a member on several boards including Gerstell Academy, Sinclair investment holdings, Cunningham Communications, and the Nextgen Foundation Charitable Trust, of which he is the founder.

The Sinclair Challengers

On July 2, 2017, John Oliver, host of *Last Week Tonight*, aired a segment uncovering how the Sinclair Broadcast Group issued directives to air must-run segments across its stations. Oliver asserted Sinclair, the largest owner of local broadcasting stations in the United States, was requiring anchors to deliver must-run segments—segments that stations are required to run during the regular local news broadcast. Oliver supported this assertion with a 30-second clip cutting to Sinclair stations across the country where local anchors read from identical scripts. Oliver was not the first incumbent actor in the free press to question Sinclair ownership and reporting practices.

In a 2004 interview with David D. Smith, *Washington Post* reporter Ahrens (2004) questioned Sinclair's directive that stations air *Stolen Honor: Wounds That Never Heal*—a controversial documentary critiquing John Kerry's service during Vietnam—during prime-time programming. Smith claimed that Sinclair had no political agenda and denied accusations that he controls content on local stations. Ahrens pointed to Sinclair's growing station acquisitions and noted how a Kerry electoral victory would tighten Federal Communications Commission guidelines making station acquisitions more difficult. And ultimately, Sinclair responded to incumbent pressure and broadcasted clips of the documentary rather than airing the documentary in its entirety. Such investigative reporting by incumbent challengers thrust Sinclair from the shadows, revealing the organization's content control and ownership strategies. In a 1995 *Baltimore Sun* interview Smith is quoted as saying that he and his brothers try "to maintain as much anonymity as we can" (Kurtz & Ahrens, 2004, p. 01A). As we look deeper into Sinclair's network of key players, a more plausible reality suggests that striving for anonymity strategically masks Sinclair's political agenda.

An examination of the executive board within the Sinclair organization and records of their financial contributions provides insight into the political agendas of those controlling the direction—and the message—of the institution and its local news stations. In a 2017 conversation with the *New York Times*, Scott Livingston, Sinclair's vice president for news, stated, "We work very hard to be objective and fair and be in the middle. . . . I think maybe some other news organizations may be to the left of center, and we work very hard to be in the center" (Ember, 2017, para. 12).

Boris Epshteyn's "Bottom Line": An Analysis

According to a 2018 article published in the *Baltimore Sun*, "Bottom Line" must-run segments escalated on Sinclair stations in the months following the inauguration of President Trump (Zurawik, 2018). Incumbent media outlets criticized Sinclair's decision to increase airtime for "Bottom Line" segments, claiming these segments trended toward slanted journalism. Scott Livingston—then vice president of Sinclair News—dismissed this criticism, emphasizing these segments are labeled as commentary (Zurawik, 2018). "Bottom Line" segments aired on Sinclair stations for the first 2 years of the Trump administration with no counterpoint to Epshteyn's commentary. Furthermore, Epshteyn's title *chief* political analyst (our emphasis) suggests his authority within the Sinclair network regarding U.S. politics and policy. In our analysis of "Bottom Line" segments aired within the first quarter of 2019, we show how the themes—Trump as the champion of the working class and a victim of the left, praise for capitalism and fear of socialism, and protecting the American dream—illustrate Sinclair's strategic aims to control local station content to further the challengers' conservative agenda.

Trump as the Champion of the Working Class and a Victim of the Left

Of the 61 "Bottom Line" segments examined in this study, 32 segments included direct criticism of Democrats as opposed to 4 segments criticizing Republicans. In segments critiquing Democrats, Epshteyn calls specific attention to individual/party actions or beliefs on national, social, or international issues. Epshteyn repeatedly accuses Democrats of taking sides on policy for the purpose of undermining President Trump. Furthermore, Epshteyn juxtaposes his argument for Democratic policy driven by an anti-Trump agenda alongside Trump's victories on behalf of the American people. Such juxtaposition portrays President Trump as *both* the champion of the working class and a victim of left. In the excerpts that follow, we show how this theme is produced in "Bottom Line" segments.

First, we explore Epshteyn's construction of Trump as a victim of Democrats, their policies, and the media. Few "Bottom Line" segments in the first quarter of 2019 focused on the Mueller investigation. However, Epshteyn aired a segment on March 25, 2019, titled "President Trump Has Been Fully Vindicated" in which he stated,

> People should be very angry with the Democrats who, in an attempt to undermine President Trump's legitimacy as our

> Commander-in-Chief, pushed for an investigation which has taken almost two years and cost over twenty-five million dollars. Most importantly the Democrats have neglected to actually govern, pinning their hopes and dreams on this idea that Mueller who they revered as a savior up until now would one day somehow be able to remove President Trump from office. (Bottom Line With Boris, 2019k, 00:26).

In this excerpt, Epshteyn argued Democrats neglected administrative duties in favor of "undermining President Trump's legitimacy." Removing Trump from office is the Democrats' primary objective and has cost the American people time ("almost two years") and money ("over twenty-five million dollars"). Epshteyn portrays Democrats operating with a vendetta rather than attentive to constituent concerns.

Epshteyn points to Democratic policy flaws, inconsistencies, and criticism of President Trump, calling out the most egregious offenders by name. In Excerpt 2, Epshteyn casts congressional Democrats and Speaker Nancy Pelosi as agents singularly motivated to thwart Trump's legacy:

> If congressional Democrats' obsession with senselessly obstructing President Trump had not delayed it, this week we would have heard the President's State of the Union address. Unfortunately, House Speaker Nancy Pelosi refused to negotiate on funding enhanced security at our southern border so the President's State of the Union address will come a week later than it was intended to be given. (Bottom Line With Boris, 2019b, 00:04)

This excerpt again portrays Trump as a personal victim of Democrats in Congress and their "obsession with senselessly obstructing" him. Speaker Pelosi is accused of unwillingness to negotiate—which links Democrats' personal obstruction to obstruction of policy. However, Democrats are not the only group

Epshteyn accuses of undermining President Trump. His representation of media coverage often casts Trump as the victim of unfair, biased journalism as seen in Excerpt 3:

> Unfortunately, this spirit of bipartisanship has been largely missing as many on the left and those in the media have put their love of our great country second to their personal hatred of our president. Despite all of that, President Trump is still getting results. (Bottom Line With Boris, 2019f, 1:10)

In Excerpt 3, Epshteyn constructs a love/hate duality to argue nefarious intentions in the media's coverage of President Trump. Note a lack of attention to media coverage on domestic issues or foreign policy. For Epshteyn, and for Trump, this is *personal.* Simply, one cannot love the United States if one disagrees with this president. In this excerpt, Epshteyn questions the journalistic integrity of media outlets critiquing this administration, stating attempts to defame this president in the media supersede commitment to quality, balanced reporting. Epshteyn asserts that despite opposition, "Trump is still getting results." In the following excerpts, we demonstrate how Epshteyn represents Trump as a champion of the American people. Excerpt 4 is taken from a "Bottom Line" segment on the Trump administration's response to veteran suicide:

> These men and women signed a blank check with their lives on the dotted line. It is disgraceful that President Trump has had to clean up the mess left behind by prior administrations. I am glad that our veterans remain a top priority for the Trump administration and I look forward to seeing our veterans receive the amazing care that they deserve. (Bottom Line With Boris, 2019i, 1:12)

Epshteyn simultaneously praises Trump's efforts while castigating "the mess left behind by prior administrations." Trump, in this scenario, is the champion of a group that has been forgotten by others, portraying him as compassionate and attentive toward a deserving group of people. A similar representation of Trump as a champion for the safety of all Americans can be seen in Excerpt 5 in which Epshteyn praises Trump for his stance on immigration at the U.S.–Mexico border:

> I believe that the President is fully within his rights to use a national emergency to protect America amid a humanitarian and security crisis at our southern border. . . . So much for speaker Pelosi gloating that she would not give the President more than one dollar for a barrier at the US Mexico border. Here's the bottom line: This is a political win for President Trump and most importantly a win for the American people. The overall result will be that the barrier will continue to be built which is the key to ending the illegal immigration, drug trade and human trafficking at our border. (Bottom Line With Boris, 2019e, 1:07)

In this description over the contested wall at the southern border between the United States and Mexico, Epshteyn represents this moment as a "humanitarian and security crisis." This language invokes the possibility of risks to human safety, thus meriting the need for protection. Ultimately, Trump—and, by proxy, the American people—emerge as victors in a struggle with "gloating" Speaker Pelosi. As we consider these production moments, representations of Trump as victim and champion paint a powerful picture of a leader triumphing over adversity for the good of the American people while simultaneously casting doubts about the intentions of his opposition.

Praise for Capitalism and Fear of Socialism

Praise for capitalism and fear of socialism was identified throughout "Bottom Line" transcripts as binaries representing left-leaning versus right-leaning ideology. In Excerpt 6, Epshteyn comments on the unrest in Venezuela. He cites socialism as the root cause of Venezuelan violence and poses capitalism as the ultimate solution:

> Venezuelan socialist dictator Nicolas Maduro's government has followed the disastrous policies of his predecessor, Hugo Chavez. They have ruined a once oil-rich economy, caused starvation and a terrible migration crisis all in the name of socialism. The Trump administration has imposed sanctions against Maduro and his inner circle in order to weaken the regime. That is the regime that has attempted to silence the opposition through violent oppression and censorship. But once quiet protest against Maduro and socialism has grown louder. . . . In response, the Trump administration has put in place even harsher sanctions. Here's the bottom line: I applaud the Trump administration for continuing to take bold action against the Maduro dictatorship in Venezuela. More countries should renounce the Maduro regime and support the opposition. Maduro should step down so that Venezuela can be reborn as a thriving capitalist country. (Bottom Line With Boris, 2019d, 00:02)

References to Venezuela's economic potential as "a once oil-rich economy" point to missed opportunities to take advantage of the prosperities within the capitalist system. Citizens have suffered atrocities "all in the name of socialism." The solution provided by capitalism indicates an end to the "violent oppression and censorship," suggesting a better quality of life for all Venezuelans. The Venezuelan crisis reemerges in Excerpt 7 as a cautionary tale in which Epshteyn warns audiences of the false promises of socialist approaches to education, health care, and environmentalism:

> Democratic socialists such as Alexandria Ocasio-Cortez and Bernie Sanders are promising free education free health care and a disastrous Green New Deal all at the expense of hard-working Americans. Yet, these democratic socialists turn a

> blind eye to examples of the destructive power of socialism in places like Venezuela where the rancid ideal of socialism has suffocated the South American country. (Bottom Line With Boris, 2019j, 00:48)

Again, Epshteyn argues the dangers of socialist programs "at the expense of hardworking Americans," implying socialist systems advantage undeserving recipients of social programs on the backs of entitled, hardworking others. Excerpt 7 underscores the "costs" of socialism in Venezuela as a cautionary tale to Democratic socialists. Excerpt 8 shows how Epshteyn draws upon the idea of deserving versus undeserving citizens in his critique of social security expansion:

> Many Democrats are embracing a very familiar song and dance. They plan on growing the size and scope of the federal government by giving out free handouts in the form of things like student loan forgiveness, free higher education, and in some cases, a living wage for those unwilling to work. Democrats expect for the American people to take these handouts and ask the important questions such as: Is this sustainable later? (Bottom Line With Boris, 2019h, 00:05)

These excerpts demonstrate Epshteyn's depictions of socialism and capitalism as being tied to costs and benefits for hardworking Americans. Epshteyn praises capitalism as an international solution to violence, censorship, and poverty and as a way to protect and prevent the potential exploitation of those deemed "deserving" of protection. In contrast, Epshteyn's descriptions of socialism are characterized by fearful scenarios in which individuals lose their freedoms and hard work is no longer valued. In essence, socialism is presented as something to be feared, a force thwarting the potential for individuals to attain the American dream.

Protecting the American Dream

Within the data set, we found that the theme of "protecting the American dream" was an important concept entangled in notions of choice and individualism. In Excerpt 9, Epshteyn provides an excerpt from an interview conducted with Secretary of Education Betsy DeVos in which school choice, vouchers, and charter schools are presented as vehicles for attaining the American dream:

> **Epshteyn:** What do you say to that criticism that most of the school choice programs in the country are targeted to families that don't have means?
>
> **DeVos:** That our low-income kids who are vulnerable that they're the ones that are benefiting the most. Those that have the economic means today are able to make choices by paying tuition or moving to places where the schools are good.
>
> **Epshteyn:** So, functionally in real basic language how does a school choice program work?
>
> **DeVos:** So we talked about charter schools which are alternatively organized public schools—there are vouchers, there are tax credit programs, there are education savings accounts, there's virtual schooling, just to name the main ones.
>
> **Epshteyn:** Here's the bottom line: Providing families with more choices allows them flexibility in their pursuit of the American dream. School choice programs are yet another way that we can intelligently invest in our nation's future. (Bottom Line With Boris, 2019a, 00:51)

In this interview excerpt, DeVos provides school choice as the remedy for the failing U.S. public schools. DeVos argues that "kids who are vulnerable . . . are benefiting the most." The assertion is that school choice programs provide access to the "pursuit of the American dream." Protecting the American dream involves protection from politicians who may not have "America's best interests at heart." In Excerpt 10, Epshteyn criticizes congresswoman Alexandria Ocasio-Cortez (AOC) for her call for Amazon to reconsider its move to New York. In his critique of AOC, Epshteyn situates Ocasio-Cortez, and "her dangerous socialist ideals" in opposition to the prosperity and possibility of the American dream.

> Alexandria Ocasio-Cortez called for Amazon to reconsider coming to New York. It would appear that encouraging businesses to come to New York and invest in the local economy is not a priority for Ocasio-Cortez. Amazon also had plans to invest heavily into providing technical education to New Yorkers but, nope, not a priority for AOC. She's busy spending her time proposing disastrous policies like those outlined in her Green New Deal or the green new disaster. Good news if you're a constituent of hers, she's only going to advocate for ways to improve your livelihood if they advance her dangerous socialist ideals. I'm of course being Sarcastic. If the progress championed by those on the left means denying access to better education and higher paying jobs for American citizens, we should all quickly denounce it. Here's the bottom line: One has to wonder whether Alexandria Ocasio-Cortez and her comrades have America's best interests at heart. She seems hyper focused on ensuring that people become dependent on the federal government when she should be helping the American people achieve their version of the American dream. (Bottom Line With Boris, 2019g, 00:19)

In this excerpt, protecting the American dream is positioned against government expansion. AOC is criticized for her socialist ideas "ensuring that people become dependent on the federal government." The American dream, in this case, can only be realized through corporate growth and the possibilities it brings to individuals. Epshteyn relies on coded rhetoric referencing "Alexandria Ocasio-Cortez and her comrades." The term *comrades* and its historical ties to communism and socialism—concepts frequently conflated by the right—function as a scare tactic positioning socialism as something that is squelching the American dream. Excerpt 11 extends our understanding of the American dream recognized through a shared sense of American identity as Epshteyn reviews the highlights of Trump's State of the Union address:

> Choosing greatness was the theme of President Trump's State of the Union address. The President certainly delivered a strong, authentic and unifying speech. President Trump made a plea for Congress to come together and support the administration's common-sense immigration reform proposals, including a barrier at our southern border. President Trump outlined foreign policy achievements in North Korea and assured the American people that we can maintain our allies while simultaneously standing up for American values. The president also touted the healthy U.S. economy that has added 5.3 million jobs and has brought about the lowest unemployment in half a century. (Bottom Line With Boris, 2019c, 00:01)

Protecting the American dream speaks to a hegemonic understanding of a singular, American identity. Epshteyn points to the "unifying" nature of Trump's speech, indicating that, if Congress comes together under the support of Trump's policies, this will "assure the American people" that American values are protected. The excerpts conclude with evidence to support citizens' trust in such policies with references to the promise of prosperity through added jobs and low unemployment.

Must-run segments such as "Bottom Line With Boris" illustrate how Sinclair challengers work to destabilize the local news, disseminating conservative ideology masquerading as news on local stations across the United States. Together with its long history of station acquisition, Sinclair has redefined the field and positioned itself as an incumbent in the field—where local news is neither *local* nor *news* but has become something more akin to conservative propaganda. This is particularly problematic when audiences may not recognize segments as inherently biased as they are couched within local evening news broadcasts. These strategies work in tandem educating citizens on national issues through local broadcasting. In the age of Fox News, one may wonder why citizens should be concerned with another iteration of conservative slanted journalism. Citizens tuning in to Sinclair stations hear local news stories but are also exposed (either intentionally or accidentally) to conservative bias on national issues. Although other news outlets have critiqued Sinclair's station acquisition practices, Oliver's segment drew national attention to Sinclair challengers, casting the Smith brothers out of the shadows. In response to incumbent criticism of its conservative-leaning coverage, Sinclair announced the premiere of "Cross Point With Ameshia Cross," a left-leaning political counterpoint to Epshteyn's "Bottom Line" commentary. The following section examines how Sinclair skillfully uses left-leaning rhetoric and the illusion of diversity through "Cross Point," which serves as another strategy that shifts the field further from incumbent journalistic standards toward a conservative neoliberal agenda.

Counterpoint: Where Is It?

In January 2019, Sinclair announced a new addition to its political commentary team to provide another perspective to the issues discussed in Boris Epshteyn's "Bottom Line with Boris" (Sinclair Broadcast Group, Inc., 2019). Sinclair hired left-leaning activist and former Obama campaign supporter Ameshia Cross to host a political commentary segment titled "Cross Point With Ameshia Cross." "Cross Point" segments are comparative to "Bottom Line" segments in length, tone, and structure. Response to Sinclair's decision to air "Cross Point" indicates the hopeful possibility that Sinclair was making attempts to provide balanced commentary. This moment can best be understood as Sinclair challengers' response to incumbent claims of conservative bias. Sinclair challengers are jockeying to maintain stability in their field by compromising around this point of contention (Fligstein & McAdam, 2012). What could be construed by Sinclair challengers as compromise is just another iteration of conservative talking points masked behind the illusion of balanced perspectives.

"Cross Point" segments provide significantly less airtime across Sinclair-owned local news channels. In an analysis of all 190 Sinclair-owned stations, approximately 164 provide news coverage. "Bottom Line With Boris" is aired across 89% of Sinclair stations providing news coverage as compared to 33% that air "Cross Point." "Cross Point" commentary is always accompanied by "Bottom Line" must-runs while 54% of "Bottom Line" segments are aired across local stations unaccompanied by "Cross Point." This illustrates an uneven distribution of commentary programming and casts doubt around Sinclair's intentions. We now turn toward an analysis of "Cross Point"/"Bottom Line" paired commentary.

"Bottom Line" segments follow a regimented structure in which Epshteyn takes up a political scenario, provides brief context and commentary and concludes with a nutshell statement reiterating his political stance. "Cross Point" mirrors "Bottom Line" in duration and structure with one notable exception—featured segments conclude with a 10-second rebuttal from Boris Epshteyn and an audience teaser for his conservative commentary. Excerpts 12 and 13 illustrate this structure, in which political commentary provided from opposing camps reifies a conservative agenda. In Excerpt 12, Epshteyn disputes Cross's claims supporting resistance to the Trump presidency. In Excerpt 13, Epshteyn takes issue with Cross's support of New Zealand's response to gun control following the March 2019 mass shooting in Christchurch.

> **Cross:** Let's get to the point: Celebrating American greatness and those that helped shape our country is a time-honored tradition. Unfortunately, much like in 2017 many people will be hosting "Not my President's Day" rallies as resistance to this President rages on.

> **Epshteyn:** Hey, Ameshia. Despite what you and many of those on the left have to say, President Trump is getting concrete results for the American people. Coming up, my thoughts on why the Trump Presidency so far is one of the best in American history. (Idaho News on Demand, 2019a, 01:09)
>
> **Cross:** Our sympathies in times of tragedy are important. But our humanity will be tested by our willingness to put an end to gun-induced terror. The U.S. could learn vital lessons from New Zealand's leadership on gun access.
>
> **Epshteyn:** Ameshia, you're forgetting the reasonable legislation that is in Congress right now, which would strengthen our background check laws. Coming up, my thoughts on whether American politicians should point to the new gun laws in New Zealand as an example of what could be done in America. (Idaho News on Demand, 2019b, 01:09)

Sinclair's recent push toward online streaming provides users access to news commentary from "Bottom Line" and "Cross Point" on local station websites. Station websites featuring both "Bottom Line" and "Cross Point" segments provide current links to the most recently aired must-runs at the top of the commentary page. Links to that day's "Cross Point" uses the same rebuttal structure. In our survey of Sinclair station websites, we found 112 Sinclair stations airing both "Bottom Line" and "Cross Point" segments in which Epshteyn's rebuttal appears in the final seconds of the most recent "Cross Point" commentary. We found no examples of "Cross Point" rebuttals across any "Bottom Line" segments posted on Sinclair station websites.[6] Whether accessed online or on television, Sinclair operationalizes race and gender in these production moments to dismantle political views opposing its conservative agenda. Cross is used as a prop to uphold right-leaning commentary in which a White male conservative commentator always has the last word.

Conclusion

As the nature of news and media consumption has changed over time, new strategies are being forged to continue promoting conservative causes. In this chapter, we argue that Sinclair's attempts to (a) monopolize local broadcast markets and (b) manage news commentary through must-run segments results in nationalized local news that supports a conservative political agenda. We situate the Sinclair Broadcast Group and its actors as challengers to incumbents in the free press in which challengers contest the parameters around what is considered newsworthy (slanted political commentary) and how it is produced (must-run segments). Sinclair challengers push the boundaries of journalistic integrity and balanced reporting favoring conservative slanted political commentary disguised as local news.

Strategic action and actors in the Sinclair Broadcast Group represent the most recent attempt to nationalize local news during the last two decades. Sinclair's shell-game acquisition of stations and must-run strategies demonstrate the challengers' attempts at consolidating local news ownership and content. Challengers jockeying for policies favoring consolidation and content control create a climate in which Sinclair controlled must-runs became possible. An examination of Sinclair's station acquisition strategies beginning in the mid-1990s, as well as its use of must-run mandates, points to Sinclair's intention toward conservative-slanted journalism, despite claims to the contrary. Our analysis of 61 "Bottom Line with Boris" must-runs looks to the most recent iteration of Sinclair's long-held strategy to nationalize local news around a neoliberal, conservative agenda. Sinclair's response to the incumbent critique of biased journalism—"Cross Point with Ameshia Cross"—shows how challengers wield social skills imbued with the language and optics of diversity to craft production moments that further dismantle journalistic standards and promote conservative propaganda disguised as local news.

Must-run segments like "Bottom Line" nationalize local news, influencing audiences through conservative political commentary on national issues. The Sinclair message reaches households across the nation as citizens tune in to local news broadcasts. In an era in which most people get their news via local television newscasts (Mitchell et al., 2016), Sinclair's consolidation and control over local content are particularly problematic. These segments impose conservative agendas on a range of national issues served to audiences under the guise of local news as they villainize conservative opponents, critique their stances on national issues, and push the success and protection of free-market capitalism, its policies, and its advocates. News media present a vital component in conservatives' long-term strategy to win an ideological war to preserve their own financial interests. The Sinclair Broadcast Group illustrates an example of such strategies in the case of the must-run segment "Bottom Line with Boris."

What's Next for Sinclair?

In December 2019, the Sinclair Broadcast Group announced its decision to pull both "Bottom Line with Boris" and "Cross Point with Ameshia Cross" commentary segments, claiming "it would use the time devoted to Epshteyn's and Cross' commentaries for more investigative reporting" (Farhi, 2019b, para. 5). News outlets speculate criticism over the tenor and substance of Epshteyn's segments sparked Sinclair's decision to pull the must-runs. Indeed, Sinclair's must-run strategy and Epshteyn's "Bottom Line" segment specifically thrust Sinclair from the shadows, making it impossible for Sinclair to operate beneath the radar. Pam Vogel, deputy editorial director at Media Matters, has been tracking Boris Epshteyn's political commentary segments since June 2017. Although Sinclair's decision to remove "Bottom Line" segments might be considered a victory favoring investigative journalism over biased, right-wing propaganda, Vogel (2019) cautions readers to remember Boris Epshteyn and his political commentary are part of a farther-reaching Sinclair strategy to undermine journalistic balance and integrity. She writes:

> Bullies don't usually just give up randomly one day; sometimes their tactics just change. What if this time around, the propaganda becomes better, more charismatic, less clumsy—easier to watch but harder to notice? (Vogel, 2019, para. 19)

In April 2019, Sinclair Broadcast Group hired Eric Bolling, previous host of the Fox News program *The Five* to host a weekly one-hour broadcast titled *America This Week*, calling him Sinclair's "chief political anchor" (Farhi, 2019a). Bolling, known for his conservative political commentary, authored the *New York Times* best-selling *Wake Up, America*. In a 2016 interview with *Politico*, Bolling said he wrote the book because he felt "a need to kind of pull the country back towards the center from how far left President Obama has been pulling us" (Allen, 2016, para. 3). Bolling's 2017 book, *The Swamp: Washington's Murky Pool of Corruption and Cronyism and How Trump Can Drain it*, unabashedly supports pro-Trump policies. Bolling is one of three Fox News alumni joining the ranks of the Sinclair Broadcast Group. In March 2019, Sinclair added former White House advisor and Fox News commentator Sebastian Gorka and former Fox News reporter James Rosen as content contributor and Washington bureau reporter, respectively. Despite Sinclair's decision to discontinue Epshteyn's must-run segments, changes in programming that involve hiring individuals known exclusively for conservative-slanted commentary signals only a superficial rebranding of image, not content.

Fligstein and McAdam (2012) note "one way to make sense of the state of the field is to examine the kinds of actions in which groups are engaged" (p. 174). With this in mind, how might we make sense of local news given Sinclair's recent programming decisions? Perhaps not much has changed. Sinclair's must-run commentaries continue disguising right-wing propaganda as local news while acquisition and consolidation strategies ensure Sinclair Broadcasting reaches the widest viewership possible. What is next for Sinclair looks to be the same conservative ideology simply repackaged to be more desirable to its audience, where entertainment reigns supreme and confidence in reliable journalism remains shaken.

References

Aalberg, T., Blekesaune, A., & Elvestad, E. (2013). Media choice and informed democracy: Toward increasing news consumption gaps in Europe? *The International Journal of Press/Politics, 18*(3), 281–303. https://doi.org/10.1177/1940161213485990

Ahrens, F. (2004 October 26). Sinclair chief denies political agenda. *The Washington Post*, p. 01E.

Allen, M. (2016, June 28). *Fox host Eric Bolling's mischievous book dedication.* Politico. https://www.politico.com/story/2016/06/fox-host-eric-bollings-mischievous-book-dedication-224870

Archer, A. M., & Clinton, J. (2018). Changing owners, changing content: Does who owns the news matter for the news? *Political Communication, 35*(3), 353–370. doi:10.1080/10584609.2017.1375581

Arendt, H. (1978, October 26). Hannah Arendt: From an interview. *The New York Review of Books.* https://web.archive.org/web/20170222205715/http://www.nybooks.com/articles/1978/10/26/hannah-arendt-from-an-interview/

Balcerzak, A. (2018, April 3). *Sinclair-related political money goes mostly to Republicans. But Democrats get cash, too.* Center for Public Integrity. https://publicintegrity.org/federal-politics/sinclair-related-political-money-goes-mostly-to-republicans-but-democrats-get-cash-too/

Bottom Line With Boris. (2019a, January 29). *Bottom Line With Boris—School choice* [Video]. YouTube. https://www.youtube.com/watch?v=zIJtiUAmF3k&t=39s

Bottom Line With Boris. (2019b, January 29). *Bottom Line With Boris—The State of the Union that wasn't* [Video]. YouTube. https://www.youtube.com/watch?v=u7mRWtAkOno&t=54s

Bottom Line With Boris. (2019c, February 6). *Bottom Line With Boris—State of the Union reaction* [Video]. YouTube. https://www.youtube.com/watch?v=XaFRq7iGlbo

Bottom Line With Boris. (2019d, February 11). *Bottom Line With Boris—Venezuela uprising* [Video]. YouTube. https://www.youtube.com/watch?v=FCuJq8WJa9U

Bottom Line With Boris. (2019e, February 15). *Bottom Line With Boris—National emergency on the border wall* [Video]. YouTube. https://www.youtube.com/watch?v=1khtU_bYsuo

Bottom Line With Boris. (2019f, February 18). *Bottom Line With Boris—President's Day* [Video]. YouTube. https://www.youtube.com/watch?v=pukhLN7F2PI

Bottom Line With Boris. (2019g, February 21). *Bottom Line With Boris—Amazon HQ2* [Video]. YouTube. https://www.youtube.com/watch?v=9iAaX12qs7E

Bottom Line With Boris. (2019h, February 27). *Bottom Line With Boris—Social Security* [Video]. YouTube. https://www.youtube.com/watch?v=rav7Z6KGfT4

Bottom Line With Boris. (2019i, March 12). *Bottom Line With Boris—Veteran suicide.* YouTube. https://www.youtube.com/watch?v=koJ-7gkn-YQ&t=10s

Bottom Line With Boris. (2019j, March 14). *Bottom Line With Boris—Socialism* [Video]. YouTube. https://www.youtube.com/watch?v=cQsAadJLoU4

Bottom Line With Boris. (2019k, March 25). *Bottom Line With Boris—President Trump has been fully vindicated* [Video]. YouTube. https://www.youtube.com/watch?v=rsU8xUz9Uh8

Boulianne, S. (2011). Stimulating or reinforcing political interest: Using panel data to examine reciprocal effects between news media and political interest. *Political Communication, 28*(2), 147-162. doi:10.1080/10584609.2010.540305

Cunningham Broadcasting. (n.d.). *About us.* Retrieved March 5, 2019, from http://cunninghambroadcasting.com/about-us

Ember, S. (2017, May 13). Sinclair requires TV stations to air segments that tilt to the right. *New York Times.* https://www.nytimes.com/2017/05/12/business/media/sinclair-broadcast-komo-conservative-media.html

Farhi, P. (2019a, April 5). That Fox-y feeling? The nation's largest TV station owner hires some familiar Fox News names. *The Washington Post.* https://www.washingtonpost.com/lifestyle/style/that-fox-y-feeling-the-nations-largest-tv-station-owner-hires-some-familiar-fox-news-names/2019/04/04/0db479c4-5632-11e9-9136-f8e636f1f6df_story.html

Farhi, P. (2019b, December 11). Sinclair TV drops pro-Trump commentator Boris Epshteyn and says it will add investigative journalism. *The Washington Post.* https://www.washingtonpost.com/lifestyle/style/sinclair-tv-drops-pro-trump-commentator-boris-epshteyn-and-says-it-will-add-investigative-journalism/2019/12/11/d380f2c8-1c47-11ea-87f7-f2e91143c60d_story.html

Fligstein, N., & McAdam, D. (2012). *A theory of fields.* Oxford University Press.

Frenkel, S., Conger, K., & Roose, K. (2019, January 31). Russia's playbook for social media disinformation has gone global. *New York Times.* https://www.nytimes.com/2019/01/31/technology/twitter-disinformation-united-states-russia.html

George, L. M., & Waldfogel, J. (2006). The "New York Times" and the market for local newspapers. *The American Economic Review, 96*(1), 435–447. http://proxy-remote.galib.uga.edu/login?url=http://search.ebscohost.com/login.aspx?direct=true&db=edsjsr&AN=edsjsr.30034376&site=eds-live

Hayes, D., & Lawless, J. L. (2018). The decline of local news and its effects: New evidence from longitudinal data. *The Journal of Politics, 80*(1), 332–336. doi:10.1086/694105

Idaho News on Demand. (2019a, February 18). *Cross Point With Ameshia Cross* [Video]. YouTube. https://www.youtube.com/watch?v=Tq_80sF1Dr4

Idaho News on Demand. (2019b, March 26). *Cross Point With Ameshia Cross* [Video]. YouTube. https://www.youtube.com/watch?v=ZbTCsoQ911Y

Kurtz, H., & Ahrens, F. (2004, October 12). Family's TV clout in Bush's corner: Sinclair orders 62 stations to air anti-Kerry film. *Washington Post*, p. 01A.

Last Week Tonight. (2017, July 2). *Sinclair Broadcast Group: Last Week Tonight With John Oliver (HBO)* [Video]. YouTube. https://www.youtube.com/watch?v=GvtNyOzGogc&t=724s

Lee, A. & Chyi, H. (2014). Motivational consumption model: Exploring the psychological structure of news use. *Journalism and Mass Communication Quarterly, 91*(4), 706–724.

Mitchell, A., Gottfried, J., Barthel, M., Shearer, E.(2016, July 14). *How Americans get their news.* Pew Research Center. https://www.journalism.org/2016/07/07/pathways-to-news/

Mondak, J. (1995). Media exposure and political discussion in U.S. elections. *The Journal of Politics, 57*(1), 62–85.

Nelson, J. L., & Taneja, H. (2018). The small, disloyal fake news audience: The role of audience availability in fake news consumption. *New Media & Society, 20*(10), 3720–3737. doi:10.1177/1461444818758715

Noam, E. (2009). *Media ownership and concentration in America.* Oxford University Press.

Prior, M. (2005). *News vs. entertainment: How increasing media choice widens gaps in political knowledge and turnout* Blackwell Publishing. doi:10.2307/3647733

Prior, M. (2013). Media and political polarization. *Annual Review of Political Science, 16*(1), 101–128.

Saldaña, J. (2009). *The coding manual for qualitative researchers.* Sage Publications.

Shaker, L. (2014). Dead newspapers and citizens' civic engagement. *Political Communication, 31*(1), 131–148. doi:10.1080/10584609.2012.762817

Sinclair Broadcast Group. (n.d.). *History.* http://sbgi.net/history/

Sinclair Broadcast Group, Inc. (2019, January 23). *Sinclair Broadcast Group taps Ameshia Cross to anchor new commentary segment, 'Cross Point'.* Cision PR Newswire. https://www.prnewswire.com/news-releases/sinclair-broadcast-group-taps-ameshia-cross-to-anchor-new-commentary-segment-cross-point-300782875.html

Statement of Commissioner Michael J. Copps Dissenting in Part and Approving in Part, in the Matter of: Various Applications for Assignment of License and Transfer of Control of Certain Television Licenses to Sinclair Broadcast Group, Inc. and Glencairn, Ltd. (2001). https://transition.fcc.gov/Speeches/Copps/Statements/2001/stmjc133.html

Strömbäck, J., Djerf-Pierre, M., & Shehata, A. (2013). The dynamics of political interest and news media consumption: A longitudinal perspective. *International Journal of Public Opinion Research, 25*(4), 414–435. http://proxy-remote.galib.uga.edu/login?url=http://search.ebscohost.com/login.aspx?direct=true&db=fsr&AN=92875558&site=eds-live

Telecommunications Act of 1996. https://www.fcc.gov/general/telecommunications-act-1996

Vogel, P. (2019, December 13). *Sinclair's right-wing propaganda will outlast Boris Epshteyn.* Media Matters for America.https://www.mediamatters.org/boris-epshteyn/sinclairs-right-wing-propaganda-will-outlast-boris-epshteyn

Zurawik, D. (2018, December 14). Sinclair 2018: Even having a friend in the Oval Office couldn't save this troubled year. https://www.baltimoresun.com/opinion/columnists/zurawik/bs-fe-zontv-sinclair-bad-year-20181211-story.html

Endnotes

1 A must-run segment is any segment the parent company, in this case Sinclair Broadcasting, requires each of its local stations to air. The segments are produced nationally but run on the local news stations.

2 Epshteyn's YouTube channel can be found at https://www.youtube.com/channel/UCmu23xO_RNF6Q1EPnDoC32A> Since Sinclair's decision in December 2019 to discontinue Bottom Line with Boris, all content from the Bottom Line with Boris YouTube channel has been removed.

3 Designated market area (DMA) is a geographic area that defines television and radio markets in the United States. These market boundaries are used to measure television viewing by Nielsen. There are currently 210 DMAs in the United States. Most DMAs are defined by large metropolitan areas.

4 Per 1991 FCC guidelines, television corporations were permitted to hold no more than 39% ownership of the stations in a single DMA.

5 Local marketing agreements (LMAs), also called joint share agreements, are contracts in which a company agrees to manage the operations of a business owned by a different company.

6 When users select a single "Bottom Line" segment, the segment is followed by a stream of auto-played "Bottom Line With Boris" commentaries. Selecting single "Cross Point" segments *also* produces a stream of "Bottom Line With Boris" commentaries.

CODA

BRIGETTE HERRON, *University of Georgia*
KATHLEEN DEMARRAIS, *University of Georgia*
JANIE COPPLE, *University of Georgia*

> For far too long, generosity has been allowed to serve as a wingman of injustice; giving back disguises merciless taking; making a difference becomes inseparable from making a killing—sometimes literally. It is high time to reject these alibis for treachery. (Giridharadas, 2019, para 19)

For many years in the United States, conservative philanthropies and organizations have proven relentless in their support for free-market capitalism and corporate profit by any means necessary. As discussed in Chapter One of this volume, tax money that should support the public good is lost to Big Philanthropy. Because of U.S. tax rules and the strategic use of donor-advised funds allowing foundations to increase the flexibility and impact of their giving as well as remain anonymous, these foundations have the means, the tax shelters, the political support, and the public relations/image management strategies to outcompete any individual. Known as philanthrocapitalism, this form of giving has impacted all areas of American life thus undermining the public institutions of a healthy, functioning democratic society.

The enduring conservative philanthropic and organizational strategy discussed in this book, joined along the way by neoliberal and corporate interests, is still having a profound impact on human lives around the world. In the era of the Trump administration, we have seen this conservative ideology in the form of tax cuts for the wealthiest Americans and corporations despite persisting U.S. debt in the trillions. This long-standing conservative movement in the

United States, as laid out in the Powell Memorandum (discussed in Chapter Two) and enacted by organizations such as the Federalist Society and the Institute for Justice (Chapter Three), has enabled wealthy conservative philanthropists to get wealthier and shelter their wealth as a result of massive tax breaks. Although wealthy philanthropists use tax shelters and are perceived to serve the public good through giving, in fact, this system allows them to maintain a benevolent public image while setting national agendas that affect the public with no federal oversight. Over the past decades, these conservative strategies have created systems of privatization and the perception that public institutions are not working, thus altering the landscape of education in the United States, from K–12 schooling, colleges and universities, and campus organizations to community education through local news.

Conservative philanthropists have choices and access that extend far beyond what is afforded to the average American. With unlimited resources to support causes most important to them, they siphon benefits from the public good to serve the bottom lines of their associated businesses and corporations. They fund politicians who will continue to support the conservative party line. In some cases, non-anonymous giving by donors can assist with improving their public image through a process of "reputation laundering" (Scutari, 2020, para 17). In this book, we explored the impact of these unrestricted activities of conservative philanthropies and organizations on multiple aspects of public life and policy in the United States.

As we began writing the coda for this volume in the early spring of 2020, our worlds came to a halt with a global pandemic, the spread of the novel coronavirus (COVID-19). Early in the crisis, when preventative steps were crucial to prevent the spread of the virus, the Trump administration dismissed the severity of the situation, despite dire warnings from the World Health Organization and the Centers for Disease Control and Prevention. The stock market plummeted to record lows not seen since the Great Depression, and this market instability caught the attention of the Trump administration to take the global pandemic seriously, but the damage was already done. In the aftermath of a slow response to curb the spread of the outbreak, we noticed how drastically our current political system, informed by conservative strategy and neoliberal sensibilities, had failed us as a society. The virus brought the implications of a long history of conservative strategy to light for U.S. educational policy and practice. As was true before the global pandemic, the wealthy seemed protected while the most vulnerable were left to fend for themselves. Economic relief was first proposed for corporations in the airline and cruise industries. Eventually support was suggested in the form of a stimulus for all Americans, but it would also likely include massive tax relief for large corporations. As we write this, the situation is still unfolding.

With "shelter in place" advisements sweeping the country, schools, businesses, colleges, and universities shut their doors. Those who were lucky went online, and many parents of K–12 children became responsible for facilitating their children's new online education overnight. It remains to be seen whether this massive shift in responsibility for education delivery will garner support for the vital work that public schools and their teachers have been performing (and for providing a steady source of nutrition for children in addition to education). However, it is just as likely the crisis will be co-opted by disaster capitalists as a new model of educational freedom, as seen in the Chapters Four and Six of this volume in the cases of the DeVos family's interventions in education policy and the top-down reforms disguised as grassroots initiatives in New Orleans' K–12 schools, respectively. Because we know our history, we should be prepared for what might come next.

As the health crisis has ramped up in the United States in recent days, we have seen the limits of our for-profit health care system. Limited intensive care unit beds, insufficient numbers of respiratory masks, and inadequate testing measures are the result of a system of privatization that has consistently taken money from the public good and used it to help corporations profit. The movement toward privatization, which has been a key goal for conservative philanthropies and organizations and backed by corporate greed, takes away resources from hospitals and schools. The dangers of privatization allow the interest of an elite few to promote and spread their vision of how the world should be without democratic oversight and taking advantage of vulnerable members of society (seen in this volume through the cases of Catholic school funding, the Walton Family Foundation's impacts on colleges and universities, and conservative philanthropies influence over historically Black colleges and universities). The situation was made all the worse by the spread of politicized misinformation, utilizing the same networks of conservative influence that have been described in Chapters Nine and Ten (from radical-right campus organizations to for-profit news networks such as Sinclair).

With all the shortcomings of a philanthrocapitalism magnified during this time of crisis, many are wondering where to go from here. First, it is important to pay attention to the history of this strategic network of conservative philanthropy and organizations and closely monitor how they might utilize the vulnerabilities Americans are facing as a way to profit and further undermine democracy. By working to understand their long-term strategy and complicated networks, educators and concerned citizens will be prepared to recognize deceptive language and resist the onset of opportunistic disaster capitalists (see Klein, 2007). Second, we agree with Saez and Zucman (2019) that a vast overhaul of the tax codes is needed in order to stop the accumulation of wealth through tax havens and loopholes. Even if the United States was not in its current economic downturn, the ability of corporations and big business to benefit from tax relief and avoid paying their fair share is unconscionable. Third, we have to fight for nonprofit, publicly funded news sources and truly nonpartisan journalism to provide accurate information and promote the well-informed citizenry that is essential to democracy. To accomplish this, we must fight against media that promotes misinformation or, as in the case of the Sinclair Broadcast Group (Chapter Ten), masquerades as local news. Finally, we have to exercise our civic duties to vote against candidates who support the interests of big corporations and tax cuts for Big Philanthropy. This includes paying attention to how the courts are staffed with judges and working to finally overturn Citizen's United and a conservative activist court (see, e.g., Lithwick, 2020). It is up to each of us, individually and collectively, to remain well informed; participate in healthy, respectful dialogue; work to push reforms to benefit public institutions and the public good while limiting tax benefits for the rich; and, quite simply, to vote for candidates who are able to push these democratic reforms.

References

Giridharadas, A. (2019, May 16). When your money is so tainted museums don't want it: Nonprofits should not allow themselves to be used by the wealthy to scrub their consciences (Opinion). *The New York Times*. https://nytimes.com/2019/05/16/opinion/sunday/met-sackler.html

Klein, N. (2007). *The shock doctrine: The rise of disaster capitalism*. Picador.

Lithwick, D. (2020, March 13). Former judge resigns from the Supreme Court Bar. *Slate*. https://slate.com/news-and-politics/2020/03/judge-james-dannenberg-supreme-court-bar-roberts-letter.html

Scutari, M. (2020, April 22). A spectrum of excuses: Eleven reasons why organizations don't return toxic donations. *Inside Philanthropy*. Retrieved from https://www.insidephilanthropy.com/home/2020/4/22/a-spectrum-of-excuses-eleven-reasons-why-organizations-dont-return-toxic-donations

Saez, E., & Zucman, G. (2019). *The triumph of injustice: How the rich dodge taxes and how to make them pay*. W. W. Norton.

AUTHOR BIOGRAPHIES

JAMIE C. ATKINSON is an assistant professor in the Department of Reading, Foundation and Technology at Missouri State University, where he also serves as the program coordinator for the Masters of Arts in Teaching Program. Jamie's research focuses on how sociopolitical dynamics and ideologies combine to drive state-level educational policy making. This work includes examining the rapid rise of neotribalism and how political ideologues utilize education policy and curriculum as a tool to divide. An additional aspect of his work focuses on the use of critical self-analysis and personal narratives—critical autoethnographic approaches—to develop future educators' philosophical understandings. More generally, Jamie examines sociopolitical, historic, and philosophical foundations contributing to critical democratic understandings in teacher education. His teaching experience spans middle and high school, undergraduate, and graduate levels. Jamie's most recent journal article has been published in *Democracy and Education.*

T. JAMESON BREWER is an Assistant Professor of Social Foundations of Education at the University of North Georgia. His teaching experience spans from the middle school, high school, undergraduate, masters, and doctoral levels. Broadly conceptualized, his research focuses on the impact of privatization and marketization of public education by way of school vouchers, charter schools, alternative teacher certification, and homeschooling. His scholarly work has been published in the peer-reviewed journals, *Education Policy Analysis Archives, Educational Studies, Critical Education*, the *Peabody Journal of Education*, *Critical Questions in Education*, the *International Journal of Play, Urban Education*, and *Policy Futures in Education*. His work has also appeared at the National Education Policy Center, the *Progressive Magazine*, the *Huffington Post*, the *Washington Post*, and *Education Week*. Follow him on Twitter: @tjamesonbrewer or read more at: www.tjamesonbrewer.com

KRISTEN BURAS is an associate professor in the Department of Educational Policy Studies at Georgia State University. She is the author of *Charter Schools, Race, and Urban Space: Where the Market Meets Grassroots Resistance,* which chronicles a decade of education reform in New Orleans. Buras is co-author of *Pedagogy, Policy, and the Privatized City: Stories of Dispossession and Defiance from New Orleans.* She has worked extensively with communities in New Orleans and is contacted regularly by school board members, teachers, parent groups, and journalists for her expertise on the "New Orleans model" of education reform and its effects on local communities. She is founder and director of the New Orleans–based Urban South Grassroots Research Collective for Public Education and was granted the Distinguished Scholar-Activist Award by Critical Educators for Social Justice of the American Educational Research Association.

KEVIN J. BURKE is an associate professor in the Department of Language and Literacy Education at the University of Georgia. His work in teacher education sits at the intersections of religion, curriculum, and queer theory. He is particularly interested in the ways in which religion exists and persists in public education in the United States, critically examining Catholic schooling and reconsidering theology as a language and structure to think differently in the social sciences. His most recent book, co-edited with Mary Juzwik, Jen Stone, and Denise Davila, is titled *Legacies of Christian Languaging and Literacies in American Education: Perspectives on English Language Arts Curriculum, Teaching, and Learning* (Routledge, 2019) and examines a range of Christian literacies underlying the schooled experience in U.S. public education. He is series editor of *Critical Perspectives on Religion and Education* with Myers Education Press.

JANIE COPPLE is a PhD student in the Qualitative Research and Evaluation Methodologies program at the University of Georgia. Prior to PhD studies, Janie worked as a middle grades classroom teacher and curriculum coordinator. She is a recipient of the University of North Carolina at Greensboro's Inspirational Educators Award and the University of Georgia's College of Education Research Scholar's Award. Janie's research interests include the role of philanthropy in secondary and higher education, as well as adolescent and family experiences with puberty and sexuality. Janie's current publications can be found in *Qualitative Inquiry, The Qualitative Report,* and *African Studies Quarterly.*

KATHLEEN DEMARRAIS is a professor in the Department of Lifelong Education, Administration, and Policy at the University of Georgia (UGA). With a background in sociology and anthropology of education, she serves as a qualitative methodologist in UGA's Qualitative Research Program. She has a long history of teaching qualitative research methods and mentoring doctoral students. Her research focuses on qualitative methodologies, critical qualitative research, qualitative pedagogy, and the teaching of qualitative research methodologies. A key research strand includes the history and funding of conservative philanthropists in the United States and their impact on educational policy and practice. In addition to numerous article and book chapters, her books include *Foundations for Research: Methods of Inquiry in Education and the Social Sciences* (with S. Laplan); *Inside Stories, Educating Young Adolescent Girls (*with P. O'Reilly, & B. Penn); *The Way Schools Work: A Sociological Analysis of Schooling* (with M. LeCompte); *Life at the Margins: Profiles of Diverse Adults* (with J. Merrifield, D. Hemphill, &B. Bingman); *Teach for America Counter Narratives: Alumni Speak Up and Speak Out* (with T. J. Brewer); and *Philanthropy, Hidden Strategy and Collective Resistance: A Primer for Concerned Educators* (with T. J. Brewer, B. A. Herron, J. C. Atkinson, J. B. Lewis, and J. Dayton). She was honored by her undergraduate alma mater, East Stroudsburg University, with the 2017 Excellence in Education Award for demonstrated superior teaching ability and extraordinary commitment to students at the elementary, secondary, or college level.

BRIAN W. DOTTS is a professor of educational foundations in the College of Education, University of Georgia. Brian's research focuses on this history of American education, civic virtue, philosophy of education, multiculturalism, constitutional law, education policy, and the privatization of public schooling. Brian is a member of the University's Graduate Faculty and Honors Program. Brian is author of *Educational Foundations: Philosophical and Historical Perspectives*, published by Cambridge University Press in 2018. He is co-editor of and contributor to *The Elusive Thomas Jefferson: The Man Behind the Myths*, published by McFarland in 2017, and he is author of *The Political Education of Democratus: Negotiating Civic Virtue During the New Republic*, published by Lexington Books in 2012. His current book project focuses on the development of social and legal constructs in a pluralistic society. Brian has published in the following academic journals: *Educational Studies*, the *Journal of Educational Foundations, Education & Culture, Multicultural Education, Democracy and Education*, and the *Journal of Philosophy and History of Education.* Brian serves as an editorial board member for the *Journal of*

Educational Foundations and as a faculty editorial board member for the *Education Law & Policy Review.*

BRIGETTE HERRON holds a PhD in adult education from the Department of Lifelong Education, Administration, and Policy at the University of Georgia. She is from Athens, Georgia, and holds graduate certificates in women's studies, interdisciplinary qualitative studies, and global health. Her scholarly research interests include transnational and justice-oriented feminist pedagogy in adult and higher education, examining the influence of philanthropy and dark money on curriculum and pedagogy in higher education, and teaching and researching with qualitative research methodology. Recent books include *Philanthropy, Hidden Strategy, and Collective Resistance: A Primer for Concerned Educators* (with K. deMarrais, T. J. Brewer, J. Atkinson, & J. Lewis) and *Neon Side of Town: The Story of the B-52s* (with S. Creney).

JAMIE B. LEWIS is an associate professor at Georgia Gwinnett College and Chair of Studies for Educational Foundations. She received her Ph.D. in Social Foundations of Education from the University of Georgia. She completed both a J.D. and M.A in Urban Multicultural Education from the University of Tennessee and a B.A. in Political Science from Hollins University. Her scholarly work has been published in the peer-reviewed journals of *Educational Studies, Critical Education*, the *International Journal of Qualitative Studies in Education*, and *Qualitative Inquiry.* She is a co-author of *Philanthropy, hidden strategy, and collective resistance: A primer for concerned educators.* Her areas of interest are the legal history of school desegregation, the intersections of life histories and genealogical research, and the history of Native American education. In addition, her research explores issues related to the sociocultural and political contexts of education with regard to the current legal terrain of accountability and the privatization of schooling in the United States.

E. ANTHONY MUHAMMAD is an Assistant Professor of Educational Research at Georgia Southern University. He earned his doctorate in Qualitative Research Methodologies from the University of Georgia. As a critical qualitative methodologist, his research combines qualitative methodologies and critical frameworks in an effort to educate, emancipate, and transform. His research interests include the phenomenology of the black lived experience, philosophical hermeneutics, and the intersection of racial and religious alterity. E. Anthony holds a bachelor's degree in Psychology from Southern University and A&M College and a master's degree in industrial organizational psychology from the University of Baltimore.

AMY E. SWAIN is a teaching assistant professor in the Department of Special Education, Foundations and Research at East Carolina University, where she teaches courses in the social foundations, diversity and social justice, and international comparative education. She has worked in and with public schools for the last sixteen years and has taught at every level of education from elementary school to university. Her research focuses on social and racial justice in education, the punitive nature of schools, and most recently, rural education. Her work has been published in *Educational Studies*, *Qualitative Inquiry* and *The Urban Review*.

INDEX

1%, the, 2-3, 13-14
501(c) (3), 5-7, 13-14, 83, 210
501(c) (4), 5-7
527(f), 7
990s (990 tax filings), 7-8, 64, 77, 153, 159, 160, 174
1895 Bakeshop Act (NY), 48

A
A Nation At Risk, 29, 87, 94
accumulation by dispossession, 34, 124, 146
Act 35, 123, 126
Alabama A&M University, 197
Alexander, Lamar, Senator, 131
Alliance Defending Freedom, 84-85, 92-95
Alliance for Catholic Education (ACE), 104-106, 111, 114
Alliance for School Choice, 62, 80, 83, 168
alliances, 121, 146, 231
alt-right, 57
American Enterprise Institute for Public Policy Research (American Enterprise Institute), 28, 55, 63, 81-82, 85, 108, 113, 132
American Indian Movement (AIM), 25
American Legislative Exchange Council (ALEC), 28-29, 66, 73, 83
American political process, 155
American politics, 40, 68Alt-Right, 57
Anderson v. Town of Durham, 68, 70
Argentina, 177
Arizona, 59, 61, 62, 63, 68, 99, 110, 158, 162, 172-173
Arizona Christian School Tuition Organization v. Winn, 59, 68, 70
Arkansas, 153, 160, 163, 167, 172, 173, 174, 175, 176
    Bentonville, Arkansas,166
    Siloam Springs, Arkansas, 175
Arkansas Teacher Corp Art Fellows Program, 175
Armstrong, Samuel Chapman, 191
Arnold Foundation, 120, 123, 134, 141
art education, 153-154, 160, 166, 167, 168
art museums, 153, 160, 166-168
Asociación de Maestros v. Departamento de Educación, 67-68, 70
Aspen Institute, 108, 111, 123, 129, 150
astroturfing, 121
Atlanta, 123, 145, 147, 196, 200, 219
Austrian economists, 21

B
Bagley v. Town of Raymond, 68, 70
Baldwin, William, 192
Ballmer Foundation, 120
Bannon, Steve, 57, 217
Barr, William, 41-42, 75
Betsy DeVos, xiv, 18, 62, 79, 80, 82-87, 89, 91-95, 103, 197-198, 245
big philanthropy, 1-2, 177, 259, 262
    role of, 4
    donor-advised funds, 11
    Philanthropy Roundtable, 187
Bill and Melinda Gates Foundation (See also Gates, Bill and Melinda), 61
black education, 122, 152
Black Leadership Summit, 185
black middle class, 127
Blaine Amendments, 61-62, 73-74
Blanco, Kathleen, Governor, 126-127, 150
Bloom, Allan, 45
Bloomberg, Michael, 6
Board of Elementary and Secondary Education, in Louisiana, 123, 127
bold plan, 120-121, 136, 151
Bolick, Clint, 58, 61-63, 70
Bolling, Eric,
    America This Week, 253
    Wake Up, America, 253
bottom-up initiatives, 119-120
Breitbart News, 57
Bring New Orleans Back Commission, 127, 147
Broad (see Broad Foundation)
Broad Foundation, the (see also Broad), 1, 123, 129, 156, 158, 169-170
Brown, John III, 173, 175
Brown v. Board of Education, 80, 93
Buckley, William F. Jr., 86
Buffet, Warren, 6

Bullock, Scott, 63
Burger Court, the, 51, 68
Burwell v. Hobby Lobby Stores, 49, 71
Bush v. Holmes, 68, 71
Bush, George W., 43, 63, 108, 123, 125, 148

C
Cain v. Horne, 68, 71
Calabresi, Steven, 44, 54
California, 63, 166, 168, 172, 173, 176-177
Callahan, David, 2, 155-157, 159-160, 166-167, 169, 171, 172, 174, 177
 The Givers, 155, 169
 Inside Philanthropy, 169, 174
Canada, 162, 177
Capitalism, 173, 188, 205, 208, 210-212, 215-216, 233, 239, 242-244, 252, 259
Carson v. Makin, 77
Catholic Education(al) (Catholic Schooling), xiv, 97-98, 101-103, 105, 109-110, 116-117
Catholic Schools, xv, 97, 99-105, 109-113, 116
Cato Institute, 49, 55, 59, 63-64, 73
CEE-Trust (see also Cities for Education Entrepreneurship), 121, 123, 137-139, 149
Center for Academic Freedom, 85, 92
Center for Disease Control and Prevention (CDC), 260
Chan, Priscilla, 6
charitable organizations, 1-2, 6, 8, 14, 85
Charles Koch Foundation, 81, 171, 197, 217
charter schools, xv, 18, 22, 30-31, 33-34, 61, 79, 85-88, 100, 106, 108, 114, 119-137, 139-151, 153, 156-158, 160, 168-170, 178-183, 245
 "build the right conditions for", 146
 "done *to* rather than *with* communities", 139
 giving a "community" face to, 145
 "impression of imposition", 140
 leaders of Color for, 140
 leaked presentation on expansion in New Orleans, 144, 147
  incredible gains" of, 132, 134
  actors, local, state and federal, 121
  advocacy, 109, 119, 121, 123, 142, 156, 168, 182
  civil rights complaints and lawsuits, 135
  community input, lack of, 123, 127, 146
  dismal performance of, 134-135
  expansion, xv, 139, 141, 143, 145-146
  governance of, 130, 135
  grassroots resistance to, 145, 148
  investing in, 134, 140, 152
  organized by "outsiders", 138
  white exploitation and profit, 125, 143
Cheyney University, 189
Chicago, 44, 59, 60, 99, 100, 108, 157, 188
chief executive officer (CEO), 10, 45, 79, 119, 120, 123, 169
Children First America, 79
Chile, 20
Chittenden Town School District v. Dept. of Educ., 68, 71
Choice Regulation Watch, 171
Cities for Education Entrepreneurship (see also CEE-Trust), 121, 123, 137-139, 149
Citizens for Strong Schools, Inc. v. Florida State Board of Education, 68, 71
Citizens United, 29-30, 50-51, 69
Citizens United v. Federal Election Commission, 29-30, 33, 50-51, 69, 71, 77
City Education Partners, 145
City Fund, xv, 119-123, 125, 134-136, 138, 140-147, 150, 152
Clark Atlanta University, 196
Clinic on Entrepreneurship, 59-60, 75
Clinton, Hillary, 57
collective bargaining, 124, 127
Colorado, 68, 158, 164-166, 169, 172-173
 Denver, Colorado, 164
 Colorado River, the 164-166
  Colorado River Trust, 164
  Conservation Colorado, 164
  Denver Water, 164
  Gross Dam, 164
  Trout Unlimited, 164

common law of agency, 49-50
communism, 205-206, 246
communist, 25, 27, 186, 188, 205-206
communities of color, 122, 143
community-based groups, 121
community engagement, 121-123, 132-133, 137, 139-143, 145-146
community engagement partners, 142
Congress, 23, 39, 53, 67, 75-76, 91, 93-95, 125, 170, 194, 201, 213, 237, 240, 246-247, 250
Congressional Black Caucus, 170
consent, generation of, 122, 147
Conservation International, 162, 163
conservative ideology and strategy, 121
conservative, xiv-xvi, 18-19, 20, 24, 32, 40-43, 44, 51-57, 59, 61, 64, 69, 81-83, 84, 86, 89, 91, 99, 101, 103, 105-106, 108-110, 111, 120-121, 145, 155, 171, 185-186, 187, 188, 189-194
conservative movement, United States, 25, 30, 53, 203, 259
    Powell Memorandum, 259-260
conservative philanthropies and organizations, 260-262
conservatism, 17, 20, 23, 52, 189, 203, 208
Constitution, U.S., xiv, 40, 46, 49, 51-53, 63, 66, 69, 75
Coronavirus (COVID-19), 260-261
corporate personhood, 50
coup d'état of public schools, 120
Cowen Institute for Public Education, 123, 128
Cowen, Scott, 128
Cross, Ameshia
    Cross Point With Ameshia Cross 248-252
Cristo Rey, 100
Crow, Michael M., 174
Crystal Bridges Museum of American Art, 166, 167
Cunningham Communications (see also Glencairn, Ltd), 235-236, 237

D

David and Lucile Packard Foundation, 177
DeBoom v. Bergeson, 68, 71
Dell Foundation, 120
Democrats, 17, 19, 229, 239-240, 244
Denver, 123, 141, 145, 147, 164, 230
Department of Education, xiv, 68, 88, 94, 106-107, 127, 152, 194
    Louisiana, 127
    Michigan, 88
    United States, xiv, 68, 94, 152, 194
designated market areas (DMAs), 258
DeVos, Betsy, xiv, 18, 62, 79-80, 82-83, 85-87, 89, 91-95, 103, 197-198, 245, 261
Dewey, John, 33, 46
Dick and Betsy DeVos Foundation (Dick and Betsy DeVos Family Foundation), 81-83, 85-86, 93, 197-198
disaster capitalism (see also: *The Shock Doctrine),* 262
donor-advised funds (DAF), 1, 5, 8-11, 13-15, 155, 259
Donors Capital Fund, 57, 64, 77
Donors Trust, the, 57, 64, 77
Du Bois, W.E.B., 190, 192
Duncan v. State of New Hampshire, 68, 71
Dunn, William, 64, 217
dynastic wealth (family dynasties), 2, 155, 160, 177

E

EdChoice, 55, 109, 112
Edgar and Elsa Prince Foundation, 83, 85
Education Cities, xv, 121, 123, 139-142, 149
education entrepreneurs, 124-125, 128, 136, 169
Education Freedom Fund, 83, 85, 88, 94
Education Freedom Scholarships and Opportunity Act, 89-90
Education Reform Council, 79
educational freedom, 89, 92
educational policy, xv, xvi, 17-18, 20, 28-30, 32, 79-81, 87, 103-106, 109-110, 117, 261
education savings accounts, 61, 68, 90, 245
Edwards v. District of Columbia, 60, 71
Empower Illinois, 109, 112
Engel v. Vitale, 66, 71
environment, xv, 31, 55, 67, 153, 159, 161-166
    sustainability, xv, 158, 162-164, 174-175
Environmental Defense Fund, 162, 163, 164
Epshteyn, Boris, 226, 232-233, 238-248, 249-250, 252-253, 258
    Bottom Line with Boris, 226-227, 232, 238-252

Espinoza v. Montana Department of Revenue, 68, 77
ethical dilemmas,
quid pro quo, 164
executive orders, 123, 127, 150

F
faculty division, 41
fascism, 20, 207
family dynasties, 2, 155
Federal Communications Commission (FCC), 234, 238, 258
federal courts, xiv, 53, 67, 73
federal tax credit programs, 88-90
federalism, 42-43, 70
Federalist Society, xiv, 39-45, 47-48, 50-57, 62-64, 66-77, 85, 260
Federalist Society for Law and Public Policy Studies, 44
Article I Initiative, 53
Feinberg, Mike, 128
Fenty, Adrian, 157
Fidelity Charitable, 10, 14, 64
First Amendment, 35, 51, 75, 204, 220, 223
Fisher Foundation, 129
Florida A&M University, 197
Florida ex rel. Attorney General v. US Dept. of Health and Human Services, 60, 71
Florida Tax Credit (FTC) Scholarship Program, 83-84
Foundation Directory Online (FDO), 7, 55-56, 64, 159
Fox News, 203, 208-209, 217, 248, 253
free enterprise, 19, 24, 26-28, 44, 80-81, 83, 90, 186, 212
freedom, 25, 28, 40, 49, 51-52, 55, 59-63, 76-77, 79-81, 83-85, 88-90, 92, 116, 179, 185, 196, 204-207, 210, 220-221, 226, 244, 261
Freedom Restoration Act of 1993, 49, 75
Friedman, Milton, 76, 90, 94, 114

G
Gaddy v. Ga. Dep't of Revenue, 68, 72
Garriott v. Winn, 68, 72
Gates, Bill and Melinda (see also Bill and Melinda Gates Foundation), 1, 6, 61, 120, 123, 129, 140
Gates Foundation, the, 61, 120, 123, 129, 140, 156
George Mason University, 196
Germany, 21
Giacomucci v. Southeast Delco School District, 68, 72
Glencairn, Ltd (see also Cunningham Communications), 235-236
Global Governance Watch, 53
ideological inconsistencies, 45
Goldman Sachs, 169
Goldwater Institute, 55, 61, 63, 70, 72
Gorka, Sebastian, 253
Guide for Cities, 119, 122-123, 131-132, 136-137, 147-148, 150
Gulf Opportunity Zone, 123, 125
gun control, 211, 249
(see also New Zealand; Christchurch shooting)
grassroots efforts, 119, 133
Gray, Ethan, 123, 138-139, 141, 149
Great Depression, the, 47, 260
Great Lakes Education Project, 80
green philanthropies, 153, 163
greenwash, 164
Grutter v. Bollinger, 59, 72

H
Habitat for Humanity, 6
Hall, Kevin, 169
Hampton model (Hampton Idea), 191
Hampton-Tuskegee Idea, 193
Hampton University, 191, 198
harbor master, 129
Harris, David, 123, 125, 136-137, 139, 141, 146, 151
Harrison v. University of Washington, 27, 68, 72
Hart v. State, 72
Harvard University, 172, 196
Harvard Journal of Law & Public Policy, 54, 61, 70, 75
Harvey, David, 20-21, 34, 124, 150
Hastings Fund, 120, 123, 134, 141
hegemony, 145, 147-148, 208
Heisman, Eileen, 10
Heritage Foundation, 28, 55, 63, 80-81, 85, 89-90, 108, 120, 123, 125, 148, 151, 217
Hewlett-Packard, 177
higher education, 1, 31, 97, 153, 154-156, 158-163, 166-167, 170-176, 178-182, 188, 190, 193, 208-210, 221-223, 244

Colleges and Universities, 153-154, 166-167, 170, 171-172, 178-179,
Arizona State University, 162-163, 174-175
Global Institute of Sustainability, 158, 162
Global Sustainability Studies Program, 174
Executive Master of Sustainability Leadership, 174
Arkansas, University of, 108
College of Education and Health Professions, 170-171, 176
Department of Education Reform (EDRE), 108, 171
School of Art, 160, 167-168
Bank Street College of Education, 170
Cheyney University, 189
Clark Atlanta University, 196
Colorado College, 158, 172, 180
Colorado State, 166
Colorado University Boulder Law School, 166
Columbia Law School, 162
Florida A&M University, 197
George Mason University, 196
Georgetown University, 168, 172
Hampton University, 191, 198
Harding University, 173
Harvard University, 172, 196
Harvard Business School, 169
John Brown University, 173, 175
Lincoln University, 189
Marian University, 170
Mississippi Valley State University, 197
Morehouse College, 196-197
New York University, 170
North Carolina Central University, 198
Notre Dame, the University of, 63, 104-107, 109-110, 117, 172
Ozarks, University of the, 173
Santa Barbara, University of California, 166
Stanford University, 166, 173
Tuskegee University, 191-192
Wilberforce University, 189
Wiley College, 197-198
Wooster, College of, 161
Xavier University of Louisiana, 197
doctoral fellowships, 158
Historically Black Colleges and Universities (HBCUs), xv-xvi, 186, 188-191, 193-199
bootstrapping, 189
cultural traditions, 189
discrepancy in funding of, 195-196
educational models, 190-193
purpose, 189
Republican funding of, 195-198
respectability politics, 189, 198-199
state of financial affairs, 195, 196
Holmes, Oliver Wendell, Jr., 68-69, 71, 76, 151
home region, 153
Hoover Institution, 55, 61, 81
Horowitz, Michael, 53, 86,
Horowitz Report, the, 53
human capital, 120, 128, 130, 132, 134, 143
Hurricane Katrina, 120, 123, 125, 152
Hutcheson, Dorthea, 161, 175

I

I3, Investing in Innovation, 123, 129
Ideas Have Consequences (book by Richard Weaver), 45, 56, 75
impact investing, 165
incubation, of charter schools, 128, 130, 137, 144, 149
Indiana, 44, 68, 105, 108, 121, 123, 136, 138, 140-142, 173

Indianapolis, 113, 120-121, 123, 136, 128, 140-142, 145, 151
individualism, 17, 19, 28, 245
indoctrination, 188, 211-212, 214
industrial philanthropy, 190, 191, 193, 195
industrial training, 190
Institute for Educational Initiatives, 104
Institute for Justice, xiv, 39-40, 55, 58-63, 67, 70, 72-73, 75, 260
Center for Judicial Engagement, 59-60, 72
Internal Revenue Service (IRS), 1, 5-7, 10, 12-14, 64, 77
Isaacson, Walter, 127, 129, 150

J

Jacobs, Leslie, 124
John William Pope Foundation, the, 197-198
"judges project", 41
jurisprudence, 39-40, 42-44, 47-49, 51-52, 58, 67

K

k-12 privatization movement, 153, 156, 157-158,
charter school, xv, 18, 22, 30-31, 33-34, 61, 79, 85-88, 100, 106, 108, 114, 119-137, 139-151, 153, 156-158, 160, 168-170, 178-183, 245
charter school management organizations, 130, 132, 137-138, 144
Chancellor Beacon Academies, 169
advocacy groups,
Alliance for School Choice, 168
Charter School Growth Fund (aka the Charter Fund), 168-171
California Charter Schools Association, 168
Education Cities, xv, 121, 123, 139-142, 149
Knowledge Is Power Program Foundation (KIPP), 104-105, 117, 128, 168
high-stakes accountability, 153, 157
school voucher programs, 30, 61, 63, 67-68, 79, 87, 89-90, 94, 100, 105, 107, 168, 170-171, 245
Kavanaugh, Brett, 54, 72, 74
Kerry, John, 237-238
Keyser Investment Group, 236
Khan Academy, 61
Kingsland, Neerav, 119-121, 123, 132-134, 137-139, 141-142, 144-145, 147, 150
Kirk, Charlie, 213
Knowledge Is Power Program (KIPP), 104-105, 117, 128, 168
Koch family, the (Kochs), xv, 1, 28, 55, 57-58, 81, 105, 155, 160, 171, 177, 196-200, 202
Koch brothers, Charles and David, 1, 28, 55, 57, 58, 81, 155, 160, 171, 177, 196, 197, 198, 203
Koch money, 199
Kopp, Wendy, 111, 117, 128

L

laissez-faire free-speech principles, 50
Landrieu, Mary, Senator, 131-132, 150
language of choice, 125, 143
Lawyers Division, 41
Legacy Foundation Fund (aka Resource Legacy Fund), 177
Leo, Leonard, 41, 56, 71, 74
Levy, Robert, 59, 63, 73
The Dirty Dozen: How Twelve Supreme Court Cases Radically Expanded Government and Eroded Freedom, 59, 73
libertarianism, 44, 47-48, 52, 56, 59-60
liberty of contract, 48-49, 77
Lincoln University, 189
Livingston, Scott, 238
local actors, 121, 125
local marketing agreements (LMAs), 235, 258
local news vs entertainment, 228-230, 253
Lochner v. New York, 45, 47-48, 73
logical realism, 46
Los Angeles, 63, 170
Louisiana Federation of Teachers v. State, 68, 73, 126-127, 150, 152
Louisiana Federation of Teachers, 68, 73, 126-127, 150, 152
Lynde and Harry Bradley Foundation, 55, 57, 197-198

M

Magee v. Boyd, 68, 73
Magerman, David, 58
Manhattan Institute, 55, 63, 107-108, 112
Mann, Horace, 80-81
Massachusetts, 172, 173
McConnell v. Federal Election Commission, 59, 73

McConnell, Mitch, 41-42
McIntosh, David, 44, 71
media consolidation, 226-231
Media Matters, 252
  Pam Vogel, 252-253
Mellor, William (Chip), 58-59, 63, 72-73
Mercer Family, the, 72, 55, 57-58
  Rebekah, 57
  Robert, 57-58
Meredith v. Pence, 68, 73
metaphysical certitude, 46
Mexico, 162, 177, 242
  environmentalism, 162, 177
  immigration, 242
  US-Mexico border, 242
Mind Trust, xv, 120-123, 135-137, 141-142, 144-146, 151
missionary philanthropy, 190-191, 193
Mississippi Valley State University, 197
Morehouse College, 196-197
Morency et al v. State of Nevada, 77
Mueller, Robert, 239-240
  investigation, 239-240
must-run segments, 226-227, 236-238, 247, 250, 251-252, 258

N
Nagin, Ray, Mayor, 127
Nashville, 123, 145, 147
National Black College Week, 194
National Catholic Educational Association, 101
National Federation of Independent Business v. Sebelius, 43, 55, 60, 69, 74
National Philanthropic Trust, 8-10, 14, 55
National Rifle Association (NRA), 217
National Wildlife Federation, 162
Nativity Prep, 100
natural gas and fracking industry, 164
Nature Conservancy, 163, 164
  Little Rock, AK, 162
  Arlington, VA, 162
negro (Black) philanthropy, 190
neighborhood public schools, 127, 135, 143
neoconservatism, 19, 20, 23-26, 45
neoliberalism, 19-23, 24, 26
  neoliberal, xiv, 18-19, 22-23, 31-32, 53, 80, 97, 103, 107-108, 110, 188, 248, 251, 261
  neoliberal ideology, 18-20
network analysis, xv, 122
New Deal, the, 40, 46-47, 59, 70, 243, 246
New Jersey, 141, 145
New Jersey's Children's Foundation, 145
New Leaders for New Schools, 123, 128
New Left, the, xiv, 18, 23-25, 27, 29-30, 32, 186,
New Orleans, xv, 119-152, 261
  all-charter-school district, 120, 125, 128
  as national model, 99, 120, 150, 152
  charter school expansion, xv, 139, 141, 143, 145-146
  closure of public schools, 135, 148
  composition of teachers, 127, 129, 130-131, 135
new philanthropic power elite, 2, 155
New Schools for New Orleans, xv, 119-120, 123, 129-131, 136, 147, 149, 151
New Teacher Project, The, 128-130, 151
New Zealand, 249-250
  Christchurch shooting, 249-250
Newark, 123, 145, 147
Newark Charter School Fund, 145
NewSchools Venture Fund, 123, 129, 132
Newsmax, 57
Niehaus v. Huppenthal, 68, 74
Nixon, Richard, 25, 186, 193
No. 86 Project, 54
No Child Left Behind, 87
nonprofit organization(s), 5, 82, 84, 210
non-profit scholarship granting organizations, 89
North Carolina, 26, 68, 176, 198
North Carolina Central University, 198

O
Obama, Barack, 60, 84, 194, 208, 215, 248, 253
  Obamacare, 60-61
Obergefell v. Hodges, 51-52, 71, 74, 77
objectivism, 58
Ocasio-Cortez, Alexandria, 243, 246
  Green New Deal, 243-244, 246
Oliver, John, 237, 248
open meetings law, 124
opportunity trust, 145
Otis, Lee Liberman, 44

P
p-12 (see also: k-12), xvi, 1, 155, 175, 236
  philanthropic investment in, 171, 174, 177
Packard, Lucile and David, 177
parent education, 119, 132-133, 145

Patient Protection and Affordable Care Act of 2010 (Obamacare), 60-61
patriotism, 205-207
Pelosi, Nancy, 240, 242
Pennsylvania, 68, 108, 176, 189
philanthrocapitalism, 4, 13, 15, 259, 262
philanthropic foundations, 1-2, 82, 169
Philanthropy Roundtable, 29, 80, 81, 114, 187
  fifth strategy, 188, 198
Plato, 46
  theory of the forms, 46
political correctness, 208
political epistemic community, 52, 59, 66
Pompeo, Michael, 54
Pope, John William, 197-198
Powell, Lewis F. Jr., xiii, xv, 17-18, 24-30, 32-34, 36, 53, 81-82, 94, 186-188
  The Attack on American Institutions, 28
  The Ideological Assault on America, 28
Powell Memorandum (Powell Memo; Powell Manifesto), xiii, xv, 17-18, 24-30, 32-34, 36, 53, 81-82, 94, 186-188, 199, 260
President Johnson's Great Society initiatives, 25
Prince, Edgar, 79, 83, 85
private foundation(s), xiv, 6, 8, 103
privatization, of schools, xiv, 29, 35, 39, 67, 69, 79, 81, 83, 87, 103, 119, 121, 142, 145-146, 153, 156, 158, 260-261
pro bono project, 54
Proietti, Annie, 169
Professor Watchlist, 218-220
progressivism, 47-48, 51, 59, 70, 80
property taxes, 6
public charity, 6
public good(s), 1-3, 11, 22, 144, 187, 259-261, 263
public relations strategies, 179
Puerto Rico, 67-68, 73-74, 90
  Financial Oversight and Management Board, congressional, 67
  Puerto Rico Oversight, Management, and Economic Stability Act (PROMESA), 67

Q

Quakers, the, 189

R

Race to the Top, 87, 123, 129
radical left, indoctrination, 212
radical right, 111, 155, 203, 262
Rand, Ayn, 58, 64
Reagan administration, 29, 32, 44, 58
Reagan Ranch Center, 86
Reagan, Ronald, 29, 32, 44-45, 58, 64, 86-87, 193-194, 213-214, 216
Recovery School District, 123-124, 148, 151
Red Scare, the 25, 205
Regulatory Transparency Project, 53
Rehnquist Court, 68
Reiss, James, 127
relativism, 46, 76
Republicans, 19, 194-195, 203, 209, 229, 239
resistance, 25, 138, 143, 145-146, 157, 249, 265
Rethink New Orleans, 135, 142, 146, 151
Rhee, Michelle, 108, 157
Richard and Helen DeVos Foundation, 55, 82-85
Richardson v. State, 68, 74
Rob and Melani Walton Foundation, 162-163
Rob and Melani Walton National Teachers' Academy, 174
Rob and Melani Walton Sustainability in Science and Technology Museums Program, 175
Robert Wood Johnson Foundation, 10
Roberts Court, 68
Roe v. Wade, 59, 74
Roosevelt, Franklin Delano, 46, 48
Roosevelt, Theodore, 192
RootEd, 145
Rosen, James 253
Ruddy, Christopher, 57
rugged individualism, 17, 19, 28

S

Salvation Army, 6
San Antonio, 123, 145, 147
Sanders, Bernie, 243
Scaife Family, 53, 55, 81, 155
Scaife Foundation, 53, 55
Scalia, Antonin, 39, 52, 54, 74, 76
school board partners, 142
school choice, xiv-xv, 29, 40, 61-63, 66-69, 71, 73-75, 79-80, 82-83, 87-94, 103-105, 108-109, 112, 114, 143, 158, 168, 171, 245, 254
school performance score, 126

school privatization, xiv, 39, 69, 83, 87, 121, 146
Schwartz v. Lopez, 68, 74
Second Morrill Act of 1890, 195
Second Vatican Council, 98
Senate Public Charter School Caucus, 131
Shafer, Kevin, 123, 141-143
Shaheed-Diallo, Kameelah, 119, 121, 123, 141-142, 144
Shelby County v. Holder, 43, 69-70, 74, 76
shell strategy, 235
Shock Doctrine, The
  Klein, Naomi, 67
Silicon Valley Community Foundation, 61
Sinclair Broadcast Group, xvi, 226, 252, 262
  history of, 233-236
  organization of, 236-237
  acquisition strategies (see also media consolidation), 227-231
single-issue charities, 9
Smith family
  Julian Sinclair Smith, 233-234, 236
  David D. Smith 227, 233-235, 236, 237
  Frederick Smith, 227, 234, 236, 237
  J. Duncan Smith, 227, 234, 236, 237
  Robert E. Smith, 234, 236, 237
social welfare organization, 7, 14
socialism, 206, 233, 239, 242-244, 247
soft rule, 121
Southern Poverty Law Center, 84, 94, 135, 152
Spellings, Margaret, U.S. Secretary of Education, 126, 152
Spelman College, 198
spokespeople, 141, 145
St. Joseph Abbey v. Castille, 60, 75
St. Jude Children's Research Hospital, 6
St. Louis, 123, 145
stakeholder trainings, 133, 145
Stand for Children, 140
State Attorney General Guide, 54
State Courts Guide, 54
  student division, 41
State of the Union address, 240
State of Washington v. McCleary, 64-65, 70
states' rights, 42-43, 52, 70
Step Up for Students, 83-85, 88, 94, 103, 114, 117
strategic action fields (SAFs), 226, 231
  incumbents, 231-232
  challengers, 231-232
  social skills, 232
strategy, xv, 2, 10-11, 49, 81, 119, 121-122, 130, 132, 138, 140-141, 143-145, 155-156, 165, 171-172, 175, 177, 188, 193, 198-199, 213, 226-227, 235, 248, 251-252, 259, 261-262
Strauss, Leo, 45
student work study, 68
Students for Education Reform, 205, 217
Summit Christian Academy v. Meotti, 77
Sustainability Solutions Services, 162-163, 174-175

T

takeover of schools, 123-125, 131-132, 142, 145-147, 151-152, 198
talented tenth, 190
tax codes, 1-2, 5, 11, 262,
  U.S. Federal, 1
tax exemptions (tax-exempt), 1-2, 5-7, 11, 64, 154
Tax Justice Now (taxjusticenow.org), 12
tax scholarships, 30-31, 67
Taxpayers for Public Education v. Douglas County School District, 68, 75
Teach For America (TFA), 31, 101, 104, 117, 123, 127-129, 157, 169, 217
teacher education, 31, 98, 136-137, 157-158, 170, 175
teacher termination, 102, 123, 127, 131, 135, 148, 158, 206
TeachNOLA, 123, 128, 130
Tennessee, 131, 176
The Revisionaries, 30
think tanks, 1, 26, 28, 54, 64, 81, 89, 97, 101, 108, 120, 156, 171
Thomas et al v. Douglas County BOE, 68, 75
Thurgood Marshall College Fund (TMCF), 196-198
top-down reforms, 119-147, 261
Trump, Donald J., 11, 41-42, 53, 57, 73-74, 76, 88, 91-92, 94, 103, 112-113, 185, 193-194, 200-202, 207-208, 210, 213, 215, 217-219, 223-224, 227, 233, 238-250, 253, 256, 260
Tulane University, 123, 128
Turning Point USA (TPUSA), xvi, 82, 185, 201, 203, 207, 212, 214, 217, 221-224
  history of, 208-216
  funding and network, 217-218
  (see also Professor Watchlist)

Tuskegee University, 191-192

U

ultra high frequency (UHF) stations, 234
United States Conference of Catholic Bishops (USCCB), 101, 109, 115
United Way, the, 6
University of Arkansas, 108, 158, 160-161, 167-168, 170-173, 175-176, 179, 182
University of Chicago, 44, 59-60, 75, 112-113, 188
United Negro College Fund (UNCF), 170, 196-198
University of Notre Dame, 63, 104, 114, 172,
Usdin, Sarah, 128-129, 132, 134, 138, 152
U.S. Chamber of Commerce, 26, 32, 55
  Education Committee, 26
U.S. Commission on Civil Rights, 63
U.S. educational policy and practice, 261-262
U.S. tax code,
  regulations, 4-6,
  shelters, 260
  tax breaks, 260
U.S. Treasury, 2
U.S. v. Miller, 59, 75

V

Venezuela
  Maduro, Nicolas, 243
Voting Rights Act of 1965, 43, 63, 76
vouchers, 30, 61, 63, 67-68, 79, 87, 89-90, 94, 100, 105, 107, 168, 245

W

Walgreen Foundation, 188
Walmart, xv, 153, 155, 160, 163-165, 167, 169, 178, 179
Walton Arts Center Council, 166-167
Walton Family, xv, 6, 81, 105-106, 117, 153-155, 160-161, 164-165, 168, 170, 173, 175, 177-178, 196-197, 200, 217, 262
Walton, Alice Louise, 161, 166-197
Walton, Ben, 161
Walton Penner, Carrie, 161, 168-170
Walton, Helen Alice, 160, 161, 173
Walton, James, 161
Walton, Jim Carr, 161,169
Walton, John Thomas, 161
Walton, Lukas, 161
  Walton, Melani Lowman, 160, 162, 163, 174-175
  Walton, Rob (aka Samuel Robson Walton), 161, 162, 163, 174-175
Walton, Sam, xv, 153, 155, 159-160, 162, 166, 173
Walton Family Charitable Foundation, 175-177
Walton Family Foundation (WFF), xv, 81, 105, 108, 117, 153-183, 196-197, 200, 217, 262
Walton International Scholarship Program (WISP), 174
Warren Court, the, 51, 68
Washington (state), 59
Washington, Booker T., 190-193
Washington, D.C., 60, 75, 86, 90, 94, 123, 131, 141, 157, 172
  D.C. public schools, 90, 131, 157-158
water privatization,
  private water markets, 153, 164
wealth inequality, 2, 11
Weaver, Richard, 45-47, 56, 58, 75-76
  Ideas Have Consequences, 45, 56, 75
  "spoiled-child psychology", 46
  "the crisis of our times", 47, 76
West Coast Hotel Company. v. Parrish, 45, 48, 76
West Michigan Aviation Academy, 86
white flight, 99
white missionaries, 189, 195
  aim of, 189
white philanthropic control, 122
white privilege, 80-81
Whitehouse, Sheldon, 39, 42-43, 57, 76
Wilberforce University, 189
Wiley College, 197-198
Windgate Charitable Foundation, 172, 175-177
World Health Organization (WHO), 260

X

Xavier University of Louisiana, 197

Y

Yale University, 39, 44, 68
Young America's Foundation, 86, 93, 95

Z

Zelman v. Simmons-Harris, 59, 62, 76
Zuckerberg, Mark, 6